Street Kids: The Tragedy of Canada's Runaways

In cities across North America, teenage runaways are struggling to stay alive. Some don't make it to adulthood. Some do, but their lives rarely rise above the despair that brought them to the streets in the first place. A few manage to beat the street, to get their lives back on track. In this disturbing account Marlene Webber draws on extensive interviews with these kids to explore the realities of street life, its attraction, and its consequences.

Street kids like to project an image of themselves as free-wheeling rebels who relish life on the wild side. All brashness and bombast, they strut around inner cities panhandling, posturing, and prostituting themselves. Labelled society's bad boys and girls, they often live up to their image. But as sixteen-year-old Eugene tells us, the street forces bravado on homeless adolescents, 'but underneath, a lot of kids are plenty scared.'

Eugene is only one of many street kids who talked to Webber in major cities across Canada. She lets her subjects tell their own stories; their voices are sometimes brave, sometimes bitter, often heartbreaking.

Common elements in their personal accounts suggest why increasing numbers of teenagers – especially girls and relatively rich kids – now flee their families. Common threads in their lives on the street help us understand why even the most determined young people are daunted by the overwhelming odds stacked against their getting out.

Webber cuts a comprehensible path through the tangle of forces, including family breakdown and social-service failure, that accelerate the tragedy of Canada's runaways. She suggests measures that might help more of them beat the streets.

Marlene Webber is a writer living in Toronto. She is co-author, with Tony McGilvary, of *Square John: A True Story*.

D1231249

MARLENE WEBBER

Street Kids

The Tragedy of Canada's Runaways

UNIVERSITY OF TORONTO PRESS
Toronto Buffalo London

© University of Toronto Press, March 1991
Toronto Buffalo London
Printed in Canada
Reprinted in paperback May 1991

ISBN 0-8020-5789-6 (cloth)
ISBN 0-8020-6705-0 (paper)

Canadian Cataloguing in Publication Data

Webber, Marlene, 1947–
    Street kids

    Includes bibliographical references.
    ISBN 0-8020-5789-6 (bound) ISBN 0-8020-6705-0 (pbk.)

    1. Runaway teenagers – Canada. 2. Homeless youth –
    Canada. I. Title

HQ799.C2W42 1991   362.7'4   C90-095663-1

The photograph on the front cover and all photographs throughout the book are by Daniel Gautreau and are reproduced with permission. The photograph on the back cover, by A. Stawicki, is reproduced by permission of the Toronto *Star.*

This book has been published with assistance from the Canada Council and the Ontario Arts Council under their block grant programs.

Contents

To Canada's runaway, throwaway, and lost kids struggling, against all odds, to beat the street.

Acknowledgments

To all the street kids and adult survivors of the streets who shared their private torments, my heartfelt, yet wholly inadequate thanks. Some of you will recognize yourselves in these pages. Others may feel disappointment that your stories are not recorded here. Although you may not see them, your contributions infuse this book. Your anger, frustration, despair, and dreams drove every line.

To all the streetworkers and child advocates who educated me to the issues, who walked me through their streets, and who connected me with young experts on life on the skids across the country, my thanks. There are too many of you to name, but I must mention those who contributed far more than a stranger dared hope. In Victoria, Dean Fortin at the Association for Street Kids (ASK), Judy Walsh of the Kiwanis Youth Shelter, and My Lipton from AIDS Vancouver Island. In Vancouver, Marie Arrington of Prostitutes and Other Women for Equal Rights (POWER), Richard Dopson at the Study Project, and Pablo Bazerque from the Downtown Eastside Youth Activities Society (DEYAS). Chris Lundquist at Alternatives in Action (AIA) provided invaluable assistance. In Regina, Donna Beatle and Merlin Longman at Beat the Street; in Winnipeg, Ruby Brass and Doug Ince at Beat the Street; in Toronto, Tracy Lequyere and especially Rick Parsons, co-founders and past directors of Beat the Street. Staff person Carol Parsons was a great help too. In Montreal, Robert Paris at Projet d'intervention auprès des mineurs[res] prostitués (ées) (PIMP). In Halifax, Father Peter McKenna, and Carol Wambolt at Stepping Stone.

A number of strangers chance delivered to my project contributed in myriad ways. Toronto Community Liaison for Project DARE, Pat Ford, reviewed a portion of the manuscript, and his critique helped me reshape one chapter. Rod Cohen, a youth-worker from Toronto, led me to outreach workers in other cities. Susan Tuck, a University of Toronto graduate student, ferreted out some disturbing facts buried in libraries. Mercifully, Stephen Endes appeared at the last minute when the research wasn't finished but the deadline was encroaching. Gillian Walker, a professor of social work at Carleton University who read an early draft, left her mark on my thinking about so-called family violence. Christine Femia-Wiseman, ex-prostitute and past director of Toronto's Street Outreach Services (SOS) for young prostitutes, came through when my manuscript needed an insider's assessment.

When it needed another writer's assessment, Alison Griffiths was there as always, giving more than I should have asked for and more than her schedule allowed.

Others deserve thanks as well. Jack Pearpoint, past president of Frontier College, which sponsors Beat the Street as a partnership, agreed to give me access to the program. Marsha Forest, director of the Centre for Integrated Education, helped me untangle some thorny theoretical questions. Judy Steed, always a treat to have in your cheering section, also contributed in practical ways.

Friends, particularly Fiona Griffiths, humoured me through the heart-breaking aftermath of long interviews with throwaway kids. The late Tony McGilvary, much in my thoughts throughout this project, prodded me along with midnight calls from Vancouver. From time to time, Jack Bond gave me a boost, always when it was most needed.

Janet Menard, a welfare director, kept my mailbox full of useful tidbits. Sherri Gershuny clipped newspapers when I was on the road. Eve McDermott let me turn her living-room into an office when I was in Halifax. My sister-in-law, Jean McClelland, managed to pry open an important Halifax door that was closed to me. Cape Breton farmer and writer David Newton alerted me to aspects of this book that might rankle certain readers. I tried to include explanations to forestall them.

Other friends, though not directly involved with this project, were none the less generous with their interest and encouragement. I hope they know how much I appreciate them.

Allyn Gandall, Co-ordinator of the Community Support Program at Covenant House youth shelter in Toronto, assisted with research and advice. (Allyn has since become director of Our House, a new Calgary safehouse for kids.) Virgil Duff, Managing Editor of the University of Toronto Press, was enthusiastic from the first page. Editor Beverley Beetham Endersby worked wonders.

Deep gratitude goes to my parents, Ethel and Harvey Webber, for their abiding interest and encouragement. Last, but foremost, I thank my mate, David Carter, who kept the discussions lively, the coffee strong, and the heart tender.

I also gratefully acknowledge financial assistance provided by the Canada Council, the Ontario Arts Council, and the City of Toronto through the Toronto Arts Council.

Street Kids

Introduction

After *Runaways: 24 Hours on the Streets* aired in September 1987, alarmed Canadians jammed CBC telephone lines with calls and flooded the desks of newspaper editors with letters, generally registering horror at the televised images of emotionally racked, penniless, and homeless adolescents on the streets of our major cities.

My own reaction to the documentary was mixed. On the one hand, and all to the good, I felt that the exposé might help dispel whatever remained of Canada's mythical image as a country benevolent towards it most vulnerable citizens. On the other hand, *Runaways* focused on the sensational, offering pictures of kids selling their bodies, sleeping in parks, and shooting themselves up with cocaine. The program left an overriding impression of weak, culpable teenagers who, with one or two exceptions, were doing little to improve their lot. The underlying causes that compel kids to run away and the failure of child-protection services were all but ignored.

Two of my streetworker acquaintances fumed about the documentary. They agreed that it might be used successfully to raise consciousness and money, but these were not reasons enough, they felt, to freeze kids on film as losers. Aside from omitting last names, no attempt had been made to protect the participants' identities.

Although the runaways took part voluntarily, I, too, wondered how able they were to protect their own interests, or understand the consequences of not doing so, when offered a moment of fame on the box. At the same time, I knew that their stories, woven into a social and economic fabric, were important. Not long after the show aired, I decided to write about street kids across the country with the aim of exposing the problem without exposing its casualties.

It seemed a natural subject for me to pursue. I had recently finished collaborating on *Square John*, the story of an eccentric flimflam man who, after twenty-two years in prison, turned himself around and founded a successful job-finding organization for ex-cons, run by ex-cons. Researching that book, I'd met young men and women who had done time not only in prison but also on the street.

Among others, I'd met Tracy Lequyere and Rick Parsons, ex-offenders and ex–illiterate street hustlers. In partnership with Frontier College, a national adult-literacy organization based in Toronto, these two brash, beefy-looking guys had established Beat the Street, a literacy program for street youths in Toronto, Winnipeg, and Regina. Their unorthodox approach – using literate street kids to tutor less literate ones – was working wonders with school-shy drop-outs, kids they call 'school push-outs.' Beat the Street was using the kids' world, the street, as a classroom. Tutors were building curriculum based on their students' everyday reading challenges, from job and welfare applications to street signs and menus.

Tracy and Rick agreed to arrange for me to meet the particular kind of adolescent I was interested in: those able and willing to talk straight about themselves and life on the downtown track. I wanted to connect with juveniles and young adults who had already unravelled some of the confusion and torment in the kitbag of dark secrets that every street kid carries.

I wanted to bypass young people who had not yet unearthed their demons. I did not want to do the harm some journalists do: barter with street kids, using the interest and attention they crave to gain their confidence and get my story, then leave them exposed and alone, with no one to pick up the pieces.

Trust, almost non-existent on the street, was the primary obstacle to my research. Meeting interviewees through outreach workers helped me gain credibility, since some kids trust, if only a smidgen, some streetworkers. When the rapport was right, kids usually introduced me to one or two of their friends. So, kids led me to other kids, just as streetworkers in each city led me to their colleagues in the next.

As it turned out, Beat the Street staff helped me arrange such a large pool of interviews in three cities that stories garnered from their students predominate in these pages. You will see, however, through profiles of kids I met via other social agencies, that nothing unique distinguishes the young people connected with Beat the Street. Themes that pervade their lives occur commonly among young urban nomads.

Meetings took place on the kids' timetables and turf. Most often we met on the downtown strip, in cheerless restaurants that ply coffee and beer. The minority of youths who had a room of their own, however temporarily, extended me the hospitality of meeting in their overpriced slums. The shortest interview lasted one hour; the longest, thirteen hours, spread over two weeks. Typically, an interview took place in two meetings of about two hours. By 'interview,' I mean only that time when the tape was running. With some kids, I spent many informal hours; with others, it was all business.

I met and spoke with scores of street people during my field research. No youth panhandling on a street corner got a loony from me without answering a barrage of questions. Formal interviews were done with twenty-nine runaways, or, more aptly in many cases, throwaways forced out of their homes. All were living a homeless life, literally on the street, or a precarious life, barely off the street in a string of shabby rooms, in Halifax, Toronto, Ottawa, Winnipeg, Regina, Vancouver, or Victoria.

Interviews slated for Montreal collapsed when two English-speaking kids didn't show. Street kids don't have stable lives anchored by appointments, so no-shows understandably occurred in other cities as well. But in Montreal I hadn't arranged back-up interviews. A French youthworker, who had walked me through Montreal's street scene, consented to interview French-speaking kids for me. At the last minute, a crisis – the daily fare of streetwork – pulled him away from a day of appointments. We planned to reschedule, but money tightened and time closed in. Time and money constraints also precluded my conducting field-work in major midwestern cities, such as Calgary, where the problems I was examining are also acute.

In addition, I interviewed nine ex–street people who have moved a significant distance from the skids but whose street experience has indelibly coloured their lives. My youngest potential interviewee was fourteen; however, she escaped from a Montreal detention centre a few days before our tentative meeting was confirmed. As a result, the youngest participant was sixteen. The oldest was thirty-three, and most were in their mid-teens to mid-twenties. Given the age range, the expression 'street kid' seems odd, especially since the street expunges all trace of childishness, whether related to age, inclination, or immaturity. However, 'street kid' captures a concept: young, homeless, and trapped.

Profiles included here reflect a cross-section of the stories I heard. None is a composite. All use invented names. Where any risk that adolescents from small towns might be identifiable from such details as home towns and parents' occupations, those facts were changed.

While the extended anecdotes at the heart of this study are typical street stories, they do not represent all subgroups of dispossessed youth. Missing, for example, are accounts from gang members of various national origins, including Southeast Asian, whose paths were perhaps determined by colonial occupation, imperialist war, and immigration trauma rather than by Canadian socio-economic conditions and personal circumstances. Missing, too, are accounts from Nazi skinheads and from bikers. These groups make up part of the street scene, but are more elusive, more dangerous, and more closed-mouthed.

The group I was interested in is the teenagers we all see – if our eyes are open – on inner-city and some suburban street corners: kids who can't go home on the last bus.

'Don't you find it depressing meeting all those hard-luck kids?' people asked me. Of course, it was wrenching being privy to so much pain. The misery I witnessed and heard about invaded my dreams. Twice I awoke in sweaty terror from nightmares in which I was being victimized by pimps, tricks, and pushers in convoluted replays of incidents kids had described to me. Twice I felt fear in the flesh. Two of the kids I met were time bombs of inchoate hatred and rage. By no means exceptional among street youths, these two live in an emotional blender that is bound to blow its lid one day, unleashing fury, against others or against themselves. As they spoke, I feared for them – and for me.

The street is a factory of depressing stories. But depression was not my predominant response. Rather, I felt anger, and hope – anger at the injustices done to children, adolescents, and young adults by the warped values of our social system; by killer poverty in the midst of plenty; by destroyed and destructive families, especially those grounded in male violence; by incompetent schools; by ineffective child-rescue and -rehabilitation bureaucracies; by the whole tangle of forces tightening around certain young, vulnerable Canadians.

Odd as it may seem, I culled hope from these stories. Most are more remarkable for what has been overcome than for what has been endured. Kids' struggles to survive and improve against crushing circumstance testify to heroism and strength in the human spirit.

Willing though that spirit is, resolve often falters. Like all of us, street kids tend to fall back into familiar behaviours. One step forward sometimes precedes two steps back. Though some profiles in the book end on an optimistic note, the progress of real lives may scuttle happy endings. By the same token, some seemingly pessimistic paths may well veer onto a road better-travelled.

During the two years I worked on this book, I witnessed or heard about both eventualities. I saw people apparently busy rescuing themselves slip back into snorting the occasional line of cocaine or turning the occasional trick. By the same token, I saw people who seemingly didn't stand a chance but who were none the less breaking new ground.

Some readers will find certain facts in this book hard to accept: facts about male battery of women and children; about incest and other forms of sexual abuse; about poverty among women and children; about illiteracy; about homelessness – about Canada the good. Even facts culled from conventional sources such as Statistics Canada, the Canadian Advisory Council on the Status of Women, and the National Council of Welfare stretch credulity when gathered together to describe the problems that beset the young disenfranchised.

You may well raise the questions about veracity that I, too, wrestled with through my first dozen interviews. Eventually, the sheer weight of numbers and consistency of themes convinced me that the kids, far from trying to bamboozle anyone, were telling the truth.

Most of these truths could have been verified by professional helpers who have participated in the lives of most street kids. It is important to grasp that typical children of the street have not gone unnoticed by institutional systems of rescue and care. Rather, most are 'helped' kids. They, and in many cases their families, are known to social workers, psychologists, psychiatrists, and police. Some seem as much the progeny of paid professionals as of their own parents. It is little wonder they are known in the street as 'system kids.'

From the outset, I wanted this book to speak for street kids, to express their truths. Initially, however, I did consider citing parental and professional views, where access to either might be possible. With permission from my first three interviewees, all in their mid-teens, I endeavoured to meet professionals connected to them. I approached social workers, counselling psychologists, and an institutional psychiatrist for interviews, promising anonymity both for them and for their agencies. These assurances, I hoped, would free them to speak more candidly, less defensively.

After my many phone calls, careful correspondence, and considerable frustration with the child-protection bureaucracy, only one meeting materialized. It degenerated into an adversarial, go-nowhere stand-off. This fiasco revealed less about the competence of the individual professional than about the terrible and fundamental inadequacies of the agency where he works. Four months into the research, I had no more success with parents, many of whom, if they are still in touch with their kids, are locked into a rancorous imbroglio.

In *The Myth of Delinquency: An Anatomy of Juvenile Nihilism*, a Canadian study of incarcerated teenagers, author Elliott Leyton, who succeeded in interviewing parents, concluded that the youngsters had more insight than did anyone else into their families' dynamics and into the source of their own misfortunes. As this project took shape, I adopted Leyton's conclusion as my premise.

Sure, some of the kids I met overdramatized, trying to redeem a life-style even they see as squalid. Some tried to make themselves appear kindly, heroic, sought-after. These kids are survivors, street hustlers; the gift of gab, after all, is part of their game. Their posturing, however, often melts away if you are able to reach something inside them.

In that regard, I was often lucky. Maybe the kids sensed my genuine interest in them as individuals. Maybe they sensed that I might believe them. Whatever the currents that connected us, most of the young people were frank with me, and the more I heard, the more committed I became to allowing them their own voice here, undiluted by others' qualifiers.

You may wonder why these youngsters would open up to me, a stranger, or why they would agree to meet with me at all. The majority said they agreed because they wanted to help other potential runaways who might read this book. They wanted to let kids at risk of running away know that they understand why some kids have to flee their families. Not one street person who participated advised kids to stay home. At the same time, none invited newcomers to the street. Rather, they beseeched troubled young people to seek alternatives, though most interviewees were at a loss for specific suggestions. A remarkable number of those I interviewed, reduced to transient lives and self-absorbed in dense despair, none the less expressed quixotic dreams of helping others. A minority said they agreed in order to help themselves; 'talk therapy,' one young woman called it.

Besides these genuine reasons, I think other unconscious agendas also drove their co-operation. For one, the tint of fame, the same reason street kids might face a TV camera, no matter how stigmatizing. I realized how much fame figured into it when, after an interview, a young man introduced me to a buddy. 'This is the lady I told ya about that's gonna write a book about me!' he boasted. (I carefully explained to every participant that I would be interviewing many people but using only some stories and no real names.)

I also suspect that a few kids opened up to punish their parents or caretakers. An experienced streetworker suggested that some go on TV to humiliate fathers and father figures who raped or beat them. An anonymous appearance in a collection of stories may not do much for revenge, but it helps. Finally, an interview means positive, personal attention – a momentary illusion in which nobody's children get to feel like somebodies.

Aside from prison inmates, few social groups feel angrier than street kids. Many I spoke with were full of hurt and hate. They loosed their vitriol indiscriminately against the world. Most spared only their biological parents, for whom they feel love-hate, from total damnation. Generally, they expressed disdain for substitute caregivers, such as foster- and group-home parents. They talked about most authority figures who touch their lives as being enemies.

With few exceptions, these kids tend to experience professional intervention as oppression more than as assistance. Their stories are laced with incidents of indifference and outright negligence – sometime criminal neglect – on the part of public child-protection agents.

For these disinherited youngsters, individuals, not systems, fail. Kids do not protest the existence of underfunded, understaffed, sprawling, and anonymous human-service bureaucracies in which workers – both the 'good' ones and the 'bad' ones, as street youths describe them – are saddled with impossibly large 'caseloads' and impossibly restrictive mandates. Hungry, homeless, hurting kids do not stop to think that they are up against agencies that can't even begin to meet their material, let alone their spiritual, needs. All they see is adults who deny them a living allowance for a room of their own or entry to a job-training or a drug-treatment program. Kids do not see that devoted professionals often find themselves defeated by the same systems that deny people the help they need.

Even if the professionals kids summarily condemn had the support of social agencies with realistic resources and workloads, the task of reparenting these adolescents would try the most caring and skilled counsellors. To heal these kids, to help them build lives, social services would have to ensure unconditionally loving, one-to-one relationships in long-term, supportive environments.

The pre-conditions necessary for reclaiming shattered lives are almost completely absent from Canada's protection services for children, leading kids to blame individuals who, to them, personify the system's failure.

While I was researching this book, I was less shocked by what I found in the street than by what I learned in my own circle.

Once acquaintances (all women, in their twenties, thirties, or forties) understood the nature of my research, they wanted to tell me their stories. After the tenth confession of incest and other forms of child abuse, I stopped keeping count. For example, two of three virtual strangers with whom I shared a long-distance car pool exposed emotional scars left from experiences with foster homes, group homes, an adoptive home, and a 'deranged' natural mother.

These stories also came up in all the likely places. A Halifax streetworker I met by chance while waiting for a no-show interview sketched her story: a victim of incest from age six; the perpetrators, her father and three male relatives. She ran away, and buried the memory – a necessary amnesia. Went to college, became a social worker, worked with kids. Married. Lived happily until she fell 'addictively in love' with a pimp – 'I had to be with him; I had no idea why.' Worked the streets for him out west for two years – 'I was six years old again, doing what Daddy wants.' Eventually she was rescued by a friend, saved by therapy.

Closer to home, a young friend smashed through the psychological wall of a necessary amnesia. She'd always known that her father, a rampaging drunk, had battered her and her mother, who had escaped to an early death. But, until recently when 'flashbacks' began, she hadn't known – not consciously, that is – about the incest.

This year, the teenage daughter of a friend hit the street. When my friend's fourth marriage crumbled, she turned to a therapist. Together, they unlocked a key to her pattern of destructive adult relationships: incest, buried in the subconscious for thirty-five years.

After scores of interviews with kids and young adults and informal discussions with streetworkers and child advocates across thousands of miles, I am left with two images branded on my mind's eye.

One is a cherubic blond boy with a Dutch cut. Although he was thirteen, slumped on a cot behind bars in a cell at Willingdon Youth Detention Centre in Burnaby, BC, he looked no more than ten or eleven. I did not speak with this child; I just caught a glimpse of him. I found out that he is a runaway, and 'delinquent'; he was in detention on remand (court date postponed) for alleged minor property theft. He comes from a home where neglect is known to occur and paternal abuse is suspected. His father remains at home, while the child begins what may well become a life of punishment and crime. 'Oh, that one,' said his keeper when he noticed where my gaze had strayed. 'He still has bright eyes, but they won't last long.'

The other image is of Crystal, whom you will meet in these pages. I see her – an ex–illiterate 'junkie whore' from a family destroyed by alcohol and drug addictions – buzzing around her sunny apartment in Regina, waving her newly earned university graduation certificate.

Sadly, Crystal's success is exceptional. By escaping the gutter, she defied the odds. Her struggle and her triumph, however, powerfully symbolize hope for kids bereft of success models – kids like the blond boy behind bars. In street parlance, Crystal is a hero. She proves to otherwise lost kids that maybe, just maybe, it is possible to beat the street and forge a new beginning.

1

Street Kids

Canadian streets destroy kids. Some are casualties of pimp violence and trick violence and pusher violence. Some are poisoned by drugs. All of them die at least a little from despair and broken hearts in a community where 'friends are just dudes ... who haven't hurt you yet.'[1]

Life on the streets is a scavenger's existence, a restless hunt for cash or for anything that can be converted into cash or a bed or a meal or drugs to sustain the hunter for one more day. The inner-city corridor staked out by homeless people is not just another neighbourhood marked by familiar daily and seasonal rhythms. First snow does not signal time to take goose-down parkas to the dry-cleaner. It triggers fear: of numbing cold, of constant fatigue because it is too risky to allow yourself sleep in a frost. At best, winter means frost-bite. At worst, it means freezing to death near an open-air 'heater,' the exhaust vent from an apartment- or office-building furnace.

For most Canadians, neighbourhoods, demographics aside, offer comforts of the known and predictable. For Canadians on the streets, nothing is certain except danger and change. Within any twenty-four hour period, life can be turned upside-down. A drug deal sours. Someone gets knifed, killed perhaps. Suddenly, police swarm the parks and bars. Suddenly, everyone is on the lam from the law, until someone gets arrested. A kid punches someone out, or rips someone off, and lives are suddenly at risk. The word goes out on the street's mighty grape-vine. Kids get 'shut down,' the most dangerous consequence of all, because they lose the protection of their group.

The street, reflecting and exaggerating backward ideas from the larger society, is rife with racism, homophobia, and sexism. Highly stratified, its organization revolves around subgroups: hookers and pimps; pushers and users; derelicts and drunks; bag ladies; bikers; ex-cons; ex–psychiatric patients; skinheads, punk-rockers, new wavers; and a maze of neo-Nazi and anti-racist sects. After school, and from Friday night until Sunday night, 'weekend warriors,' suburban gawkers and thrill-seekers, join the mêlée. Big-time gangs with a rep for violence are also out there, alongside juvenile panhandlers and petty offenders.

It's a complex scene. Friendships are fast and superficial. Loyalties shift. There is a constant influx and outflow of players.

Some community lines are fluid; others, rigidly divisive. Anger is endemic. Turmoil is not always created from within; pressures from outside the street community frequently descend on it. Ratepayers in newly gentrified city centres organize to clear hookers from 'their' sidewalks. Developers decide to upgrade a crumbling downtown block. When fire marshals accommodate the developers by condemning rooming-houses and cheap hotels, these buildings disgorge welfare recipients, poor working people, transients, and runaway kids into the streets. With nowhere else to go, the kids hang out in malls, where shopkeepers anxious about losing customers encourage police to slap kids with tickets for loitering. Since they can't afford the fines, the kids are forced to run from the law or go to jail.

The street offers no privacy, no individual space, and no stability. The only staples are danger, disease, despair, and the desperation of life on the edge. Health care, which has to do with self-care, access to services, and a life with plans, is practically absent. Unless delivered to hospital emergency departments by ambulance, homeless individuals typically receive no medical treatment. Most don't seek it. Some feel their lives aren't worth caring for. Many feel health practitioners don't see them as human beings worthy of service.[2] Besides, they can't afford prescription drugs. Street people, especially the kids, also steer clear of professionals they fear might try to force them to go home or into institutions.

With increasing numbers of kids moving in, first-come inhabitants are caught in a never-ending 'push-push' squeeze, forced to compete for ever-shrinking territory in the inner city. Young transients just keep moving, stay a while wherever chance delivers them, then move on to chance's next stop, likely the tenderloin track in another big city.

Eugene: Victim of Racists and Homophobics

'Are you sure you want to do this?' I asked Eugene periodically. Although he'd answer 'yes,' I was never sure he meant it. He hedged or half-answered most of my questions, even though he knew the answers, and had found them through the anguish of facing up to his life. Eugene is only sixteen but has the perceptiveness and self-knowledge of someone twice his age. A thinker, sensitive and broad-minded, he has an understanding of the world that stretches beyond his own skin.

Eugene is very black, very tall, and very lean from the erratic eating patterns of panhandlers. He sniffles a lot. 'You live on the street, you get colds and flu all the time,' he says apologetically. Despite obvious unhappiness, he affects an upbeat, breezy style. On the street, Eugene is an enigma, the type of teen you'd expect to meet in an alternative school rather than on the skids; he seems too soft for the street's imperatives.

Rejection has hardened him a little. He tasted it first at home, in a Toronto suburb. His father, an electrician, and his mother, a secretary, have, by Eugene's account, a good relationship. 'They discuss problems, work things out between them and make compromises. They are very straightforward, reasonable people ... except when it comes to me. I've got some clues, but I'm not really sure why my parents don't want me ... It's a constant source of pain and confusion.' He looks away, fighting a lump in his throat.

Eugene remembers the first sting of rejection he felt. In grade five, a teacher called him 'dyslexic.' 'Words were just a senseless jumble to me. I couldn't "see" words, only letters. Instead of helping me, the teachers ignored me. I couldn't go home for help because my parents are very strict. My sister was one of the school brains, and my parents expected big things from me too. Even though I was just a little kid I knew they wouldn't understand that it wasn't my fault.

'I begged my teacher not to tell them that I was supposedly dyslexic. I was scared they'd punish me bad for having so much trouble learning. Not that they were violent; I got the occasional strapping but nothing more than you'd expect from a strict Christian family that believes in discipline.'

His parents, of course, knew that Eugene was failing. 'My dad's idea of helping me was to watch over my shoulder while I did homework. I got so frustrated at school, and at home where no one understood my problem, that I started fighting with everyone.'

Alienation from teachers, fights with classmates, and tensions with his parents escalated. 'Everyone wanted to get rid of me, so

I got shipped to a private school for grades six and seven. Actually, it was better there. With help from a real good teacher, I finally started to unscramble the jumble.'

But when Eugene went back to public school in grade eight, the old school-yard troubles flared. 'The kids thought I was dumb, and they called me names. I started fighting again, not just to defend myself but to protect my sister's reputation from stuff boys said about her. You know what teenage guys can be like.

'My parents were convinced that I was an uncontrollable "problem child." I'm not saying that I was an angel; I was a very mixed-up, frustrated kid, mostly because of my school problems. I needed help, not punishment.'

His father phoned the Children's Aid Society (CAS). 'Then the real trouble started. The first foster home I went through was okay; they didn't beat me or hold back on the food. It's just that the family's kids got treated much better than us foster kids. We got blamed for everything that went wrong or went missing.'

What happened in the other two foster homes and one group home where he was later placed? Although he introduced the subject, Eugene refused to talk about it. Several days later, when I broached the topic again, he opened up a bit, telling an abridged story of abuse that involved 'drugs, restraints, and knives.' Eugene claimed that, in various combinations, foster fathers, natural fathers and sons, and older foster boys sexually abused younger foster children. 'Actually, in the group home, the house parents weren't involved. The older guys were doing it to us younger boys. I don't know for sure, but I think the house parents knew what was doing down and didn't care.'

Did he ever report any of this to his CAS worker?

Eugene laughs. 'Of course. First place it happened, I asked to be moved, but it was a complete waste of time. My worker told me I shouldn't make false accusations about people that were good enough to take me in when my own family didn't want me!'

Why would Eugene now tell only a censored version of what happened to him in these homes? Embarrassment? The pain of remembering? 'No. The truth of what went down is too horrible for straight people like you to believe. If I tell you what really happened, and if you write about it, then people aren't going to trust anything I say. I'm just a dumb street kid, a liar, a "problem child" as my parents say. Who's going to believe me? Even if they believe it, they'll figure it's my fault. So, you might say I'm cutting out the dirtiest bits so people will believe the rest of it.'

During the year Eugene spent in CAS care, he went home to visit occasionally. More often, he went AWOL and was picked up by police and delivered back to his group home. His father visited him there at Christmas. 'He embarrassed me very badly. He let the other kids know that he didn't exactly think I was a red-blooded, all-American boy.'

'What do you mean? Does your father think you're gay?'

'Well ... maybe.'

'Are you?'

'No ... ah ... My dad just couldn't accept me the way I am, that's all.'

Eugene couldn't accept the sexual abuse and the restrictive atmosphere of the group home. Just after his fifteenth birthday, he ran away and has been on the street ever since.

'I spent the first six months walking the streets all night. I slept only in the daytime; I was afraid to sleep when it was dark because it's too dangerous for a guy that people think is gay. I know I come across like a sensitive type and I'm black to boot – two marks against me. Down here, anyone different is in danger: gays, blacks, Indians, mixed-race people. Everyone on the scene plays tough because the street makes us pretend. But, under- neath, I think a lot of kids are just as scared as me.

'You don't dare show the fear. If you seem weak, you get beat up. I've been kicked around and threatened by skinheads, and by other guys who've really been hardened and who've learned from the street how to hate.

'Black people get little-enough respect anywhere. Down here it's worse because all the sores of the society are real raw. I get called "nigger" so much that my life begins to feel like one long racist joke. That's part of the reason I steer clear of the shelters. They're full of bigots and they're too violent. If you don't fit in, you're harassed.'

Now Eugene sleeps in abandoned cars and boarded-up build- ings, or 'crashes' with friends. He panhandles spare change for

food and washes in public bath houses such as O'Neill's on George Street. Since he doesn't have a drug habit to support, he can stay alive, albeit wafer-thin and sickly, on nickels and dimes. 'I was only into drugs seriously for about three months and I never once had to buy them. There was always some pusher around passing out treats so maybe you'd get hooked or peddle drugs for them. Maybe I would have gotten hooked, but I wasn't in the street four months before I watched a buddy croak on an overdose. That finished it for me.'

What does he want from life? 'I haven't got much going for me, to tell the truth. But I've got one thing: Beat the Street [a literacy program for street kids]. I'm working on grade-ten English and math. You go along at your pace in a friendly situation with lots of help. Right now, my goal is to get on student welfare, get a place to live, and finish high school.'

Beyond that, Eugene isn't sure where he's headed, but he wants to 'be in a position to help other abused kids. Maybe become a streetworker, but not a social worker. They never helped me much.' He says that whatever he ends up doing, he wants to fight for human rights. 'We all have to fight – street kids, handicapped people, psychiatric patients, women, gays, and especially people of colour like blacks and Indians. Discrimination has taught me that we've got to fight because no one gives you your rights, you've got to grab them.'

Charlie: A seesaw of defeat and hope

Charlie was practically born a street kid, forced from an early age to hustle his living from the street. There is nothing in his past except three generations of welfare, alcoholism, and soul-destruction to help him construct a better future.

He looks and plays the victim's part. Long and skinny, with pointed features and a thin moustache, at nineteen he has the awkwardness of a younger teenager, pimples and all. Jittery, he rubs his hands together, grins in jerky little flashes, twitches constantly, and picks his pimples raw. His intense brown-black eyes dart away from contact, staring at nothing in particular, but not missing a thing. He flicks his Bic on and off, click, click, click, through hours of interviews.

Charlie's memory is murky. He stumbles over the sequence of sore spots that subsume his life. He calls all the places where he stayed 'foster homes,' even though all but one were detention centres and group homes to which he was court-ordered for stealing. He's clear, however, that these 'foster homes' – with one exception, where he was well-treated – 'were just like prison.'

Investigate the details of his story and some would probably not check out. He seems confused about who did what to whom, and when. He may himself have committed cruelties similar to those he recalls being done to him. His lying is probably not deliberate. Rather, he seems genuinely muddled. But through the confusion of his grisly account, recurrent themes emerge. They include the mental and physical violence his mother subjected him to and the rapes his stepfather perpetrated against him. They also include the labelling and 'dumping' he suffered at school, and the failure of child-protection services to rescue him from any of this.

His monologue is condensed from a long and tangled tale.

I spent most of my childhood locked in my bedroom. The door was bolted. The room was bare and cold. It was just an empty room. I slept on the floor. Even in winter I had no covers because my mother wouldn't give me any.

My parents got divorced when I was about two. From when I can remember, she made me feel the marriage broke up because of me. 'You're just like him,' she used to say. I guess she treated me so bad because I reminded her of my father. Her boyfriend knew about the starvation and the beatings but he didn't care because he done worse.

I think I was four when the rapes started. He never stopped doin' it till I left home for good at age fourteen. I told her what he done to me, but she said I was a liar and locked me in my room. I broke the bedroom window and ran away so often that she took to boarding it up. When I was able to escape from the house, I'd run to my dad's new family, but he couldn't do nothin' to help me because his wife hated my guts. They were on welfare, my dad had a heart condition, and they had a pile of kids, so I didn't blame him for taking me back to her. I know in his heart he wanted to help me, but what else could he do?

After he'd take me home, I'd just run away again, steal food, or anything I could sell to buy food. I'd break into other kids' lockers at school and rip off their clothes and ghetto-blasters. I've always had trouble with the law; I don't know how many times I been to juvenile court. Even when I lived at home, I had to steal to eat because there was no food in the house. Her mother's allowance went on booze for her boyfriend and drugs for both of them – grass, hash, coke, angel dust [PCP]. I'd steal the drugs and try them out in the bathroom at school.

When she was in a good mood, I'd get to party with everyone, drinkin' mostly – with my mother's boyfriend, my uncle, my grandfather. I'd drink with my own dad when I visited him, too. There were always home brews around, especially at my grandfather's. He loved me more than anyone, but he's always been an alcoholic. He drinks every day, anything he can lay hands on – shaving lotion, bitters, it don't matter. When I was still a little kid, supposed to be drinking milk, he'd give me beer; there was never nothin' else to drink in his house or mine.

I didn't do too good in school. Too weak to concentrate. I remember passing out from dizziness; it was the hunger, I guess. Besides, we were always moving, so I was always changing schools. Every move, they'd start me in grade one again. I think I was in grade one for four years.

One teacher was nice to me. He fed me and gave me some clothes. When I got home, my mother ripped the clothes up and told me to wear them tore up like that. Only other gifts I ever got were from my dad on Christmas and birthdays. She'd destroy or sell anything he gave me, including a TV. That teacher wasn't the only one that figured out how I was being treated. Neighbours used to call the CAS. Then the CAS would phone her to say they were coming. She'd clean the place up, get some food in the cupboards, take the locks off the bedroom door. Only time I could count on eating was when the social workers were coming.

I remember one time in particular that the social workers came. I was about eight. About a month before, a kid in my class must have guessed that I was real hungry because he took me home. When his parents saw the shape I was in, they kept me for a week but I guess they didn't call the cops or nothin'. When I went home, she beat me very bad, then locked me up for weeks until some friends of hers called the CAS, but they never did nothin', never took me away. I don't know why, maybe because of the show she put on when they came.

She didn't go any easier on me as I got older. Well, she did change – got rougher, started beating me with a whip. Then, when I was about fourteen, she called the CAS herself. The first foster family they put me in was real nice. I arrived near Christmas. Even though they didn't have much notice that I was coming, they managed to buy me presents. That summer they even bought me a dirt bike. They really liked me, but they couldn't put up with the stealing, which you can't blame them for. I had to steal to buy cigarettes and booze and drugs, which I was used to havin' by then.

I spent the next year with my dad [probably on a juvenile-court custody order after stealing from the foster family] and his new family. His wife didn't beat me, but she called me down to every low thing. 'You're slow, you're stupid, you're useless,' that sort of stuff. She made me take care of the younger kids.

After my father's place, I got sent to a foster home [a CAS group home]. It was like a prison for CAS wards. They got a school just for the kids in the home where they didn't teach you nothin' because they think we're all dummies. The discipline was very strict, and we were kept very poor. It's hard on teenagers not to have any change for cigarettes or other things you want. My dad, when he visited, gave me cash so I could buy a few treats at the store, but the house parents used to fine us for breaking house rules – five dollars a shot – from the fund where they said they kept our money till we would be released. In the end, I stole a van and ran away, and I never got my money back.

I hate the Aid [Children's Aid Society]. With the worst passion. All I ever wanted from them was to be returned to the first foster family that treated me like a human being, but instead they got me thrown into 999 [Queen Street Mental Health Centre] after I lost my temper at one of the workers and kicked him in the mouth. I admit, I got a violent temper, but no one deserves that joint. They drill you with questions and pump you with drugs; they don't treat you like a person with problems. I didn't tell them nothin', and eventually, after about three months I think, they let me go.

I ran away from everywhere practically from the time I could walk, so it's hard to say when I became a runaway. I was about sixteen when I started living full-time in the street downtown in Toronto – in parks, abandoned warehouses, bus shelters, hallways of office buildings.

Daytime, I'd hang out at drop-in centres, or sit on the sidewalk outside stores, watching TV through the windows. I'd eat at soup kitchens and, in the winter, sleep at hostels: Seaton House, Sally Ann, Under 21, Dixon Hall, the lot. I hate hostels because of the cockroaches and curfews and body lice. After sleeping at hostels awhile, I'd have to get that green gunk from the clinic to get rid of the lice.

Even though sleepin' in the street is better, you're always scared of gettin' mugged, stabbed, or killed maybe. You can fall asleep on a park bench and never wake up again. It happens all the time, but because it's street kids gettin' shivved [knifed], no one cares.

I'd get odd jobs and panhandle. Once I sold chocolate bars door-to-door for some handicapped organization. I made forty cents on every two dollars' worth I sold. Then I got a job at the Oshawa Food Terminal, which was great because I could buy my drugs from the truckers while I was workin'. I earned up to fifty dollars a day on that job; every penny went for drugs and booze. But the drugs and booze and street life were really messin' me up. I was dizzy and weak a lot. I knew I was sick but I didn't know exactly what was wrong.

Charlie's health had deteriorated so badly by the time he was seventeen, in summer 1986, that he could barely walk. At the time, he was living at the Markeen Hotel, a dive and welfare hotel where CAS paid his rent. During that period, Charlie stumbled into outreach workers from Beat the Street. That chance meeting was the beginning of a process that would help him gain some basic skills – Charlie could read a bit but couldn't write a word – and feel a first glimmer of self-confidence.

It wasn't easy for him to work at learning. At first, even with the support of another street kid who was tutoring him, he resisted. 'I didn't want to try to read and write because I didn't want to get put down. That's what education does to you,' Charlie says. But with empathy from others who'd endured put-downs in school, Charlie eventually warmed to the idea of learning. With constant support from peers, and with Beat the Street's method of using the street as a classroom, he began to read street signs and store signs. 'It feels so good now not having to ask strangers to read subway signs. I always hated asking. And I hated not being able to read newspapers. Now I can read the *Sun*. I like the stuff about education, and the Sunshine Girl, and the horoscopes.'

Beat the Street helped him with other needs too. When he turned eighteen and lost his CAS allowance, staff helped him apply for $375-a-month student welfare. With a buddy, Charlie rented a room in Toronto above a restaurant near Parliament and Dundas.

His room is worse than the restaurant, though the restaurant is about as bad as they come. The smoke-clogged air is charged with the anger that sparks from desolate lives. A very young girl – maybe thirteen – in skin-tight jeans and high-heeled white boots staggers towards her booth to the catcalls of toothless old men.

Arguments rage between people. With so many people berating one another, it is difficult to tell who is cursing out whom. Women at the greasy arborite tables are as drunk or stoned as the men, and as tough-looking. There are as many tragedies in this room as there are people. Charlie lives with this, in a small room at the top of the dun-coloured, rickety stairs. It is after midnight when I see his place for the first time. It's difficult to get a close look because there are no lights; the electrical outlets don't work. Light from a street lamp struggles through the greasy windows and through a hole where one of the panes is broken.

Three cockroaches are squashed on the turquoise wall, probably killed days earlier by a shoe. The peeling grey floor feels spongy underfoot, with valleys in the sagging floor-boards. The only furniture in the room is a cluttered kitchen table and a junky bedside table littered with half-empty bean cans. Nearby, a one-burner hotplate sits on an inverted white plastic pail. 'Can't do much cookin',' Charlie says flatly, 'because there's no electricity. Sometimes we run a cord from the ceiling fixture in the hallway, but first we got to turn off the hall light and make sure nothin' else is on in the other boarding rooms. Otherwise, all the power blows.'

Two stained pillows lie on shabby blankets crumpled on the floor – beds to Charlie and his roommate. 'We ordered welfare beds when we moved in three months ago. The worker said she'd put through a rush order, but we got no beds yet.' In one corner, a few sad-looking clothes hang on bent wire hangers. In another corner, a gurgling rad throws off a thin whisper of heat. 'My roommate hardly ever comes in because the room is so bad,' Charlie confesses, embarrassed.

Every month the landlord collects $300 for this room and for each of the six or seven like it in the building. There is easy money to be made from homelessness.

'What did your welfare worker say when she saw this room, Charlie?' I ask.

'She asked to see our rent receipt to make sure we were using our cheque to pay the rent. We gave her the receipt and she left. Didn't say nothin'.'

Charlie's room, however, isn't much worse than the room his grandfather rents for $400 dollars a month just blocks away on the run-down side of River Street, across from renovated Victorian homes on the fringe of trendy Cabbagetown. The hallway in Charlie's grandfather's boarding-house is putrid from fresh animal faeces and stale cigarette butts ground into the stairwell carpet. (I count ten rooms on two floors and hear sounds emanating from the basement. Somebody is making at least $4,000 a month from this tenement.) Grandfather's room has a filthy stove, a rusty sink, and pile of broken-down furniture.

The frail-looking man lies in bed, chain-smoking and flicking ashes into an overflowing bottle cap as he stares at a sitcom braying from a snowy black-and-white TV. The television is propped precariously on top of his rattling fridge. The old man is jovial. He seems pleased to have unexpected midnight visitors. He apologizes for not having drinks to offer us. He mumbles something about his daughter being Charlie's 'good mother,' and says Charlie is a 'good boy' who gets him groceries when he's sick.

Because he has 'a place' and isn't worried where he'll sleep this crisp autumn night, Charlie can do what he does most nights, prowl a small patch of the downtown corridor bounded by Gerrard, Yonge, Dundas, and River streets. He bums spare change, and when he has a few coins in hand goes into the nearest pinball arcade to play games. Or he drops into hang-outs, perhaps one of the all-night donut shops full of lonely, luckless men who live on sugar and small talk. Charlie mixes easily with ne'er-do-wells.

Later, on his rounds, he makes a stop at the kind of restaurant where most patrons have the black eyes and battered faces of men who fight and stumble a lot; the kind of restaurant where a twenty-dollar hooker patrols the dark hallway downstairs, outside the men's room, turning a two-minute trick to pay for the cold chili and warm beer she left on her table upstairs – the kind of place you wouldn't be in if you had any choices.

Warmed by coffee and cheered by the live entertainment – an old salt strumming Hank Williams favourites – Charlie goes back out into the cold to bum more change. Now and then he spots a truck unloading in a laneway. 'Let me unload that station wagon for ya,' Charlie implores the receiver. No luck. Farther along his route, in another laneway, he tries again to get a job hand-bombing (off-loading) delivery trucks. Again, no luck. At the Pinball Spot, a known pimp and pusher cracks (talks) to him, trying to sell him drugs. Charlie doesn't have the money; perhaps he doesn't have the interest either, since he claims he's clean.

'What would you rather be doing tonight than this, Charlie?' I ask.

'Sittin' home, watchin' TV – if I had a home or a TV.'

UPDATE: BEAT THE STREET GRADUATION CEREMONIES, 17 NOVEMBER 1989

I don't recognize him at first, but at second glance, I realize it's Charlie. He looks good, changed from our first meeting about a year ago. Well-groomed, dressed in a slick black shirt and tailored denims. Standing tall, he looks me in the eye and smiles. The jitters are still there, but much less so.

'Great to see you looking so good!'

'Everybody says that.' Charlie beams. He introduces me to Clayton, a paunchy, fiftyish-looking father figure. Clayton does most of the talking. He says he met Charlie when they were both renting rooms in the dismal place I visited. He shares a little about his own background. Orphanage-raised, he became a runaway and was a street hustler for many years. He knows Charlie's terrain well. Clayton has a twenty-year-old son who's on the streets now, though he just shakes his head in bewilderment when I ask why. 'I don't know. Maybe it was his upbringing, maybe it was the house rules. It's hard to raise kids.'

Clayton says he may not be able to help his own son, but perhaps he can help Charlie. 'You're wondering what's in it for me, right?' he asks.

'I see myself in these kids. I look at Charlie and I see myself when I was on the corner; I don't want him to have to go through what I went through.' Clayton is not prepared to expand on what he went through, but, whatever it was, he claims it's the reason he befriended Charlie and took him into his family. His family includes Clay's girlfriend and his ten-year-old daughter. He makes a number of disparaging remarks about his daughter 'turning out just like her mother,' but refuses to be more specific. It is a conversation with many blanks.

In addition to giving Charlie free room and board, he's helped him enrol in Futures, an upgrading program. A condo superintendent, Clayton is also training Charlie in janitorial work. Charlie boasts that he is now an assistant superintendent. For spending money, Charlie collects the small government stipend Futures students earn.

As we part, Charlie jokes about juggling his invitations to Christmas dinner – from Clay's family, from his grandfather, and from some friends. 'Sure is a lot better than last Christmas, eh?' He smiles at me.

Commonalities among Uncommon Kids

Each street kid is an original with individual persona, miseries, memories, and dreams. Sprinkled among their qualities, one finds, are the same human fortitude and frailty, intelligence and stupidity, generosity and mean-spiritedness, high-mindedness and gutter morality distributed randomly throughout the population. However, like members of most identifiable groups, no matter how heterogeneous, most street kids also share certain traits. About a dozen common threads run through the backgrounds, attitudes to life, self-perceptions, and desires of those interviewed for this book.

Betrayal is the most common experience among them. Like Eugene and Charlie, many street youths feel profoundly betrayed by significant adults, usually one or both parents, or surrogate parents assigned by the state. More often than not, runaways are throwaways, the refuse of families that, far from nurturing their young, at best ignore them, at worst, abuse them.

In the worst-case scenario, prevalent on the street, kids have had scarring experiences of both emotional and physical violence.

In this way, they have been well-initiated into the violence of street life. It is exceptional to find a teenager living downtown who has not witnessed a friend's death, often in his or her arms. Street kids know death and, as you will learn from their testimonies, some regard it as a liberator.

Although most have confronted, at a very early age, serious issues and challenges, street kids seem remarkably innocent. A bizarre blend of naïvety and maturity, they live fast-forward lives, while their mental and emotional development lags far behind. The result: unbalanced, distorted growth.

The imbalance usually begins at home. No matter what the particular family story, kids typically believe that one parent is a demon and the other a saint. As each story unravels, it usually emerges that the good parent, normally the mother, is being victimized as well. Often, to reassure themselves that one parent loves them, kids invent powerlessness for the good parent. Whether that parent is helpless or complicit, kids overlook her failure to rescue, empathizing with her real or imagined paralysis of fear.

This good guy–bad guy, female-male division is not universal. Eugene, for example, believes both parents ganged up on him, though he seems to feel his father's rejection more. Charlie, abused by his mother and neglected by his father – an atypical scenario – loves and forgives his ineffectual, non-rescuing parent.

Perhaps no one more clearly exemplifies the need to forgive the parent-accomplice than does Elly Danica, a Canadian writer whose father raped her and pimped for her when she was a little girl. Danica dedicated *Don't: A Woman's Word*, her brave public confession of her private humiliation, to (among others) her mother – a woman who was aware of the family's terrible secret, yet silently colluded. Danica believes that her mother had no choice but to comply.

While many street kids paint the family portrait with one villainous and one innocent parent, the finished picture usually reveals a parental style. Most often, rigidity, non-negotiable rules, strict demands, and high expectations govern that style, though the adult authority cannot or will not model how a child might achieve the standards required. These overly rigid families, like Eugene's, and rancorous families figure high on the list of grievances street kids vent.

Evelyn Lau, whose experiences are recorded in her autobiography *Runaway: Diary of a Street Kid*, is a perfect example. According to Lau, her parents fought incessantly, and they suffocated her with attempts to control her. Feeling disregarded and disrespected, Lau fled her family at age fourteen, preferring two years on Vancouver streets to the stranglehold her family tried to exert.

Coming from strict backgrounds, as many do, runaways add their voices to the street's chorus of hatred against anyone, whether parent, parent surrogate, or public agent, perceived as trying to control them. 'Perceived' is the critical word here, because many prostitutes, virtually enslaved by pimps, don't perceive their masters as controllers. From a distance, street kids understandably appear inexplicably wild. Close up, however, they prove to be wildly irrational for a reason. Theirs is not reflex rebellion, not an irresponsible demand for freedom. Rather, they react against constraints that remind them of the homes or institutions they have fled.

Although many street kids act cocky and self-assured, rock-bottom self-esteem usually lurks beneath this veneer. Most of the kids hate themselves. Devalued by their families, alienated by schools that may have treated them as failures and trouble-makers rather than as kids needing help, they learn their lessons well. Something is obviously wrong with them, they reckon; otherwise, they wouldn't deserve such hellish lives.

Guilt is typically their closest companion. Elly Danica captures the sense of guilt pervasive among incest victims and common among street kids who have been abused in other ways as well. Of one night, when she was eleven years old, after her father and his well-heeled, paying guests had used Elly for a pornography shoot and gang-bang, Danica writes:

I kneel beside the bed, blanket around my shoulders, I pray to be forgiven my sins. I pray that mother mary will understand why I had to let him do those things to me. I didn't mean to let him. I didn't want to let him. I know I did, but it was so he wouldn't hurt me anymore. I pray to be forgiven, and that she will understand that I don't have the courage of a martyr. I don't like to be hurt. I can't stand it when he hurts me. I am so afraid. I hope she will ask her son to forgive me for being a coward. I hope I didn't commit a mortal sin because I couldn't make him stop.[3]

The street is awash in Elly Danicas, convinced they are wicked children because they have been so abused. No matter which social class street kids come from, they tend to feel responsible for the crimes others perpetrated against them. Even non–street kids from privileged families, as Warner Troyer found in his study of 'divorced kids' (children of divorced families),[4] assume that family breakdown is their fault. Anger against themselves for being so bad forms the emotional corner-stone of their lives.

Elly Danica did not run away, though she desperately sought solutions by appealing to priests and relatives who could have, but did not, rescue her. Other kids deal with their splintered worlds by running away. Feeling bereft of personal power within their families, they lunge for control by fleeing.

Ironically, they run away to save themselves, yet typically end up in as much – if not more, albeit different – trouble as they were in at home. From the outset, runaways are endangered by the fact that they have almost nowhere to go. Without a network of safe, welcoming refuges across the country, they gravitate into the streets.

Unable to fathom the maelstrom of emotions percolating inside themselves, many kids succumb to flash-point tempers. The tempers flare without warning when kids reach breaking-points they don't understand. Their terrible hurt expresses itself as terrible anger, most often destructive to themselves and sometimes to others as well.

Only a thread separates victim from perpetrator. While most kids come to the street as victims, many can survive only by becoming perpetrators of crimes. Most of these kids have never known anything but violations of their person; oppressing others presents itself as a natural way of behaving. As Evelyn Lau discovered, 'You learn selfishness on the streets by beginning to understand how ugly other people can be, and realizing that the only way to survive is to take as much as you can get.'[5]

To be street smart is to distrust everyone. 'You have to watch your back, or you will get beat up or sliced [knifed]. You cannot trust anyone on the street,'[6] said one young man, reciting the code that echoes along the downtown track. 'The code is very simple: intimidate or be intimidated, seduce or be seduced, get over on or be gotten over on, do it to somebody else first – and make sure you get paid. Don't believe anybody.'[7]

Despite distrust, and despite betrayal by the most important adults in their lives, street kids routinely desire family reconciliation more than they savour revenge. The majority of youths interviewed for this book, though sometimes torn by love-hate conflicts, hunger to go home again, if only to visit, in peace and with dignity. Eugene, for example, flummoxed by what went wrong, is fixated on his family. Until he reconnects with his parents in a way, however tenuous, that makes him feel accepted, he may not find a moment's peace. Even Charlie wonders where his mother is and, despite the evidence of his tortured time with her, clings to the apparent fiction that she cares about him.

Surprisingly, most kids crave a conventional family. They dream of creating an idyllic nuclear unit with themselves as perfect partners and parents. To chase away the emotional havoc gnawing away at them, they imagine the fantasy family they never had. Most street girls seem to want, more than anything else, to have babies. Practically every young woman who contributed to this study had given birth by her mid to late teens. Their babies were fathered by boyfriends – often homeless adolescents like themselves – or by pimps – posing as boyfriends. Most became pregnant neither through ignorance of birth control nor by accident. The majority ultimately gave up their babies for adoption – often after a failed attempt to keep and look after the infants – or lost them involuntarily when children's aid societies intervened. Yet, most girls began their pregnancies in the thrall of a family fantasy.

As you will see from their stories, getting their lives together almost invariably means the pursuit of prosaic goals, from high-school diplomas or trades training to decent jobs and decent wages. In the street kid's mind, a satisfying life usually shapes up in the form of a suburban bungalow shared with a husband or wife and 2.5 kids. On the whole, street kids don't measure up to their misbegotten image as free-wheeling revellers who love life on the wild side.

Not only do many of these kids ache to tame their own turbulent lives, they also brood about misfortune in the lives around them. At least half of the young people questioned spoke at length about their desire to help others. Many dream of becoming a youth worker, a plan they rarely attach to formal education. Rather, they talk about helping from the heart. Like Eugene, they invariably separate the social work they want to practise from conventional social work, which they disdain. Given their antipathy to helping professionals, and the broken trust most have suffered, the degree to which street kids believe in human kindness is astounding.

Other studies have found the same caring inclinations among dispossessed people. When the authors of *Street People Speak* asked adult males, average age thirty-three, living on Toronto streets what wishes they most cherished, they were astonished by the number who counted among their priorities the desire to help less-fortunate people. With only three wishes, two-thirds of the men had at least one wish for the world at large or for people other than themselves.[8]

Unlike Eugene, however, most street people express their concern in apolitical terms. They talk about helping others in the way they desperately wish someone would care about them, as individuals. Consumed by the struggle to survive day-to-day, most have little intellectual room for big ideas of human rights and social justice. Beyond saving themselves, they cleave to dreams of rescuing some other disposable child shucked off by society and family.

Why Kids Run Away

Public and expert opinion offer a hotchpotch of views as to why kids run away from home.[9] Some see adolescent runaways as incapable, dropping out or running away because of personal inadequacies. Others hold the family unit responsible for the youth's flight from home and school. Still others believe that kids run away because parents neglect or abuse them, and because child-protection agencies fail to mend broken families or to find workable alternatives for their kids.

None of these conventional explanations is wrong. But taken singularly or together, they do not explain why so many kids are on the street. Blaming the child harkens back to more socially unconscious times. Yet, in a way, blaming the victim has its merits. It is true that runaways, unlike kids who stay put in families where they are deeply unhappy, refuse to adjust, and choose, instead, to flee. In this sense only, there is something 'wrong' with runaways; they are, indeed, stubborn and rebellious. Their non-conformity drives their attempt to rescue themselves from intolerable circumstances, however dead-end their efforts.

The idea that families are responsible is, in the immediate sense, valid. Like Eugene and Charlie, all the youths interviewed fled families they describe as seriously impaired. Though ·the nature and degree of dysfunction varies, all the kids felt spurned. Not one ran from a family where the child felt loved, wanted, and safe. All claimed that various caregivers, usually male, abused them. Survivors of incest and other sexual violations, plus survivors of an imaginative menu of physical and emotional tortures, occur as commonly as drugs in the street. As you will see, family violence, most often a euphemism for male violence, constitutes the main well-spring of adolescent grief that triggers running away.

It must be underscored, however, that not all street kids have been raped or beaten by their fathers or father figures, neglected by their mothers, or abandoned by their siblings and extended families. Kids end up on the skids for a constellation of reasons, sometimes despite the best efforts of their parents. From the child's vantage point, his or her parents' best may not be good enough. It is one thing for adults to feel satisfied that they did the best they could for the child. It is quite another for a child who feels unloved to be able to rationalize parents' limitations.

Finally, among conventional explanations for why kids run away is the charge that child-protection services don't work for most troubled kids, neither salvaging families at risk nor rescuing and repairing damaged youngsters. Journalist Martyn Kendrick, himself a graduate of protection and corrections, has shown the system to be fundamentally flawed.

In *Nobody's Children: The Foster Care Crisis in Canada*, Kendrick describes how the state fails to provide children in care with the one thing they most need – love.[10] Instead of guaranteeing them a human touch-stone in the form of at least one reliable, loving adult, the system, by design, guarantees only transience. It shunts kids through a series of temporary, often incapable, families instructed not to bond with their young charges.

In addition, it is common practice for a string of professionals to manage each 'case,' leaving kids adrift with no social worker to call their own. The street, Kendrick argues, has become an integral part of the system, just another predictable stop along the circuit of care. It is not surprising, therefore, to discover that many, maybe most, street kids are products of the child-protection system. Among those interviewed for this book, only a fraction had not experienced the state's help.

All the partially true explanations ignore the economic, social, and moral foundation on which faltering families, failing schools, and inept social and correctional services totter. These explanations skirt the imperatives of private profit and patriarchy that govern our society, as if fall-out from both did not affect how human services are conceived and funded or how families function. This book roots itself in the belief that it is impossible to understand the phenomenon of street kids within the myopic context of disabled social services and distressed families.

Society's failure to nourish families, the failure of some families to nurture its kids, and the failure of helping agencies to take up the slack is a chain reaction. It begins in the very fabric of the economic and social order, in the values and priorities that order weaves. Families and safety nets are simply most visible in a chain of failings that predispose some kids to a lifetime of trouble in which running away is only one stage.

Although these are times of great prosperity in Canada, greater wealth for the few at the cost of greater poverty for the many hardly constitutes true prosperity. Economic Council of Canada research has shown that middle-income earners (today in the $30,000 to $60,000 range) are decreasing. In 1967, they constituted 27.4 per cent of the population. By 1986, they had shrunk to 21.5

per cent. The council also discovered that labour income per worker was 2 per cent higher in real terms a decade ago than it is today.[11] Poverty, not wealth, has trickled down.

The upsurge in homelessness, especially among the young, is only one measure of the decline abundance has heralded. Poorest families, though the most besieged, are not the only victims of our chaotic economy. People previously able to make a get-by living have inherited pressures that have always pinched the poor: the exorbitant cost of necessities, and the frustrations of not being able to afford the stunning array of products advertised as the substance of a worthwhile life. Mother-led families in particular reel from the impact of overwork, underpay, high costs, and the paucity of affordable, adequate childcare.

While youngsters from the poorest and most pressured families seem to predominate on the streets, affluent kids are not immune. Adolescents from ostensibly solid, able, loving families in all social classes now funnel into street life. A minority of kids who hide out full-time downtown come from rich homes. More often than not, neglect, physical abuse, or incest lurks in their background. Their parents, often professionals, present a polished image, making it hard for outsiders to suspect them of terrible misdeeds. None the less, their offspring, if they are on more than an adolescent lark, usually have horrific tales to tell.

Like all families, those of street kids reflect the values abroad in the larger society. No family can operate as a cosy vacuum sealed off from forces shaping the world outside its door. Given the strains of modern life, especially the uncertainties of work and relationships, it is little wonder, therefore, that many families are shaky. Even otherwise unremarkable families polarized in tugs of war over the kids and property as the unit breaks up are not always able to communicate love and keep the kids within the fold.

If a society invests billions to promote escape, excess, and self-indulgence, it should come as no surprise when some families fall prey to demoralization. If patriarchal society socializes males to covet power, then denies most except rich men access to any real power, it does not surprise when some males pummel women and molest children. If the culture, driven by profit and patriarchy, worships power and often eroticizes violence, what surprise can the results bring?

The existence of street kids is inextricably linked to male violence, and to sexism and racism. Solving the problem of street kids is, therefore, inseparable from the task of expunging these toxins from society. It is also inseparable from the challenge of eradicating poverty and unemployment. It cannot be tackled in isolation from the need to re-create schools and human services. In sum, creating economic and social conditions that foster healthy individuals may be the only way to ensure society will stop neglecting and abusing children and spitting them into the street.

In the absence of a just, egalitarian social system driven by human needs rather than by private profit, quick fixes for complex problems remain elusive. However, successful approaches to helping some kids beat the streets are accessible. This book's conclusion tackles the question of how to rescue runaways before the street ensnares them. It suggests what can be done to reclaim some young lives seemingly lost in a wasteland of pain.

2

Destroyed and Destroying Families

Jessie: Fat, ugly, and stupid

We meet in an office at her Halifax group home, superficially a typical house in an ordinary neighbourhood, substantially a mini-institution. Trim, in tight jeans, Jessie sits across from me, fidgeting in an overstuffed old chair. A conventionally pretty, baby-faced blonde with startling brown eyes, Jessie could have stepped out of *Seventeen* magazine. Obviously bright, she is easy to like. I have to suppress a laugh when she confesses that she sees herself as fat, ugly, and stupid. She does not see in any mirror, including the mirror of her mind, what others see. Rather, Jessie sees the picture her parents projected of her.

Jessie is the elder of two children from a comfortable middle-class family in rural Nova Scotia. According to Jessie, her father, a store manager, is an alcoholic ('he drinks every night and all weekend'), a 'mind-bender,' and a beater. Her mother is a 'slave ruled by him. Sometimes she cried when he beat me, but because she couldn't stand up to him, she ended up on his side. When he wasn't around, I felt we had a warm bond between us, but I could never trust my mother because, the minute he entered the room, she'd turn into his slave again.'

It was after a family feud. Jessie was seven years old, sobbing 'You don't love me' to her parents, when her father first beat her. 'After that, he never stopped; he beat me almost daily. He'd beat me with a closed fist or his belt, mostly on my face. One time, on Hallowe'en, the bruises were so bad that my mother made me wear a costume and put pancake make-up on my face before I left for school in the morning, even though we weren't supposed to dress up till afternoon. I felt silly sitting in class, the only kid in a costume. At lunch, she touched up my make-up and told me: "If it washes off when you bob for apples, say your face is bruised because you're allergic to make-up." '

Both of Jessie's parents repeatedly told her that she was un-loved and undesirable. 'No child of theirs could be like me. According to my father, I was just plain bad. Born bad. I didn't have to do anything to bring on a beating. Sometimes he'd invent excuses. Like, if he heard that drugs were going around at school, he'd accuse me of using them. He'd scream at me, stuff like "You worthless brat. You're going to be a drug addict when you grow up!" I didn't know what a joint was, and I hadn't even tasted liquor, but that didn't stop him from believing everything bad about me.'

Jessie says her dad beat her younger brother occasionally but reserved severe, frequent beatings for her. Her father imposed strict rules on Jessie, but none on her brother. He couldn't do wrong; she couldn't do right.

'My parents are very rigid people, and what's that word when you know everything that's right to do and believe in, and everyone else is ignorant? ... "Righteous," that's it. They're very righteous.' For Jessie's parents, everything was black and white, in more ways than one. 'My parents hate black people and tried to make us believe ugly lies. They were always telling us that black people smell, that they're dangerous, that they're killers. We lived in a small town where everyone knew everyone, and people mixed together. I had white friends and black friends. I didn't care what colour my friends were. I was just happy to be part of a group that accepted me like I was, that didn't seem to think I was fat, ugly, and stupid. If a black friend called and my father answered the phone, he'd call them "nigger" and slam down the receiver. Then he'd fly at me, hollering, "It's them or us. Choose!" '

Most of my interviews with street kids included no third parties. Interviewing Jessie was unusual because her counsellor joined us, the group home's pre-condition for our meeting. I worried that a chaperon might inhibit Jessie but, as it turned out, the strength of their relationship was a support. Her counsellor's comments about Jessie's background echoed what Jessie herself described.

The counsellor, an empathic woman in her thirties, relayed incidents when both she and Jessie had tried to involve the parents with their daughter. 'They just kept saying "no." It didn't matter whether it was material support – like paying for a train ticket for Jessie to return from Montreal one time when she ran away and the house didn't have emergency cash – or the emotional support of knowing she could turn to her family when she's feeling low. They've said "no" to every overture. Her parents contend that the courts "own" Jessie, by which they mean that she is on probation and in the care of Children's Aid.

They constantly point out how embarrassed they are by her, how they want her doings and her whereabouts kept secret.

'True to middle-class form,' the counsellor continues, 'they seem like nice people. In jargon, they "present" well. That made it harder for me to see the truth about them, but after repeatedly scraping Jessie off the floor when they've finished with her on the phone, and after my own attempts to involve them, I realized what Jessie's up against. It's heart-breaking to watch her being rejected and hurt by adults who can't meet her half-way in her attempts to reconcile ... Like all the kids here, Jess desperately wants to go home, wants to fix her family, make it right.'

I was thirteen the first time I ran. That time, I wandered around our town all night. The second night I hid in a friend's basement. On the third day, my father caught me, or maybe I let him find me because it was too scary on the street alone. My parents grounded me. For two months, I wasn't allowed to leave my room, except to go to school. After that, I ran away every chance I got. I used an abandoned ticket-booth for my hideaway. For warmth, I had a sleeping-bag. I stole groceries, cigarettes, and clothes and stashed them in my booth. Because I was alone – there were no real street kids in my town – I'd get lonesome and try to phone my brother. But, whenever I was on the run, my parents would keep a sharp eye on him to make sure we couldn't talk to each other or get together. I think they wanted to break my heart more than it was already broken.

I couldn't go to school because the police would be on the look-out for me. Instead, I'd keep on the move between malls and donut shops, and I'd hitch rides to nearby towns. Sometimes the police would pick me up and they'd ask why I was always running away. I was terrified of getting my parents in trouble, maybe even jailed, so I'd say, 'I'm just a problem child; I don't know why,' which is exactly how my parents explained it. Or they'd say that I ran because I was rebelling against rules. They didn't explain what those rules were, or how badly my dad beat me even when I didn't break them.

I'd be gone anywhere from one night to one month. It was lonely, but it was still better than home. Between runs, I'd catch up on school work enough to get passing grades.

The last time I left home, age fifteen, I took $135 from my mother's purse. She pressed charges against me. My own mother! After court, I couldn't face going home any more, so I went to Children's Aid and

they put me in a foster home. I can't describe to you how filthy that
home was, way worse than my ticket booth! If all CAS could do was
dump me in some dirty house with dirty people that didn't care, I felt
I had no choice left but to get away from my town.

Jessie hitch-hiked to Halifax, where older street-wise teenagers,
savvy at exploiting rookies, picked her up. Given her exceptional
looks, her small-town innocence, and her emotional neediness, it
is pure luck that these rounders were petty criminals but not
pimps. Had she arrived in Toronto or Vancouver, her story
would have been different.

Jessie moved into an overcrowded basement apartment (rent:
$450) with 'rats and rattling pipes, bare bulbs hanging from low
ceilings,' and was indoctrinated by her older female room-mates
into the craft of lumpen survival: shoplifting; drug-dealing; theft;
acting as a 'runner' (courier) for her pals. Jessie was still fifteen
when the police picked her and her friends up in a stolen car.

'Even though I was still a minor, they moved me from one
facility to another in handcuffs and shackles. I'd lied, said I was
nineteen, but anyone with eyes could see I was underage. I went
through their whole rigmarole without any feelings. Hard as a
rock. I'd laugh off every question, spit "I don't care what you do
to me" in their faces. In my mind, I was a "bad little criminal"
[one of her father's expressions] getting what I deserved.'

Jessie was placed on probation and permitted by the court to
live with two of her former friends, bad little criminals themselves. She ended up back in the same basement hole, in the
same life. During this period she was raped by a young man she
knew who broke into apartment when Jessie was home alone.
She didn't report the rape. 'What for? Who would believe me – a
bad kid who hangs out with fringey people?' Jessie spent her
sixteenth birthday in a correctional centre before being court-
ordered into the group home where she now lives.

Living in a group setting has not been easy. 'By the time I was
sent here, I had stopped caring about anything. I was using
drugs, acid mostly, anything to escape. In here, I had to learn to
live on welfare's so-called comfort allowance of twenty-two
dollars a month. I wanted to go home. I missed my brother
terribly, and I kept wondering if there was some magic that

could make my family better, like the Cosby family or something. I did go home for two visits; it was horrible as ever, and I came back here depressed.'

Since Jessie moved into the house, her life has taken on a pattern that goes something like this: with the support of a few group-home adults she 'sort-of' trusts, Jessie struggles to make it. She works hard at school. She shuns drugs and her old circle of petty offenders. Feeling better, she begins to long for her family. She calls home, or goes home to visit. Then the emotional downturn begins.

The pain of having parents who do not accept, want, or love her swallows her. Self-hate takes over. When she is down on herself, the street beckons, as do drugs and 'life on the edge.' She goes back to the street in search of a rush to transport her momentarily into an emotional high. When the hardship of the street wears her thin, she crashes and returns to the group home.

Jessie balances precariously between these two dissimilar worlds. The street world both confirms her parents' prophecy and allows her to lash back at them. The 'straight' world teases out a suspected self-worth and self-respect.

Jessie has what seems like a rock-solid support in her counsellor. Although group homes are imperfect substitutes for loving families, she is none the less in an environment that accepts her as she is, that does not blame her for the path she has strayed onto, and that supports her unsteady attempts to grow.

Genuine, not ritualized, caring surrounds her. Understandably, Jessie does not move easily into close, trusting relationships. 'I never let anyone get near me. I'm afraid that if they see the real me (the fat, ugly, stupid me), they'll back off.' While she thinks too little of herself to let anyone too close, she often thinks too much of people who don't deserve her respect. Her counsellor points out that 'Jessie needs to believe there's good in everyone, even in parasites who would use her. Her parents are extremely judgmental, so she's out to prove that everyone has some redeeming qualities.'

Jessie cuts in. 'I admit I have certain friends I like to hang out with when I'm in a wicked mood, and yes, some of them are dealers and pimps who would even have me working the streets if I was willing. In one way, I don't trust them at all, but in another way I like them. They have criminal records just like me;

who am I to judge them?' Her counsellor can always detect when Jessie is flirting with her old life because 'she becomes very hard-looking, wears gobs of make-up, and the gloomy side of her really comes out.'

Our interview is winding down when I realize how little we've spoken of sex, except for Jessie's awkward, whispered allusion to the rape. I ask about boyfriends. Her candidness evaporates. Her voice lowers, and she rivets her eyes to the ground. 'Guys only want one thing,' Jessie whimpers, 'and even though I don't get anything out of it – it makes me feel dirty and used – I, well, I go along. Maybe sex could be better, but I don't think it could ever be fantastic like it is on TV.' Questioning evokes nothing but broad statements from Jessie, but I learn that she is involved in Services for Sexual Assault Victims (SSAV) and that the rape was only one of her many unwanted experiences.

Jessie still has a long struggle ahead to achieve the stability that comes with self-esteem. But she has taken tough first steps: school attendance and good grades; more time with her straight friends, less time with her fringe friends; more acceptance of a family she cannot change. It is a beginning. 'I still don't feel very good about myself and I still get depressed. I guess there will always be ups and downs, but it's easier to get up now and to stay up.'

Dangerous Homes

Most of us think of home as a safe place. However, for many women and children, home is a minefield. Child abuse or other symptoms of serious family impairment afflict an estimated 20 to 40 per cent of Canadian families.[1] They harm children in a remarkable number of ways, ranging from neglect to physical abuse, to mental and emotional torture, to sexual travesties. It is tempting to assume that violently handled children will become more psychologically disturbed and more antisocial than will children from less overtly brutal backgrounds. Testimonies in this book and elsewhere do not support this assumption. Surprising as it may seem, neglect can be as devastating as cigarette burns and rape.

All abuse, whether emotional, physical, or sexual, is an abuse of power, a distortion of the natural authority adults possess over children. Because one controls and the other is controlled, their relationship contains a fundamental inequity that incapable or irresponsible adults can exploit. Rix Rogers, special adviser on child sexual abuse to the federal health department, has found that most abusers enjoy a position of trust with their victims.[2] University of Alberta psychology professor Dick Sobsey has found that physically and mentally disabled Canadians are two to ten times more likely than the general population to suffer abuse, often at the hands of their paid, institutional caregivers.[3] Experts agree that family insiders, plus outsiders who occupy authoritative, respected roles *vis-à-vis* youngsters – people such as priests, teachers, baby-sitters, scout masters, and hockey coaches – pose the greatest risk to children.[4]

Since 1987, that jeopardy has been dramatically illustrated in Canada with a spate of criminal charges and sex-offence convictions against priests and Protestant clergy, lay Catholic brothers, former priests and clergy, as well as a few teachers and social workers. The fiasco focused first on the recently closed Mt Cashel Orphanage in Newfoundland, but soon expanded to include Saskatchewan's Bosco Children's Homes; St Joseph's Training School in Alfred, Ontario; St John's Home for Boys in Uxbridge, Ontario; and residential schools imposed until recently on aboriginal children. Revelations of sexual, emotional, and physical brutality against children by their caregivers have now become commonplace.

Individuals charged tend to have held power over their victims, including, in one case, male social workers charged with sexually abusing female welfare recipients on their caseload. In the orphanage and residential-school situations, the alleged and convicted molesters and paedophiles enjoyed not only conventional adult authority over the children they violated, but also the protection of a hallowed institution, the church.

Snippets of testimony reported in the media from some of Mt Cashel's survivors echoed experiences and feelings many street kids express in these pages. The street kids, too, found themselves victimized by powerful adults hiding behind the bulwark of another isolated institution, the family.

To children, an abusing parent can be mystifying as well as frightening. How can it be, the child wonders, that someone who supposedly loves you and takes care of you does bad things to you? 'It is hard for us to imagine the utter confusion they are thrown into by the father who provides for, protects, loves and rapes them. How to comprehend the terror at his approach, *and* the terror that he will abandon them; or their blank despondency when the mother, the teacher, the police, the court, will not believe them, when the psychiatrist, wagging a knowing finger at them, says he's onto their "tricks." '[5]

'The incestuous relationship between father and child is particularly complex because there is more often than not a degree of tenderness, and the child is therefore driven into a perverted kind of love.'[6] The abuser's deceitful personality complicates an already befuddling reality. To make matters worse, 'the child's sense of being exploited and abused is disqualified by the adult, and the child is led to feel responsible for the abusive events.'[7] It is not surprising, therefore, that Jessie blames herself, confessing to police that she runs away because she is a 'problem child.'

Victims commonly equate love with abuse. One youngster expressed that confusion this way: 'After they used to whip me, they'd always say, "We did it because we love you" ... That confused me about what love was.'[8] According to press reports on the royal commission inquiry into the Mt Cashel charges, former resident Shane Earle testified that Brother Joseph Burke frequently and brutally beat him, then gave him a lollipop. Earle said he couldn't hate the brother because the man made him feel 'special.'

The same 'love is abuse' refrain runs through *The Violent Years of Maggie MacDonald*: 'I must have thought that the beatings that Bobby [the boy next door who fathered one of her children] gave me were love, because I remember telling a friend, "If I don't have a black eye, I don't think he cares, because it means that he's ignoring me." '[9] MacDonald, the product of a destroyed and destroying family, who later murdered two very violent husbands, says she thought of herself from a young age as a bad kid who deserved to be beaten.

While some adults defile children in every conceivable way, most children love their parents in return. Some, like Jessie, even protect them from authorities who might intervene if they were made aware of the abuse. Canadian journalist Victor Malarek, as both his autobiography, *Hey Malarek!*, and the film *Malarek* based on it reveal, was desperately attached to his drunken father, the man who lacerated his wife, shunned and terrified his two sons, and ultimately destroyed the family. Malarek is not alone in his need to love and forgive his feckless father.

It seems that abusers, consciously or unconsciously, count on their victims' deep-seated need to believe theirs is a special relationship. They exploit and pervert the genuine love their victims feel, knowing they can apologize later and emerge little worse than lapsed heroes.

Since 1987, every jurisdiction across the country, except New Brunswick, has had some form of centralized child-abuse register. However, definitions and reporting criteria vary according to jurisdiction. In addition, no centralized index of suspected and verified abuse exists. As a result, a reliable statistical overview of child abuse in Canada remains elusive.

None the less, the provincial data reveal country-wide trends. More girls than boys under age seventeen are abused (the ratio is about two to one). Girls are twice as likely as are boys to be sexually assaulted, while boys are more likely to be beaten up. Males perpetrate 70 to 85 per cent of child battery and sexual assault reported in this country. (Other researchers, such as Rix Rogers, claim that more than 90 per cent of offenders are men.) In 1987, Nova Scotia recorded a combined total of 209 cases of physical and sexual abuse; Quebec, 1,884; Ontario, 1,784; and Manitoba, 1,526. In the 1987–8 fiscal year, British Columbia recorded 26,283 cases of abuse. (This number, far exceeding those recorded in other provinces, dramatically illustrates the jurisdictional discrepancies in defining and recording abuse.)[10]

Since most abuse is hidden, we can safely assume that these numbers represent only a fraction of actual incidences. Even so, these figures are higher than those cited even four years earlier. For example, Ontario's 54 child-welfare agencies investigated about 14,000 allegations of child abuse in 1987, more than double the 1983 rate of 6,383.[11]

The 1984 report of the Committee on Sexual Offences against Children and Youth (the Badgley Report) found among its sample that one in two girls and one in three boys had been victims of sexual offences.[12] The 1982 National Population Survey found that 29 per cent of female victims were aged seven to eleven when first violated.[13] Forty per cent of confirmed sex-abuse victims treated in 1988 at Toronto's Hospital for Sick Children were age six or younger.[14] Recent research estimates that 25 per cent of females and 10 per cent of males are sexually abused at least once before age seventeen.[15]

Among street kids, the abuse count is much higher. A 1984 Covenant House study found that 73 per cent of their sample had been beaten at home. Thirty-eight per cent of the male runaways and 73 per cent of the females had been molested.[16]

A survey conducted for the Ontario Ministry of Community and Social Services suggests that physical and sexual abuse in foster homes occurs as frequently or more frequently than in the general population.[17] Children with developmental disabilities living in institutions, foster homes, and other extra-familial arrangements face heightened risk of abuse. It is estimated that up to 68 per cent of girls and 30 per cent of boys will be victims before their eighteenth birthday.[18]

Frightening data about northern native girls surfaced in 1989 in a study co-sponsored by the Northwest Territories Native Women's Association and the Social Services Department.[19] Survey results showed that eight out of ten girls under age eight are victims of sexual abuse, and that five out of ten boys the same age are molested. Most offenders are age fifteen to twenty-five, and most were victims themselves, the study says.

While some data are current and some dated, comparisons of them lead to one conclusion: there is no evidence that numbers are diminishing. On the contrary. Kids running in unprecedented numbers to the street indicate that a significant minority of families are in ruin. Street kids signal that some parents and parent substitutes, mostly fathers and father figures, are clobbering kids in their care.

Most assault takes place within the family. Among the almost 10,000 verified child-abuse cases in Ontario between 1979 and 1986, 77 per cent of perpetrators came from the immediate family, 14 per cent from the extended family. Only 9 per cent were outsiders, some known to the victim, some strangers.[20] The creepy stranger who lurks around playgrounds does exist. However, the real danger lurks closer to home.

Since men commit most of the abuse, and since they do it in the privacy of the home, it is hard to assess just how much the incidence of child abuse has increased, though reporting has soared. According to *Heroes of Their Own Lives: The Politics and History of Family Violence*, incidence has not changed much over the last century. However, social concern about violence within the family has fluctuated with the fates of feminism. When the women's movement wields influence, as it does today, concern runs high. In the past, when the movement has been weak, revelation of and protest against abuse have been more muted.[21]

Feminists point out that the home is one locus of male power and female powerlessness, and that male violence within the family is culturally accepted,[22] even though formally criminal. Among the small numbers of men charged, those convicted normally receive light sentences. For example, of fourteen cases of sex crimes against children reported in the *Toronto Star* between September 1984 and July 1985, seven offenders received jail sentences of three months or less, two to be served on weekends.[23]

Fourteen of thirty-four priests recently charged with sexually assaulting children have been convicted. One was acquitted. Another, who previously served two years for one of many charges made against him over the many years the church shuffled him from one diocese to another, died in custody. The rest are awaiting trial. Sentences for nine of those already convicted range from probation to eight months, to five years in one case. The priest who received eight months pleaded guilty to seven counts of assaulting altar boys aged eleven to thirteen.[24]

Far from receiving even light sentences, most abusive men are never caught. They carry on with impunity, protected by the sanctity of the home as a man's castle, or by the powerful respect accorded to state- and church-run substitutes. Ironically, the violence commonly uproots the victims, not the perpetrators. Male batterers episodically force women and children to flee into shelters while the men remain at home. When child-welfare authorities suspect or confirm abuse, they remove the child, leaving the criminal in the house.

Many street kids originate from this situation. Their fathers' crimes, even if detected, go un- or underpunished. Instead, kids are taken away from offending fathers and placed in other, often hostile environments. They risk ending up on the street. Their dads risk little, typically ending up in the family home.

Of course, women abuse children too. As you saw from Charlie's story and as you will see from other testimonies, mothers are as chillingly capable as violent fathers of devastating their children. In her study of violence in the family, American historian Linda Gordon encountered 'extremely violent and cruel women, as well as women whose passivity was sometimes literally murderous toward their children.'[25] Gordon describes situations evocative of Elly Danica's home where Father raped and Mother knew but didn't intercede.

No matter who abuses, the underlying dynamics remain the same. The powerful prey on the less powerful, the weak on the weaker. However, as data cited earlier show, there is no real competition between men and women as child abusers. Many men abuse women and children in their control, whereas relatively few women vent their frustrations on the only people more powerless than themselves: children. Considering women's far greater contact with and responsibility for children, especially the exclusive child-rearing burden on large numbers of single mothers, it is unfair to speak of male and female child abusers in the same breath.

Many kids don't report their abusers. Like Jessie, they may fear the consequences for their parents or for themselves. Others, again like Jessie, who don't report rape, fear no one will believe them. Yet, many cry out for help. Street kids tell of appealing to police or of being picked up by police after running away from abusing adults. Among youths surveyed for this book, many claimed they turned to authorities for protection from natural parents, step-parents, or foster- and group-home parents. Most, like Eugene, saw no evidence of being believed or protected. Rather, they ended up like Jessie: back in their unsafe families or surrogate families, delivered there by justice and childcare authorities who apparently concurred with adult claims that the kids were lying.

According to press reports, in testimony presented at the Mt Cashel hearing, victims had confided in some teachers and police officers. Apparently, even some senior social-services and justice officials had been alerted to the child endangerment kids claimed was rampant at the orphanage. Yet, no one took effective action.

That is not to suggest that child-welfare authorities do not normally investigate battery charges. They are inundated with allegations of abuse, many of which are hard, if not impossible, to corroborate. They are handicapped by miserly budgets, narrow mandates, scarce resources, and overburdened staff. Especially given the dearth of safe, loving alternative placements, the decision to remove a child can be tricky. It is particularly so in a society that idealizes the intact, nuclear family and trusts state- and church-run alternatives.

Even among child-abuse cases on the provincial registers, the journey from suspicion to proof is arduous. Legal convictions are hard to obtain because courts often consider children incompetent witnesses. By contrast, many mothers and therapists of incest victims insist that children rarely invent fairy-tales of battery and rape. (At the same time, no one can deny that false reporting by children and adults occurs – especially during custody battles – and can ruin the lives of those charged, guilty or not.)

I Am One of Them: Mothers Speak Out about Incest,[26] a video documentary, points out that, like authorities, even non-offending parents, usually mothers, sometimes doubt the children's claims. Even when incest confessions are believed, mothers often bear the blame, while most offenders go free. Mother-blaming echoes in the common questions: 'What kind of mother are you? How could *you let* your husband do that to your child?' When one mother profiled in the film reported her husband's molestation of their child, police investigated *her* background. Speaking at a Toronto YMCA public screening, the angry mother said, 'I kept saying to the police: "My daughter is the victim of a crime committed by my husband. Why are you investigating *me*?"'

Mother-blaming is traditional. 'They've been accused of sexual coldness, of being emotionally or physically absent from the home, even of knowing of the abuse and silently "colluding" with the offender in order to preserve the family. Such accusations have been built up from courts, schools, therapists, other family members, as well as from the bitter memories of incest survivors who have often spent years, even decades, repressing their terrible secret.'[27]

The suggestion that women and children invite male violence against themselves, that they are somehow responsible for the harms others do to them, is widespread. The myth of the seductive child was recently reinforced by British Columbia county-court judge Peter Van Der Hoops. He awarded a suspended sentence to thirty-three-year-old Delbert Leeson who admitted to sexually touching a three-year-old girl. The judge said the toddler had been 'sexually aggressive.' Commenting publicly after the Newfoundland priests were convicted of molesting altar boys, Nova Scotia archbishop Colin Campbell said that the boys could have said no.[28]

Imagine Charlie saying no to his rapist stepfather, or Jessie saying no to her warped father, or Gilette – who speaks next – saying no to the adults who twisted his personality. Choice is the perpetrator's prerogative; choosing to run away may be the child's only way of saying no.

Gilette: On a torturous path

Gilette wasn't yet born when hippies smoked pot and romped barefoot in public parks, their long hair and diaphanous robes swirling around them. He wasn't born when 1960s activists fought for civil rights and against America's war in Vietnam, and protested against the gospel of materialism the United States was exporting around the globe.

But his parents, like those of a significant number of today's West Coast street kids, had firsthand experience of the 1960s. Offspring of these leftover hippies – Canadian-born and American émigré – describe parents who rode the coat-tails of a movement, hedonistic revellers for whom hippiedom was a permit to do their own thing. According to their kids, they weren't so much concerned with protesting against racism or imperialism as they were with blowing their minds on psychedelic drugs. 'I think my mom stopped growing up when she started growing her marijuana plants,' Gilette says. 'She took care of her ganga better than she took care of her kids.'

Like some progeny of similar parents, Gilette ambles among the lost, nihilistic punkers who drift in a haze of hatreds, looking as ashen as holocaust survivors. They wear regulation black – from their Doc Marten paratrooper-style boots to their dyed spiked hair. Every statement they utter is as grim as their uniforms.

Seventeen, armoured with a dozen tiny gold ear and nose rings, cross-and-skull ornaments studding his black leather biker's jacket, Gilette is fairly typical. When I met this emaciated-looking young man in Vancouver in autumn 1988, he spoke about his nomadic childhood. 'Until my mom and dad split up when I was six, we travelled constantly around the interior of BC in a beat-up old pick-up. Sometimes we lived in tents. Probably didn't stay put anywhere more than six months at a time.' Why all the travelling? 'They were hippies and that's what hippies do. They grow their hair long, their weed high and wild, and they hit the road.'

Gilette does not remember family fights or tensions, 'but there was no closeness either.' He recounts his memories in monotone, his expression as lifeless as the existence he describes. 'I don't think I noticed it when my dad left us.' After the split, he, his mother, and his little sister moved to Idaho, where his 'rich grandparents – from stocks and stuff, not from working' – supported the threesome. Eventually, his mother got a job as a cook and was rarely around. 'Me and my sister had the house to ourselves. There was no discipline, but I didn't need it 'cause I wasn't a bad kid.'

Left to his own devices, Gilette spent a lot of time brooding in his bedroom and experimenting with black eye make-up. Because he thought school 'sucked,' he didn't bother to attend much and barely passed. His mother didn't seem to notice.

Mom was also blind to how bizarre his then seven-year-old sister was becoming. 'She went really strange, into multiple personalities. Over the years, she developed eighteen of them. It took a half-dozen shrinks, a string of foster homes, years of craziness, and finally hypnosis before we found out what her problem is: when she was two and three, while we were living on and off at this same bush shack, a neighbour molested her many times. She's still pretty messed-up today.'

(According to Manitoban Dr Colin Ross who specializes in treating the disorder, multiple personalities – as few as two, as many as a hundred, on average between eight and fourteen – are most common among females who were severely abused in childhood.[29] 'It is a child's creative adaptation to an unbearable situation ... a sensible and effective way of coping with abuse,' says therapist Margo Rivera.[30] By hiding in the wings of consciousness, children apparently allow another of their personalities to endure the suffering. Rivera points out that multiple-personality patients spend an average of seven years in the mental-health system before they are correctly diagnosed.)

As Gilette approached puberty, the kids' lonely lives were disrupted by a stepfather, 'a real mind-fucker of a guy.' 'He and my mother suddenly joined some charismatic church, became crazed holy-roller types almost overnight. Suddenly, everything we normally did became a crime against God. It was very confusing because they had been hippies – anything you wanted to do was cool, right – then suddenly the same things were sins.'

Gilette's affect, dead-flat to this point, suddenly flashes an edge. He shakes the chains hanging from a shoulder clasp. 'I used to wear heavy black circles around my eyes, right. I admit, I was scary-looking, but I liked it. The look suited me, fit the way I felt. This fucker thought anyone done up like me was gay.' Is he? 'No, but that didn't stop the homophobe from calling me a "fucking little faggot" and throwing chairs at me.'

Gilette looks past me, avoiding eye contact as he will during our entire afternoon together. 'I don't know if I'm gay. I try not to think about it.'

There is a lot Gilette tries not to think about. Like why he became a 'regular little kleptomaniac' who stuffed his closets full of booty for which he had no use. 'One time my newly God-fearing parents turned me in to the cops. But that was before they left the church and my psycho stepfather started growing drugs in the attic!'

Nelson, BC, their home base at that time, was not the place to revert from righteousness to marijuana-farming. 'Maybe in the 'sixties it was a community of open-minded hippies that my mom remembers, but when we moved back there, it was redneck country of loggers and miners. Pot was so plentiful that even the hardhats toked up, but they weren't going to put up with a speed-freak punker and acid head like me.' Gilette describes a series of incidents reminiscent of the 1969 film classic *Easy Rider*: rednecks in rickety trucks slinging beer bottles and slurs at non-conformists. Inside himself, Gilette felt every bit the outsider local 'yahoos' were yelping at. 'I was just a freak that had no friends and who was flunking out at school. I wanted to get the hell out of there.'

His chance came after a 'weird' visitor from Ontario befriended him. She and some of her 'well-off' crowd bought him a bus ticket to Toronto, where he moved into the comfortable High Park home of his new girlfriend. He 'crashed' there for two months until her parents returned from wintering in Florida. Then, age fifteen, he hit the downtown punk corners, became a 'stew-bum' (vagrant) living off hand-outs from friends, and from wages his girlfriend's mother gave him for doing odd jobs at their house.

'Her family was totally strange; her mom had been addicted to anti-depressants for over twenty years. This was one violent, bizarre lady.' Gilette found Toronto cold and mean. His girlfriend found her mother's erratic outbursts more and more impossible to accept. Along with another teenage girl, they decided to see if Vancouver's streets would be kinder.

His girlfriend bought their tickets for the three-day bus trip across the country. Both girls, first-time runaways, imagined police would be on their trail, so they dyed their hair a blue-and-green combo and greased it into spikes. 'They needn't have bothered disguising themselves. As it turned out, it took my girlfriend's parents three weeks to notice she was missing! By then, she was ready to go home to more torture anyway.'

When his girlfriend headed back east, Gilette reconnected with his natural father, a carpenter living with his new family in Vancouver. Though relations were cordial, things didn't work out between them.

Gilette was soon back on the street, 'squatting in doorways or crashing at a drug haven. Kids using the pad were what I'd call "doom rockers," with huge black hairdos, black make-up, totally pale and skinny. Happiness for them was a negative attitude, a six-pack or news that a shipment of coke was coming into town and they could soon shoot up. Their favourite activity was beating up guys for their air-sole boots from England. The only thing they loved was hating people and getting violent. Most of them were white, though there were a few blacks, which I couldn't understand since this is a white-power movement. Some of the guys came from super-rich families, but most were poor. In some ways, I felt at home in their who-cares attitude, but eventually it got too depressing even for me. Nelson started to look better than that scene.'

But only from a distance. When he got home, he discovered Nelson hadn't changed in his absence; his appearance was still too outrageous for a small town. At least his stepfather wasn't around to berate him. The 'jerk' had left his mother, 'run off with some lady lawyer, the best thing that could have happened to my mom as far as I was concerned.' He found his sister, three years his junior, in a foster home, 'the usual kind of sterile place with people that only want the money.' In his absence, his sister had been around the psychiatric circuit and was still a 'basket case.' By then, so was Gilette.

'I went really strange and got committed to a psych ward. I don't remember it too well. I try not to think about it. All I know is that I became odd and everyone was scared of me. But the shrinks must have thought I was sane enough because, after a month, they released me. Being a psycho case shook me up though. I couldn't get out of Nelson fast enough.'

Back to Vancouver and the 'doped-out – only psychedelics, never needles – doom scene.' Back to the boredom and the poverty. What did he do for money? This question triggers a volley of nervous twitches: pick at the chains, scratch the table, stir the coffee. Silence.

'Did you hustle?'

No answer. His eyes, like those of a dead fish, stare into some forbidden inner space.

'I try not to think about it.'

'Are you embarrassed?'

'It's embarrassing to talk about it.'

But with a little prodding, he does, in an almost inaudible whisper. 'I just want to forget about it. I don't want to think about it. It was no big deal. It's over now,' he tells himself, talking fast. 'With the tricks, it felt like I was being molested ... I don't know why it seemed that way. Why did it seem that way?' he asks himself in a reverie. 'Maybe I was molested as a little kid ... maybe the guy that did my sister ... I don't remember, I don't remember ... I don't want to think about it.' A blade of panic cuts through his calm. He struggles for control, seemingly unaware of my presence. 'Even if it did happen, it's had no lasting effect,' he consoles himself.

I feel a little panicky myself. I'd been waiting fearfully for these moments, when kids would connect with pieces of their past, when holes in the puzzle of their lives would fill in.

'Have you ever told anyone that you think you might have been molested as a child?' I ask, feeling totally inadequate.

'No, I've never talked to anyone before.'

Then he closes the subject. My mind is whirring with names of Vancouver people he might be able to talk to. I angle for the chance to support more disclosure, to suggest conditions under which he might feel comfortable going farther on the torturous journey he started that day. Try though I do, there is no getting back to it. Gilette makes sure the interview is effectively over.

After we part, I wonder about his confession. Why to me? Why now? Maybe it was safe to mention childhood sexual abuse for the first time to a stranger he knows is catching the next plane out of his life. It takes a while for the currents from our meeting to settle, but, when they do, I find comfort in thinking about the steps Gilette has already taken to emerge from his depressed stupor.

Over the last year he has stopped using drugs, he claims, gone back to an alternative school, and gotten onto a financial-assistance program that will cover tuition for a hairdressing course he plans to start two months hence. Gilette is living with a new girlfriend in a regular apartment and reconnecting with his thirty-six-year-old mother who, he says, is finally pulling her life together.

'He might be okay' I tell myself, but the after-image of Gilette, a sombre soul stumbling through a labyrinth of emotional pain, extinguishes my optimism.

Abusers and Abused

Identifying potentially hazardous families is not easy. Many families exhibit characteristics typical of harmful ones, yet are able to nurture their kids. Other families that do not fit the abusive mould mangle their young. Elements from a defined set of factors, however, appear in many cases of suspected and proved abuse.

Unstable families appear more likely than stable ones to become abusive. Instability takes many forms. It may derive from a mother who has a series of lovers or live-ins. The greater number of serial boyfriends or stepfathers, the graver the risk seems to be for children. One survey of abuse victims and runaways found the incidence of abuse among children to be about three times higher in situations where children live with unrelated males than for similar children of the same age living with biological fathers.[31]

While it would be a gross error to tarnish the image of stepfathers as a breed – some being substantially better than blood fathers – some do reject or otherwise abuse children from previous marriages. As you will see from Jarett's profile, in the next chapter, his problems began when his stepfather, who apparently adored his natural children, rejected Jarett. The man refused to speak to the boy, treating him as if he did not exist.

Emotional instability seems to occur commonly in families that abuse. Children's fortunes tend to fluctuate with parental fortunes; if adults live on the end of a yo-yo string, so may their children. Some research suggests that young parents, confounded by their own immaturity, are more likely to abuse their kids.[32] When the perfect little baby who was supposed to make life blissful messes the diapers and spoils their sleep, some teenage parents can't rein in their rage.

As testimonies in this book illustrate, stresses of all kinds permeate the histories of abusive families. Marital breakdown, financial stress, unemployment, alcohol and drugs constitute garden-variety ingredients that pepper the family's volatile emotional brew. Although these stresses may trigger destructive episodes, they can hardly be called causes of abuse per se. Drink may embolden violent men, for example, but that does not make alcohol responsible for the outburst. Clearly, many non-abusive families endure the same pressures without lashing out in damaging ways against other family members.

Beyond broad indicators, little else forewarns that a family might become dangerous to its children. A reliable profile of the potentially abusive individual is equally hard to pin down. A set of common characteristics, however, seems to recur among abusive and violent men.

One characteristic leads the list: most men who abuse children were beaten or witnessed abuse in their own childhoods.[33] Violence against women and children is learned behaviour. Violent child-rearing practices modelled by fathers often resurface in the next generation. Violent fathers/stepfathers/surrogate fathers are typically one more link in an intergenerational chain of abuse.

But, what about the other 20 per cent or so of male batterers who were neither victims nor witnesses of abuse in their childhoods? What forges them into assailants?

Those who believe the primary antagonism in society exists between the sexes argue that men learn violence from the gendered pecking-order of society at large. They learn it from advertised images of macho men and object women, and from male aggressiveness and violence celebrated in sports and culture. Others who believe the primary antagonism in society exists between exploiter and exploited argue that men learn from their experience in the market-place to oppress people less powerful than themselves. They re-enact in the home the social relations of production, becoming the all-powerful boss. Sexism and violence expressed in the culture reinforce lessons assimilated on the job.

Obviously, only some men succumb to these lessons in oppression. Those who do tend to be afflicted with low self-esteem. To overcome feelings of impotence, they reach for personal power by lording it over children,[34] and over women, too. Immature, they typically have a limited emotional lexicon in which all strong feelings express themselves as anger.[35] Both overcontrolling and overdependent, they commonly deny being abusers, by which they mean that what they did was not wrong.[36] Often enough, they defend their actions as demonstrations of love and caring for their children.

Some people assume that men who batter must be hotheads. Yet, outside the home, many of these men are perfectly controlled. At home, where they feel it is safe to let go, they release their impulses. Only under particular circumstances, with particular targets – in the home, with women and children – do these men become violent.

In *No Safe Place: Violence against Women and Children*, authors argue that the culture constantly legitimizes unfettered male authority. They describe social tolerance for male violence as covert and insidious.[37] Consequently, some men internalize the tacit encouragement sexism and violence thrive on in our society, reducing the lives of scores of women and children to confinements of fear.

Although some common traits exist, neither violent men nor abusive families are homogeneous. Nor do abused children consistently exhibit common characteristics. However, many abusers blame their acts on certain inherited traits among children.

Abusive families tend to invent scapegoats, unconsciously making one or more children the repository for unsettling business that disturbs family equilibrium. According to *The Myth of Delinquency*, many incarcerated youths come from homes where they have been assigned the bad-boy role. Generalizing from data collected over years, the National Society for the Prevention of Cruelty to Children in Britain ascertained that the singled-out child may be awkward in some way, perhaps an 'ugly duckling' or the product of an extramarital affair or a teenage pregnancy.[38] These unwanted children remind the abusing parent of an infidelity, lost youth, or rejection by their own parents or spouse.

Or, like Charlie, they remind the battering parent of the abandoning parent. Charlie's mother justified starving and beating her son by saying that the child reminded her of Charlie's father, long gone. Mother may have wanted to pummel her ex-husband but couldn't, and made Charlie his dad's stand-in.

Some parents also blame sickly children whose needs may be greater than those of their peers. 'I was the oldest and very sickly,' Shelly, a fifteen-year-old runaway, told me. 'As far as I can tell, that's why he [her father] beat me ... He was drunk a lot and half-mad all the time; I was his favourite doormat.'

In some families, particular children are targeted for beatings. In other homes, only the mother is victimized. In yet other situations, a mother and a singled-out child or children are preyed upon. The fall-out from violence, whatever its form and targets, ripples through the family, touching everyone in its wake. Research has shown that boys exposed to, but not personally subjected to violence – for example, watching their fathers beat their mothers – exhibit adjustment problems similar to those of abused boys.[39]

Many street kids come from homes in which the mother was the primary punching-bag. Like Louis, whom you will meet in chapter 5, when these kids try to intervene, they end up taking the blows themselves. Other kids hide in their bedroom, terrified, crying, pillow wrapped around their ears to muffle their mother's screams.

The extent of violence against women is mind-boggling. Men perpetrate an estimated 40,000 sexual assaults annually, or more than 100 on any given day, against women in Canada.[40] Every year, an estimated 750,000 women are battered by their mates; that means that one in ten women who live with men will become victims this year.[41] Wife assault, committed mostly in the home, accounts for one-fifth of all Canadian homicides.[42]

Even this small sample of data conveys a sense of the justifiable fear that infuses some homes. Even women who flee often carry their terror with them – fear of violent ex-husbands and lovers who may track them to new addresses.

Wife battery in Canada cuts across the usual social dividers. 'Research done over the past ten years has repeatedly shown that batterers can come from all walks of life. They may be working outside the home or inside the home. They may be unemployed or have a steady job. They may be rich or poor, well-educated or illiterate, of any nationality or race, young or old, with or without children.'[43] In recent years, increasing public exposure of marital rape and battery by affluent men has done much to quash the myth that only the downtrodden beat their wives and kids.

Heroes of Their Own Lives: The Politics and History of Family Violence argues that the arrogance and prejudices of rich benefactors, founders, and workers in early family-welfare agencies helped create and sustain the myth that poor people make bad parents and poor men make bad husbands, while the well-off are beyond reproach. In addition, the well-off can afford the cover-ups, whether lawyers or private clinics, that money can buy. Normally beyond the scrutiny of social-service agencies, they are more able to abuse clandestinely.[44]

However, gentility is not the only curtain between appearance and reality. Women are abused, on average, as many as thirty-five times before they contact police.[45] Many people cannot fathom why women stay with beaters. Their reasons are many, ranging from simple economics to complex psychologies. Women stay because they have little or no money and nowhere to go. Even working women rarely earn enough to act as sole supporters of themselves and their children. Single mothers and children make up a large proportion of Canada's poor. This fact is not lost on battered mothers; some stay because they think their kids might be better off with less poverty and more violence than with the opposite. This choice can be even more complicated when the children are not the primary victims of violence.

Women stay because of conditioning, because they are taught to judge themselves by what others – especially fathers, boyfriends, husbands – think of them. If a man thinks so little of a woman that he beats her, she learns, if only subconsciously, that she is worth nothing. So, she stays.

Women stay because they are often penalized when they seek help. As is true of children's claims, women's charges of abuse are often doubted. And, even if the claims are believed, many victims are blamed. 'What did *you* do to provoke him?' is a commonly asked question.

Women stay because they cannot count on police protection or on justice from the legal system when they seek custody and support – which many fathers don't pay even when mothers win awards. To intimidate victims into staying, abusers often force reconciliations by using children as ransom, or by threatening to kidnap or seek custody.

Fathers win [custody] because they earn more money; mothers lose because they have been forced onto welfare or because they have gone out to work, thus proving they don't care for their children. Fathers win because they have a new girlfriend or wife who can 'look after the children'; mothers lose because they have a boyfriend and are therefore immoral. Above all, fathers win because of the overwhelming male bias of the legal system.

Fathers have won custody despite non-payment of child support, lack of close relationship with the child, kidnapping, wife-beating, sexual molestation, even murder. And good mothers lose after no-holds-barred 'witchcraft' trials in which they stand accused of not mending socks, or packing inadequate school lunches. A father who does anything for his children is seen by judges as outstanding; mothers get no points for doing absolutely everything, which they are supposed to do anyway.[46]

Women stay mainly because they believe they have no choice. Ultimately, most stay out of fear – fear that their partners will hunt them down, haunt their lives, harm their parents, harm their kids – maybe kill them.

One measure of the fear and extent of abuse can be seen in the extraordinary demand for shelters across Canada. In 1985, mothers with a total of 110,000 children sought refuge. Mothers of 86,000 of these youngsters needed shelter because they had been battered. Although there were 230 shelters at that time, they could take in fewer than half the women at their doors. In other words, more than 55,000 children and their mothers were turned away.[47]

Data collected by transition houses from battered mothers reveal that many children in these families were also abused. Almost half the women said their partners were emotionally destructive to their children; more than a quarter said their partners were beating the kids. Seven per cent told shelter workers that their men were sexually molesting their children. In 11 per cent of cases, mother and child(ren) were abused at the same time.[48]

Some women also admitted to transition staff that they, too, mistreated their children. In addition to these confessions, more than half the workers reported witnessing neglect and abuse by a small minority of women residents.[49]

In recent years, many shelter staff have also noticed that the children themselves have become more violent.[50] They see little boys become aggressive towards their mother and try to control her, taking over their dad's role in his absence. They watch little girls mimic their moms by becoming submissive and withdrawn, trying to get by unnoticed.

Still, there is no equality of the sexes when it comes to violence. Men inflict most of the harm children suffer in the family. Women inflict some, but much less. More often, immobilized by fear and intimidation, they fail to rescue their endangered children. Whether wilfully blind or actively abusive, women, along with their children, are more often victims of male violence in a society that tacitly condones denigration of women and children.

Sharon: From her tough streak, her father forged a fighter

'You can't do anything right, you stupid bitch,' my mother would holler at me while smacking me across the head with her open hand. 'Stupid bitch' and 'bad girl' were practically the only words she ever said to me. I don't remember her being that cruel when I was very little though. I remember her as a perfectionist, always putting on the dog, pretending to be somebody special. Even if we were just going to a show, she'd be at her bedroom vanity, primping like she was getting ready for a fancy-dress ball.

Funny, I don't remember what she was wearing the day she collected me from the foster home. I was five years old, all dressed up in a red outfit. I don't recall much about my time with the foster family other than a vague recollection of my mother saying she'd be back to pick me up 'someday,' and me always wondering if 'someday' would come.

I was very happy to be going home to my father, a hard-slogging transport-truck driver. Although he had a violent temper and rough ways, he wasn't mean like my mother. We always had a special bond, my dad and me. Maybe our bond was part of the reason my mother hated me so much.

From age six, I did all the housework. Nothing I did, from peeling potatoes to scrubbing floors, was ever good enough. I got no thanks, just beatings and threats that she'd kill me if I complained to my father.

I'm trembling in my thin nightie as Mother opens the front door. I'm only seven, but I sense something terrible is about to happen. The first light of day is just creeping into our living-room. Blood, so much blood. Blood everywhere, even on his trouser cuffs. My dad is standing there, propped up by two big cops. His nose is off to one side of his face. Tears trickle down his cheeks. I want to run to him, comfort him. But I stand glued to my spot.

The police tell my mother, who's shrieking obscenities at my dad, what happened. 'Your old man has been on a gambling binge. Lost his shirt, even his red Mustang convertible. The guy that won beat him up. All he's got left, he tells us, is the twenty bucks the winner left in his pocket.'

I ran to my dad and threw my arms around him. 'I'll take you to the hospital and they'll make you all better,' I sobbed. We were both sobbing. 'I'm sorry, baby, I love you, I'm so sorry,' my dad kept repeating. My mother just kept screaming. I don't know what propelled me, but I broke loose from my dad's arms and ran over to her, jumped up and smacked her in the face. She started to beat me, ranting 'You bitch, you're just like him.' The cops grabbed her. 'Don't take it out on her, lady. She's just a little kid.'

From that day on, it was like something was put on us. Our lives went down the toilet faster than the booze went down her throat. Guess that gambling binge – not his first but certainly his worst – was the last straw for her because my dad lost our savings, a down payment for a house. All of us had put a lot of dreams into 'the house' – my mother because it meant she was getting somewhere in life, and me because I imagined a house would make her happy and she'd stop beating me.

Although my dad had always been a drinker and a gambler, he'd never squandered our rent or savings before. Poverty soon forced us to move to Regent Park [with more than 10,000 residents, the largest public-housing complex in Canada]. With the heart-break came more drinking for both of them. Drunk, my dad couldn't work steady anymore, so he'd work on and off. He'd sober up for work and tank up after work. The fights between them became more violent; he'd smack her around and she'd smack me around.

She needed more than his earnings and the welfare for necessities – booze, cigarettes, and the odd loaf of bread. So, she got domestic jobs in rich Rosedale homes. She got the wages; I did the labour. She'd keep me out of school, where I was in trouble anyway, to go with her to houses she had keys for, where the lady wasn't home. She'd watch the soaps *and help herself at the overstocked bars, spiking the half-empty bottles with water, while I cleaned. When she'd inspect my work, she'd complain that it wasn't good enough, smack me, and curse me out.*

The abuse was our secret; my father would never have tolerated it. With his heavy drinking and spotty work, however, he stayed home more, and she drank more. The more she drank, the sloppier she got at hiding the abuse. He must have suspected what was going on because one night they had a big fight over me.

'I'm hungry, get me some supper,' he commanded.

My mother, slobbering drunk, slurred back, 'I'm too tired. Get her' – meaning me – 'to do it.'

'You expect me to ask a little kid to get my supper?' he snapped back at her.

Before she had a chance to answer, he started grilling me. 'How much work have you been doing around here, Sharon?'

I just stood there shaking. I wanted to tell him but I was too scared. My mother sat on the couch glowering, silently daring me to defy her.

'Answer my questions, Sharon. How much? How long?'

'A lot ... a long time,' I whispered.

He had always seemed like a big man to me, but never so big as that moment. He walked calmly over to my mother and smashed her in the face. After that evening, she treated me much worse.

'You're just a little Catholic brat,' the teacher berated me for some misdemeanour in front of the class. She was black, so I blurted out 'I hate you, you fucking nigger.' Then I ran crying from the grade-school class. That's just the way it was in my neighbourhood. From kindergarten, you talked tough, looked tough, and pretended you were tough, even if you weren't. To survive, you had to.

Branded a 'trouble-maker,' I didn't know why I fought in the schoolyard or provoked the teachers. I'm just grateful to my father that he taught me to stand up for myself so I could survive a school system and a neighbourhood that crushed weak kids. When I'd come home, crying because I'd been licked by a bully, my father would literally lock the door behind me, send me back out to beat up the kid who sent me scurrying.

Over the years, a few teachers saw beyond the surface toughness and tried to help me. Most of our teachers were satisfied to label us – 'trouble-makers,' 'bad kids,' 'learning disabled,' 'dyslexic,' 'delin-

quents,' 'dummies' – and dump us in 'special classes' where they stick kids who need help. My special classes were always full of the poorest kids. The girls studied cooking and sewing. I was getting expert lessons at home, so I didn't need classes for that.

Although I wasn't learning, I never failed until grade nine. I think they just put difficult kids ahead to get rid of us. Even the caring teachers never tried to help me with schoolwork. It was as if reading and writing weren't important for poor kids.

I remember one teacher who called my mother after I'd come to school a few mornings headachy and tired. The teacher figured out that I wasn't getting breakfast. My mother, of course, denied I was hungry, but Miss MacDonald saw through the bullshit. She invented a phoney project to convince my mother I had to go to her house some days after school. The first time Miss MacDonald gave me supper, which I wolfed down, I said I'd do the dishes.

'Don't be silly. You don't have to wash the dishes.'

'Yes, I do. I have to.'

She tried, but couldn't convince me that I was entitled to a meal without working for it. I was in grade four then. Finally, she let me do the dishes. Then she tried to give me a dollar.

'I can't take money,' I protested.

'Why not?'

'Because if my mother finds it, she'll take it off me and buy something.'

'What will she buy?' Miss MacDonald prodded. 'Some beer, maybe?'

'Maybe,' I answered. She wasn't going to get me to say my mother was a lush and a beater. 'And if she doesn't take the money off me, she'll think I stole it,' I added, thinking I'd get the subject away from my mother's drinking.

'Why would she think you stole it? Do you steal things sometimes?' Miss MacDonald asked.

I don't know why, but I told her the truth. 'Only when my mother is drunk and I steal fifty cents to buy fish and chips for lunch.'

'And what does she do to you when she finds out?' she probed gently.

'She has this plastic brush and she makes me put my hands on the table so she can smash them,' I confessed to the horrified teacher. 'That's nothing. She does lots worse. And then she calls me bad names and says she'll kill me if I tell anyone.'

'But, Sharon, you must tell, and we must do something about it.'

On hearing her intention to do something, my alarm system took over. I even remember what I said: 'If you ever tell anyone what I told you, I'll make your life miserable' – repeating one of my mother's pet phrases. Eventually she promised that 'it will be our secret, but if you ever need anyone, promise you'll call me.' I promised, but never called. That's not to say I didn't need rescuing.

The crew I ran with were very rebellious. We all had hard home lives. By the time I was fourteen, sniffing solvents and stealing were everyday events. I'd sniff anything: glue, spray paint stolen from the school workshops. We'd hang out behind a church on Bleeker Street and sniff till we felt far enough away from our dead-end lives. I didn't do the heavy stuff like speed that most of my crew were doing but I was always willing to hit up the kids who were squeamish about injecting themselves with needles.

One time, I was almost forced to shoot up. Two pushers chased me and my girlfriend down an alleyway. They caught up with her but not with me. They pinned her to the ground and pumped her up with speed. I took her to the hospital; I was often at the hospital with friends who'd overdosed.

A teacher from one of my 'special classes' tried to help us off drugs. He'd come right into the back alleys to fetch us. Mr Wilson never reported us to the principal or to our parents. He was a real to-sir-with-love kind of teacher, stuck with a classroom full of troubled kids. He saw beyond the black leather shingle jackets, and the matching attitudes, even beyond the switch-blade I carried in my cowboy boot. But he was just one exceptional teacher, one short year.

After I lost two friends to overdoses, I made a stab at quitting glue. I did okay until something got me really depressed. My reflex when I was in trouble was to grab Cutex and a bag and rush out behind the church. That time, just as I was starting to sniff, my friend Cathy appeared. She yanked the bag off my face and smashed the bottle on the ground. I was on her in a flash, beating the hell out of her. I even knocked out a tooth. Afterwards, I sank to the ground and bawled.

'Why did you make me do that to you?' I whimpered.

'I just want to stop you from sniffing.'

'I beat the piss out of you and you aren't even mad?' I said, stunned.

'I'm your friend. You can't shake me that easy.'

That was the day I quit drugs for life.

By fourteen, virginity was the only innocence I had left. I would soon lose it in a rape during a baby-sitting job I took on with an older girlfriend. At least it was supposed to be a baby-sitting job, except the kid's father didn't go out. Instead, he had some rowdy, card-playing buddies in. He told us to keep the kid occupied in the bedroom while the guys played in the kitchen. They were older guys, very friendly. They gave us pop and drinks; like most teenagers, we felt pretty grown up to be drinking.

It wasn't long before I'd passed out on a bed in the boy's room. I woke up with his dad naked on top of me, raping me, his young son watching. Mad with terror, I managed to squeeze out from under him and grab the shotgun in the corner. The guy was a biker, so having a shotgun lying around was not unusual. My girlfriend, meanwhile, was being raped by two guys that had her pinned to the couch.

I was running around half naked, crying uncontrollably, waving the gun, threatening everyone in sight. The guys tried to calm me down, grab the gun. My girlfriend got hysterical. As one of her attackers inched towards me, I shot at him. As the owner, the guy that attacked me, had been claiming the gun wasn't loaded, but no one, including him, was certain. At that point the brother of the guy who raped me walked in. When he realized what had gone down, he beat my attacker half to death. I watched indifferently.

I never reported the rape to anyone. There was no point; I knew I'd be blamed. If you're from Regent Park, police either don't care or blame you anyway. I knew my mother would call me a whore. My father wouldn't blame me, but he would have killed the guy. I didn't want my father in prison. So I clammed up.

In a sense, I even blamed myself. The rape confirmed that I was no good, just as my mother had always said. Strange, but all I could think about for months after was that I couldn't become a nun because I was no longer a virgin. Not that I had any ambition to become one, but the convent was always in the back of my mind as a possible haven. My church-going mother, hypocrite that she was, had somehow put that idea into my head.

I was sure I'd never get married either because no man would want a spoiled woman. For a while after that, I hated guys. I spent all my time with girlfriends. My classy mother started calling me a 'lesie.' I'd holler back at her, 'If I hang out with girls, I'm a lesbian; if I hang out with guys, I'm a tramp. When are you going to make up your mind what I am?'

At fifteen, I failed grade nine and quit school. The only bright light in my life then was Joey, a boy from Scarborough I'd become friends with. My boyfriend I guess, but we didn't have sex because the rape, I felt, had started my sex life and finished it. Joey made me feel like a person, not a piece of garbage.

I was antsy to leave home. My parents had sunk so low that they were bringing home drunks from the street and partying on goof [cheap wine]. They were fighting constantly; cops were constantly at our door. One time I found my mother lying in a pool of blood after she'd fallen and smashed her head on a steel bed frame. My father was flapping around. I was calm. I'd gotten so used to bloody scenes that I just cleaned her up, got her to emergency, watched them stitch her up, and taxied her back home, so she could start boozing again.

At that time, I was working as a salesclerk and had saved enough for a winter coat. When I walked in with my new coat, my mother created a scene.

'Tell me, tramp, where did you get the money to buy that coat?'

'I earned it.'

'I'll bet you earned it – on your back.'

'Afraid not. I don't have your bad habits.'

I just blurted it out of anger; there was no truth in the accusation. Provoked, she tried to rip the coat off me.

'No, you don't. It's mine. I worked for it. I saved for it. I can pay my own way,' I screamed at her.

'Good,' she said, 'then why don't you pay your way out the door.'

'Great idea,' I screamed back.

'You'll find out just how great it is once you're out there on your own.'

'Lady, I've been on my own in here, so what's the difference?'

I stormed to my bedroom to pack. She was on my heels, telling me to get out with just the clothes on my back. Then she went into the kitchen and bawled. I cooled down and decided I wanted to say goodbye; I didn't want to leave like that. When I went into the kitchen, she said, 'You're leaving because you hate me, right?'

'Yes ... and no,' I confessed.

She was very small by then, all shrivelled and hunched from the drinking and fighting. This pathetic little woman let loose. She smashed me in the face, pushed me up against the wall. That was the final blow for me. I grabbed her by the throat and screamed, 'You've screwed up my life this far but you won't get the chance to screw it up any more.' When I let go, she slumped to the floor.

'I never dreamt we'd say goodbye like this,' my distraught dad said as he stuffed five bucks in my hand, the only money he had. We hugged, crying. 'I love you, Dad.' 'And I love you, baby.' I walked out the door. I wasn't yet sixteen.

Three years later. I'd taken the baby for a check-up. We'd come home to our dingy apartment in a condemned building near King and Jamieson. Joey was out, probably drinking and gambling as usual. Everything I valued in the apartment was gone: my stereo, my Elvis and Beatles record collections, even an antique radio I'd refinished. A notice for an overdue $1,000 Woolco bill sat on the kitchen table. Joey had sold everything.

When he came home a while later, he acted as if nothing had happened. 'I'm hungry, make me some spaghetti,' he ordered. Obediently, I did. When I put it on the table, he pushed the plate away. 'This is cold, you bitch, I don't want this garbage. Get it out of my face.'

I picked up the plate, and his glass of milk, and poured them over his head. 'There. Now you can't say I didn't give you supper.' Then I walked out of the room. He came raging after me, spaghetti dangling from his hair. Before he could grab me, I was back in the kitchen, a large knife in my hand.

I started stabbing the swinging door between the kitchen and the living-room. He was on the other side, holding the door steady, begging me to stop. In slow motion in my mind, I was picturing how I would kill him and carve up his face. I had snapped; it was as if all the anger of my life erupted in that one moment.

I just kept stabbing and stabbing the knife into the wood. Next thing I knew, the police were breaking down the front door. My hand was so rigid around that knife, the cops had to pry it loose. I blurted out the whole story of the violence I'd endured from Joey. It had started after we'd married and I'd become pregnant.

The lower Joey was on his gambling luck, the worse his violence. The more the baby cried, the more I got beaten. 'Why the hell is he crying?

Can't you shut that kid up? Why don't you take care of him? What the hell do you do all day – screw guys?' The more I tried to hide the welfare to buy food and clothes for the baby, the more he beat me.

He'd smash me in the face, punch me in the stomach, curse me out, throw me against the wall. He'd trash the apartment. One time after a vicious beating, he had me on the floor, his boot on my throat. 'I know you got money, you fucking bitch, so you better cough it up fast if you don't want to die.' All I could think about was being quiet so as not to wake the baby. I was constantly afraid he'd hurt our tiny son, though he never did, but I couldn't shake that fear.

After I told the cops what he'd been doing to me, they took him away. I wouldn't charge him; I was too scared what he'd do to me later.

I can still feel the relief of that moment when they escorted him out the door. I fell into a chair and cried for what seemed hours. The same line played over and over in my head: 'This is no life for Robie [the baby], this is no life for Robie.' At that point, I could think about a better life for my child, but I couldn't imagine that there'd ever be a better life for me. After all, hadn't my whole life confirmed that my mother was right? Obviously, I was bad and stupid and worthless. Next morning, I called the CAS. A worker was at my door the same day.

'I want you to take my son and place him with a good family; I can't take care of him.' Then I spilled the story of what had happened to me and why I felt giving Robie up was the only chance he had. She listened, patient and sympathetic. 'You're not an unfit mother, even though Joey says you are. It took a lot of courage, and a lot of love for your baby to call us. I won't take Robie, but I will do everything I can to help you.' We discussed how I could relocate before Joey showed up again. She found out when the cops were going to release him. The CAS worker got me everything I needed, all new things, good things I'd never had for Robie before, including a shiny new crib to replace the old dresser drawer he'd been sleeping in. She stored the stuff at her office for my move.

Before I could get us moved – and to tell the truth, I'm not sure I was ready to split – Joey came back. A changed man. Or so he claimed. I'd never seen that much apologizing and begging before. Believe it or not, I was still vulnerable to him. I still cared about him and I was still hoping that things could be good again. I agreed to stay. For about a month, everything was perfect.

Then one night, for no apparent reason – no fight, no scene, no beating, nothing – he kicked us out. Just like that. Joey stormed in the front door, screaming. 'You and the fucking kid get out. Right now.' It was around 1:00 a.m., mid-winter, sub-zero. He plucked Robie from his bed and threw him in the carriage. He helped me pack baby things and some of my things. I stuffed them around the baby and all over the carriage to keep Robie warm. Then Joey held the door open as I pushed the carriage out into the black night.

We had no place to go. By then, Joey had destroyed all my friendships. His insane jealousy and wild accusations had driven all my friends away. When my girlfriends used to call or drop by, he'd claim we were conspiring against him and making dates for me. Everyone had stopped calling.

I sat rocking the carriage in an all-night restaurant on King Street. Next morning an acquaintance came into the laundromat where I'd taken Robie to try to keep warm. She was living with a guy named Bob, who would eventually become my third husband. She took us home with her. Bob fixed it with their landlord to let me move into the vacant flat on the third floor of their house. They helped me get my few possessions from Joey – there wasn't much left, plus after he kicked us out, he shredded most of my clothes – get on welfare, and get a part-time job housecleaning.

Within a few months, I was feeling like a human being. I hoped the abuse was over.

Then came Alan, a guy who shared the ground-floor flat with the land-lord. From the beginning, I knew he was gay, bisexual really. I wound up pregnant. After my divorce came through, we married for one reason only: so Alan could do the 'right thing' for his ever-so-respectable family. We moved into the basement apartment of his mother's home.

During my pregnancy, my dad died. The drinking finally killed him – cirrhosis of the liver, the same disease that would kill my mother a couple of years later, after she told me, for the first and only time, that she loved me.

Just after Dad died, Lisa was born. Before long, both Alan and his mother were ordering me around, a real chorus, the two of them: I was a lousy mother, I was a lazy home-maker. A no-good. For me, it was old-home week. And just like I had done when my mother put me down, I swung from believing they were right and thinking I should kill myself, to believing I was a worthwhile human being deserving a better hand than the one life insisted on dealing me.

Alan and I drifted apart in the same indifferent way we had drifted together. I was so sure we'd separate that it didn't even matter to me when I found evidence of his infidelities with men. We weren't together a year when he moved out. He left a legacy, however – his friend Bob. While Alan and I were breaking up, Bob and his live-in girlfriend were also failing. After Alan left, taking his former sense of responsibility for me and the two kids with him – he made only two support payments before he disappeared for good – I shared the apartment with Bob. For a long time we were just house mates and casual friends.

Five years later. Robie is nine years old and in grade four. He asks me to help with his homework.

'But Daddy always helps you ... I'm too busy ... not now ... maybe later.'

'It's okay, Mom. If you don't know how, I can get some help at school and come home and teach you.'

I started to cry ... my son had figured out my secret; I couldn't read or write well enough to help with grade-four homework. My husband of the past five years, Bob, didn't suspect how weak my basic skills were. He thought of me as a smart, strong lady. He kept asking what was bugging me. Eventually, he badgered a confession out of me and begged me to go back to school. But in my vocabulary school meant failure. Bob volunteered to teach me himself. After he tutored me for a while, I began to make some headway, enough confidence to walk into Beat the Street, a learning centre he had tracked down.

Over the past two years, two tutors have helped me advance at my own pace, which hasn't been too slow. I only need six more credits to get my high-school diploma. I can't tell you it's been easy. But I have learned, mostly because of my family's support.

I didn't think I'd ever believe that family could mean love and support. I'm not saying there are no hard times ahead. But no one will ever be allowed to abuse me again. Bob and I have helped each other come to terms with our past. His background was way worse than mine. No one loved him. I was lucky. I had a father who loved me, even if he couldn't do much to help me, and I had a tough streak he helped me develop, so I could finally say 'Stop! No more!'

Running Away, Repeating the Cycle

Like all families, dysfunctional ones teach their children values and behaviours. In unsafe and unhealthy homes fraught with neglect, abuse, and violence, kids acquire their self-concept, outlook on life, and performance skills, as their peers do in safe homes, rich in love, nurture, and tolerance. Although many people, from most denied to most blessed, transcend their backgrounds, most of us are indelibly shaped by our beginnings, good or bad.

A large body of research shows that seriously impaired families produce seriously impaired kids, including the bulk of runaways. One study concluded that the decision unhappy kids make about whether to stay put or to run away depends on the quality of their relationship with their parents.[51] Although both runaways and non-runaways surveyed felt equally that their parents did not understand them, significant differences emerged in their perception of their families. Parents of kids who stayed home were able to communicate love and caring to each other and their kids, while parents of kids who fled did not convey empathy or respect to anyone in the family. The researchers concluded that parents' ability to express caring can compensate for the adolescent's feelings of being misunderstood.[52]

Even though adolescence seems like temporary insanity to some parents and an interlude of perfect knowledge to some teenagers, crazy-making tensions are not normally enough to provoke running away. Most healthy families that fumble through the period of adolescence emerge intact. But in already shaky families, kids' urge to escape has no buttress to keep it in the realm of fantasy. 'Children have an instinctive faith in their parents' strength and goodness and, as they grow up, try – often against considerable odds – to maintain it ... This faith, after a long period of erosion, has crumbled, and with it their central life support ... The conflict escalates until the child's pain is beyond bearing, and he or she runs away.'[53]

To the kids, running away presents itself as the only way out, the only way of saving themselves. Can anyone argue that Jessie would have been better off staying home, where she was beaten and demeaned? Should Charlie have stayed with a mother who was starving and torturing him mentally, and with a stepfather who was raping him? Was Gilette better off with his neglectful mother and abusive stepfather than he was on the street? Was home a reasonable place for Sharon to stay?

Already jaded by experiences in foster and group homes, few young people with any experience of the main child-protection agencies will go voluntarily into the system's embrace. So, instead, they run to the street where they meet others just like themselves, kids without external supports being eaten away inside by internal conflicts.

The street changes some things for them. It gets the molesters and beaters off their backs. The external form of their lives manifestly changes, but because they have internalized a distorted emotional life, things don't get better for them. Jessie gets nabbed by street-wise older girls; Charlie gets beaten down by everything and everyone; Gilette wanders around in a drugged state of nihilistic numbness, terrified of the flashbacks and confusion simmering inside him; Sharon falls in love with a series of beaters who reproduce her childhood experience of adult love.

A twelve-year follow-up study of runaways found that their problems, especially in forming relationships, continued into adulthood.[54] A thirty-year longitudinal study showed that the kids of conflict and violence-ridden families were at grave risk of engaging in criminal behaviour as adults, committing such crimes as rape and assault – crimes that had been committed against them.[55] In substance, the street changes nothing. It is home without shelter.

3

Sexually Exploited Kids

Patsy: Some tricks are closet child molesters

When I first met Patsy, she looked tawdry and garish. Thick neon-blue shadow rose to her eyebrows. Caked-on blusher masked her face. A tangle of gold chains, a shiny purple tank top, wispy peroxide-yellow hair, and a rhinestone cross dangling from one ear completed her image of tough defiance.

The next day, as we sat across from each other in the din of the Day & Night Restaurant in Victoria, a hang-out for street-battered types, Patsy seemed different – younger, softer, surprisingly spontaneous and girlish for a sixteen-year-old who had spent three years hardening on the street and on the prostitutes' 'stroll.' Her face was pudgy-round with the pebbly skin and enlarged pores of adolescence abetted by too little soap and too much make-up. From inside the rough shell a very likeable girl emerged.

Growing up, Patsy did not feel well-liked. 'The only one who liked me was my father. My mother and brothers despised me – a normal family, I guess,' she says in earnest. 'My dad loves me to death because, of six kids, I'm his only daughter. My mom didn't want a daughter. She figured a girl would end up like her – on the street, on alcohol, and on drugs. I didn't disappoint her, 'cause here I am.' She gestures with mock triumph.

From age three to eight, Patsy was molested by an older brother. He was nine when he started touching her 'down there,' usually late at night in her bedroom while their parents were 'out drinking or downstairs sobering up.' Patsy explains, apologetically, that although she resisted her brother, she didn't understand that what he did to her was wrong – even when touching escalated to penetration.

'I was seven when the rapes started ... My parents were into alcohol and my brother was into incest. As far as I knew, my family was normal and what my brother did to me was what all families did to their girls. If anything was wrong, I would have figured it was my fault anyway.'

When Patsy was eight, her mother walked in on a rape. How did she react? 'Left the room till my brother finished and we had our clothes back on. Then she came back into my bedroom, asked him to go outside. "You slut," she hollered at me. "Why are you doing this to your brother?"' As Patsy recalls the scene now, her brown eyes fire with rage, and her voice quavers.

That night, another brother told Patsy's father what had happened. 'I think my brothers knew all along that I was being abused, but they kept their traps shut – macho code of loyalty, that bullshit. Until then, my dad had no idea. The news stunned him. He cried. He's a quiet, gentle man who has to get very riled even to curse. He actually beat my brother up. My dad's reaction made me realize that maybe what was going on in my bedroom wasn't normal, and that maybe it wasn't my fault.'

'If you ever lay a finger on her again, I'll kill you,' Patsy's father threatened her brother before drowning himself in a bottle. From that day forward, her father's drinking worsened and her mother's lessened. 'She pretty much sobered up, though I don't know why, because she couldn't have cared less that I was being raped. The whole house clammed up. He [the offending brother] glared at me all the time. Everyone else dummied up. They'd be talking and they'd hear me coming down the stairs. Conversation would stop.'

A terrible secret, in which some family members had probably been silently complicit, had been opened up, and no one knew how to deal with it. Patsy's father tried. He took her to a psychiatrist. 'I remember sitting there in this big chair, feeling very small, my mouth shut. I wouldn't talk to him. I mean, he was a guy. I'd already figured out not to trust them ... not that I trusted women either.'

By the time she was ten, Patsy had discovered the pain-dulling benefits of alcohol. By eleven, she had started sniffing typists' correction fluid. By thirteen, she knew how to make the cash she needed to bribe older kids to buy her beer: just hitch-hike to the next town in the Kootenays and 'do favours for dirty old men.' By her teens, she was a seasoned runaway. 'I didn't understand why I started running away when I was seven and sleeping in the bushes, but looking back I know I ran to get away from the sex abuse. At the time, I used to say that God told me to run away. When I got a bit older and into a cult, I used to say that Satan made me do it. Now I know it was me making me run.'

When Patsy was twelve, her father, her only ally, was involved in a serious construction-site accident and was shipped in a coma to a Vancouver hospital, where he remained for over a year. The family moved to Victoria. Patsy avoided going home. She started staying overnight with friends, and sometimes in the street.

'By fourteen, I hit the streets hard. My dad had recovered and was back home, but it was too late for me. No one else in my family loved me; except my dad and one older cousin, no one had stood up for me. Even my grandmother blamed me. After the family blow-out, I ran into her at the bingo hall. When I said, "Hi, Gran," she just snubbed me, said in a real uppity voice: "I don't know who you are."

'I really hurt my dad by going to the street. He even went public to threaten my pimp. He said on TV that the only reason he wasn't hunting my pimp down was fear that I might be in danger. I hurt my dad in ways I can never replace. But my family hurt me in ways they can never compensate for, so I don't feel too guilty.'

Although Patsy hoped a street family could make amends for the hurts, the street compounded the pain, heaping more injury on a child well-primed for pimps. She was fourteen, working the streets in a mutual-protection pact with another girl, when she 'fell in love' with her first pimp.

'Tara, my native girlfriend that I shared a hotel room with, had just died, murdered at fifteen by a trick. I was heart-broken. My boyfriend [pimp number one] was a big help. I didn't know he was a pimp. No one did because he was new to Victoria and he didn't "play game" on me – no gifts, no sweet talk, none of the usual crap that comes before the sucker-punch.

'He was just my boyfriend. He kept six [look-out] on me when I was on the corner, took down licence plates, acted as my spotter [protector]. One night, he asked to borrow some money. Next night, he wanted *his* money. It took me three weeks to figure out he was a pimp, but I stayed with him six months.' Why? 'Because he was the first person besides my dad to love me, and because I was his only girl. Now he's a real player with a stable of five girls, including a couple of twelve-year-olds. Tricks just love fresh meat.'

Her 'boyfriend' took all her money. 'To hang onto any cash, I had to cheat him. I'd say I'd broken [had dates] for sixty dollars, when I'd broken for eighty.' In return for the money she supplied, he supplied beatings. 'He treated me like shit in hell. Poundings. Knifings. One time he even stuck a shank [knife] in my gut. He loved acting tough around his friends. "You're seen, not heard, bitch. Remember it!" ' Did she think he loved her? Did she feel she loved him? 'Oh yeah! It was love all right.

'After six months, he sold me ... that's right, sold me. A cash transaction. For $4,000, according to him. [To buoy her sense of self-worth, this figure may be inflated, but it's probably not far off the mark. In the street, 'fresh meat' fetches a high bride-price.] It happened when I was out on Broadway. A new player from LA was in town. I see them talking. Next thing, number one is giving me the word: "This is it, bitch, you're gone. Time for me to find myself a new ho [hooker]." '

Number two was no improvement. Patsy was his 'wife-in-law' [second-ranking girl] in a 'family' of six girls living in three rooms at the Quality Inn. Her job as second whip was to kowtow to the pimp's main lady, his 'private slave and leg-spreader.' Patsy had to prostitute, plus collect money from his other hookers.

Barely fifteen, she was already a veteran in the perversions of pimps and tricks. 'Bad dates are routine for a girl like me who doesn't listen to her gut about guys that smell dangerous. I went with – and I still go with – almost anybody. I don't care if one kills me; maybe it's more peaceful on the other side. Besides, even if you're careful, you're bound to get bad dates. I mean, just look at the bad-trick sheets [news updates on violent customers compiled and distributed by street outreach organizations]: rapes, assaults, murder attempts.'

Patsy has worked in Toronto, Calgary, Vancouver, Victoria, and Seattle. She says some places are more dangerous than others. 'Out here, in Victoria, high heels and your teeth are usually weapons enough – though they won't help if you get the guy who's going to beat you no matter what. In Vancouver and Toronto, you've got to carry a switch-blade or a gun. The bad tricks there are very violent. Calgary is mixed; it can go either way, wild or tame. They've even got a corner, under the tower at 9th Avenue, where lesbians can pick up hookers. I did it once. I got $100 for walking around with my shirt off all night!' She giggles. 'At least there's no risk of violence when girls pick you up. [There appear to be very few female tricks in Canada whether lesbian or heterosexual.]

'From men there's always the possibility of violence. In my books, all tricks are bad, really. I think most of them hate women. Dirty slimeballs, sickos. Many want you to be their little daughters. They'll say, "How old are you, sweetheart?" and I'll say, "How old do you want me to be, honey?" Most of these bums will answer "ten" or "twelve." Basically, they want to fuck their daughters. I've got a regular who brings along kiddy gear for me to prance around in at the hotel room: smocked dress, ankle sox, lollipops, hair ribbons. He likes pig-tails and freckles, so I have to put silly dots on my face with an eyebrow pencil. Closet molesters like him are common, but I prefer them to rapists who get off on smacking girls out and raping us.'

What do police do about bad tricks? 'Sometimes I think the tricks are a cakewalk compared to the cops. Some of them like beating up on street kids; they get off on it. I'm a juvey, right? You'd think they'd go a little easier on me, or try to help me get off the street. The only street they want to help me get off is theirs – like if they rough me up, manhandle me, beat me up enough, always when I'm hand-cuffed, hands behind my back – will I do them a favour and get out of town? Cops here won't even take charges from hookers on bad tricks. Only on pimps. You want to charge a pimp with living off the avails and they're all ears; you want to charge a trick with attempted homicide and they dummy up, tell you it's the price of doing business and basically what you deserve anyway! After all, you're just a worthless whore!'

Victoria was the only city where I heard this complaint, one reiterated by outreach workers and other street kids. The 'condom lady' from AIDS Vancouver Island, My Lipton, and Judy Walsh, who manages a youth shelter and does streetwork for the Association for Street Kids (ASK), said that, in practice, though obviously not in policy, police won't accept assault and rape charges from hookers. They also complained about merchants and politicians who, they claim, collaborate to rid their streets of youngsters, a don't-bother-us-just-go-someplace-else attitude.

It's easy to understand why. Government Street, the heart of the stroll, is as much a magnet for tourists as it is a boulevard of broken dreams for runaways. All roads in Victoria lead to this one short stretch of domp brick with its exclusive boutiques featuring the finest of British worsteds and native crafts. The pristine setting is anomalous, nothing like the grim decay of tenderloin tracks in most Canadian cities. The contrast here between impoverished girls leaning against lamp-posts and relatively rich tourists window shopping is jarring. Greater Victoria, with a population of around 250,000, is a provincial place where contradictions that are easier to mask in large cities become conspicuous.

One night, on Government Street, I watched a john in a sleek car pick up a child hooker. I wondered what he was buying. 'Anal sex, if he can get it,' said Patsy. 'That's pretty popular. But I don't do that. Then blow jobs, which are safest because you've got teeth and if the guy tries to choke you, you can bite. Let him try to explain his bleeding dick to his wife!' She laughs with obvious delight.

As glib as Patsy is about street dangers and death, she has to worry about protecting herself. Pimp protection is not all it's cracked up to be. How can a pimp swaggering in the street or swilling in a bar protect a girl in a car or hotel room? Patsy knows he can't. That's why she carries a knife. She says she used it 'only once – to stab a bad trick in the nuts. This guy was a real freak, assaulted seven girls in one week. When he tried to pick me up, I went along just to get our revenge, and I got it!'

Has she ever wanted to avenge the sexual assaults her brother committed? 'No. That's different. That's like carrying a grudge. A grudge is something you can't afford in the street. You can't carry around hate forever, especially for your family. Like the junkie that stabbed me in the foot. I could have killed him at the time, but I understand why he did it. He was sick. He needed money. He thought I had some. I haven't exactly forgiven him, but I don't hate him either. In his spot, I could do the same thing.'

As a self-confessed 'hype' (intravenous drug-user), Patsy could easily be in the same situation. Yanking up her shirt sleeve, she says: 'See. My track marks are already drying up, but I was hooked on needles. Hard to explain how the needle suckers you more than the drugs. It's something about seeing your own blood and having the power to push it back into your arm, to save your life or let it go out.'

By the time, barely a month before this interview, that Patsy started to exercise a different kind of power over her life by trying to kick drugs, she had spent three years experimenting with every drug available on the street. In the end, she was on an alternating regimen of cocaine and heroin, plus 'anything else you can mix up in a spoon and shoot up your arm.'

Between age fourteen and now (sixteen) she had three pregnancies from her 'boyfriends' (pimps), two of them miscarriages, and had given birth to an addicted baby who was put up for adoption. Patsy was probably facing one of three kinds of premature death: accidental overdose, deliberate overdose, or homicidal customer.

But love came to the rescue. 'One night, for no good reason, my boyfriend [pimp number two] beat the shit out of me with a pool cue at a billiard hall. I staggered out of there with blood dripping from cuts on my head. A stranger walking by ran to help me.

' "You need to get to a hospital," he said to me, all concern. "I'll take you, c'mon."

' "I can't go with you. My man's over there. He'll kill me if I go with anyone except a date."

' "Don't worry. I'll pretend to be a john."

'He took me to the hospital. After they stitched me up, I went home with him. He took care of me and tried very, very hard to get me off the street and off drugs. He even called the cops on me one time when I was crazy-high. They told him they wouldn't come, that nobody can do nothing for a junkie that doesn't want to quit.'

Patsy, eyes smiling, enthuses about her 'fiancé.' 'He's the first real boyfriend I've had, a real friend. He's twenty-two, a working mechanic, a straight arrow – no drugs, no booze, not even cigarettes – although he hasn't always been that way. When he was nineteen, he did time for armed robbery. So he knows about the kind of life I'm living.' Does he know she is still hooking? 'He knows I have no other way to live right now because he's in jail.' Jail? I though he was a straight arrow. 'He's doing four months on my beef, took the fall for my heroin-possession charge. But he'll be out by Christmas and he's going to find a clean lady. I quit junk the day he got sent away. It's the least I can do for a guy that's doing my time and who tried so hard to make me clean up.'

How serious is she? 'Dead serious. I quit cold turkey and, when the withdrawals started, I got a social worker to put me in detox for two weeks. I have to quit; I can't survive much more junk.' What about 'soft' drugs, and what about hooking? 'I'm staying clear of chemicals, but not grass or alcohol. Maybe if me and my fiancé last, I can cut back to beer and cigarettes and grass, a square life-style, in other words. As for hooking, I can't afford to quit. With my education less than grade nine, what else can I do? To tell the truth, I'll probably stay on the street until I'm too used up to pull a trick within an hour on the corner.

'But at least I'm not going to kill myself with drugs. Sometimes now I even feel like I want to live, because even if I'm not special to myself, I'm special to my fiancé.'

One cannot help but wonder how solid her fiancé is; Patsy has not been groomed for finding good men. If he turns out to be yet another frog rather than the prince she gushes over in typically teenage fashion, what then? Not only is she trying to quit drugs for him, not for herself, but she is back in an alternative school, working on her grade nine, not because she wants to but because of a bargain she struck with one of her brothers. 'He's paying me sixty dollars a month to go back because his wife committed suicide after her twin sister, a hooker, was murdered by a trick. I guess murder and suicide made him realize what danger I'm in, and maybe he wants to save me 'cause he couldn't save the other girls in his life.'

Does she want to save herself? 'Yes and no. Most of the time, I don't care about life. I still think about suicide almost every day. Death doesn't scare me. I think it will be more peaceful on the other side. Maybe over there people won't judge me for what I've done ... funny, eh? Men don't mind using you, but then they zip up their fly and treat you like a leper. They make you suck their cocks and then they call you a "filthy little cocksucker"! Do all these judges ever stop to think that I wouldn't be out here if I had a choice, that I wouldn't be fried on drugs if my life wasn't so bad? Prostitution is what you do when you can't make a decent living any other way.' Patsy suddenly looks drawn and tired, the girlishness gone from her face.

Then, as suddenly, she perks up, having reached deep, I think, into the survivor's inner reservoir that keeps kids like her alive. 'But, on the other hand, I want to live for the day when I can look in a mirror and feel conceited, when I can brag to my fiancé, "You're lucky to have me." He'll answer "I know," and that will put a lasting smile on my face.'

Jarett: In limbo between street and straight life

'I know you're about ten years older than me, so I hope you won't misinterpret it if I suggest we meet for lunch at a little café,' Jarett said when I called him to arrange for an interview. Strange comment, I thought to myself as I answered: 'Not that it's relevant, but I'm more than twenty years older and we can meet anyplace that's convenient for you.'

I first met him by chance after a high-school variety show in a typical bedroom community west of Toronto, populated by middle–middle-class home-owners. Jarett performed some of his original songs and poetry. His recital was full of allusions to street life, his lyrics and prose from a well-spring that couldn't belong to a typical suburban kid. When we chatted after his performance, I learned that he had just returned to school, newly off downtown streets where he had lived for four years.

Our second meeting took place at a terrace restaurant overlooking lush hotel grounds, the kind of setting that would overwhelm most street kids. But Jarett couldn't have been more comfortable. 'It's a sweltering day. You'd probably like to sit inside where it's air-conditioned,' he offered as I wilted towards his table. Suave kid, I thought to myself, too suave for the streets.

My interest was piqued as I watched him waltz smoothly through a ritual of getting us and his drink relocated indoors while charming the harried waitress. 'She'll have a Perrier with ice and lime,' he instructed the waitress. 'In this blistering heat,

it's the only thing.' He said it with such authority that I nodded agreement instead of admitting I'd prefer a Coke and could order it myself, thank you very much.

Jarett grew up in the neighbourhood where we met, and described his stepfather as a well-off owner of a small trucking company. Although he adopted Jarett when the boy was six, the stepfather in essence disowned him and his older sister, products of his mother's first marriage. 'He was fine with their kids – the two he had with my mom – but he hated us. No exaggeration: hate! He wasn't a beater, he was worse: an emotional blackmailer. He wouldn't talk to me at all, like I wasn't in the room. My mom was too weak to stand up to him. She was our go-between.'

Tormented by the rejection Jarett ran away repeatedly and, like so many other street kids, appealed to his 'friends in blue' for help. 'The cops always made me feel like a whiny brat when I'd complain about my stepfather. Maybe they would have taken me seriously if he'd beaten me half to death, but instead they took me home and agreed with him about what a foul-mouthed little punk I was.'

At fifteen, Jarett stopped going to the police and started going downtown instead. Today, at nineteen, he is living in limbo, 'mostly off the street' but not reunited with his family. He thinks reconciliation is impossible. He pretends he doesn't care, but hurt and love-hate colour every reference to his mother. This young man smoulders with unfinished family business.

From the moment Jarett and I met that day, I was uncomfortable – uncomfortable making eye contact, awkward with questions, unconsciously shying away from the sticky ones. Jarett was quietly forthright and loquacious, composed beyond his years.

'How did you survive four years on the street? What did you do for money?' I asked after the slow interview warmed up a little. He nonchalantly listed his sources of revenue: 'B&Es, muggings, hustling – for women, not gays – and dealing dope.'

Hustling women. In the street, Jarett used what he had – good looks that combine blue-eyed softness and square-chinned ruggedness, plus the charm of cultivated manners and an interest in the arts – to make his living. When he admitted it, I understood my discomfort; it was Jarett's manner, the way he moved, the way he looked at me: every motion, every glance was subtly suggestive. Jarett had learned to be provocative, never knowing where a meeting with an older woman might lead, open to all possibilities. There was nothing personal in it; he was interacting the way he automatically relates to all women.

'Sexual relationships are the only kind I've ever had with women,' he confessed. 'I can't get into normal relationships at all; I've only ever had one girlfriend. Otherwise, it's all been sex with friends to keep warm on a cold night, or to share a passing feeling. Looking back, I know it was never more than a fast fuck.'

After Jarett talked about his life as a hustler, it's not hard to imagine how a teenager could cynically equate relationships with empty sex. 'Mostly you have to screw rich – as in big cars, gobs of jewellery, mitts-full of cash – women in their thirties and forties who are bored with their marriages. Or you have to do it to rejects who can't get a man. Sometimes it's for a couple of lesbians that want your bod for certain acts.

'I didn't care who it was or what they wanted me to do; I'd just think about the room service and the TV I'd have to myself after the gig was over. You lay a chick, you can count on getting a hot meal and a hotel room for the night. It sure beat sleeping in the street.'

What kind of money did he make? 'Money?' Jarett laughs. 'That's what the pimp gets. By the way, my pimp's a woman, and just in case you never heard of female pimps before, there are only a few of them around, mostly hookers who tire of working on their backs and decide to get on top of the game for a change. Some guys that hustle women use a female pimp because we can't exactly stand on street corners and expect ladies to cruise by and check us out. With female tricks, business is very discrete. The pimp usually sets up the dates and collects the cash up front. Me, I get a small cut, plus maybe a tip from the date. And the drugs, of course. My pimp would give me a few hits from time to time.'

Jarett also broke into private homes 'to raid the fridge,' or he and other members of his pick-up gang mugged passers-by, or panhandled, or dealt dope on street corners. 'Until there was enough cash to score more drugs. I did every drug you can name, except heroin. One time when I was on blotters of weird-stone, as it's called in the street – it's like LSD but it's produced in a lab – I slashed myself up with a razor. It's a high that makes you feel completely invincible. I don't remember cutting myself, but I do remember waking up in hospital. Obviously, I didn't die, but death is never far from your door – not that you have a door. Street kids all know death. Death is where your friends go.'

When he hits the sad notes, Jarret's voice trails off into flat affect and detachment characteristic of street kids when they recount the deadly vignettes that make up their lives. Despite his appearance, dress, language – none of which would set him apart from a high-school-dance crowd – experientially and emotionally, Jarett hails from a distant and alien zone.

Yet, he has conventional ambitions; he is determined to finish school. Even as a street kid, he periodically disguised himself and used a phoney address to enrol in a suburban high school. 'My teachers had no idea I was living in abandoned buildings. One English marm caught on to my scam after I brought in my rough for an essay on brown-paper bags! After that, she gave me school supplies and swore not to reveal my secret.'

Jarett had good reason to hide his real address. A lot of 'chump change' went missing from locker rooms, as did lunches and Walkmans. His earnings from petty theft and occasional tricks paid for his schooling.

He wasn't caught for theft, but he was called down for being a street kid. The principal who figured it out kicked him out. 'He called me "the pied piper of an élite street gang" and told me he wanted me out because I was a "bad influence," bound to "corrupt" other students and "drag them down" to my level. Instead of admiring me for trying to get an education while I was squatting in condemned buildings – no home, no family – the guy wanted to kick me back to the streets. He didn't want "undesirables" in "his school." '

He speaks about beating the street. 'I'm one lucky SOB. Because I never got busted, I don't have a record. But I lived in such terror

of spending my life in jail that it finally drove me off the street.'
He has already taken strides 'back to civilization.' He's living as
a welcome, non-paying house guest with the family of a school
chum who knows about his past and is giving him a base for
building a future. Besides being back at school, he says he has
quit B&E's and drugs, 'except pot at parties. I've quit the hard
stuff, but it hasn't stopped affecting me. Every time I read a
paragraph and try to recall what I've read, and can't, I know
what damage the dope has done. My memory is shot.'

His plans include summer courses and a year's schooling to
graduate from high school, all in preparation for university
studies in performing arts. It sounds good.

As we part, Jarett, in his narrow black leather tie and trendy
sports jacket, tells me he has a 'date.' 'I don't have a pimp any
more, so for a ten-minute poke I can make what it would take a
week to earn in the kind of jobs high-school students get.'

At most it will take five more years before he is too shop-worn
to sell his body easily. When Jarett's flesh isn't as firm anymore,
when he isn't as pretty, his market will dry up. In the meantime,
he lives a double life as a talented high-school day student with
the night-time values of the street.

Child Prostitution

Sexual abuse of children usually begins at home. Some runaways
never escape it. Instead, they move on to the business end of
abuse on the street, where girls and boys are bought and sold. A
1987 conference on adolescent prostitution in Canada equated
underage hooking with sex abuse and charged society with
tacitly condoning this misuse of children.[1] A 1988 education
campaign by Family Services of Greater Vancouver included a
widely displayed poster that read: 'Real Men Don't Buy Kids.'
The conference and campaign message were the same. Kids do
not prostitute themselves; adults exploit them. Kids are not
hookers; they are victims.

Child prostitutes are usually adolescents, effectively without
families, forced into extremely dangerous situations to meet their
basic needs. Mostly penniless, luckless throwaways, they have

little control over their lives and few choices. Rather, they are pawns in a sordid business largely controlled by pimps and pornographers who treat kids like commodities, selling them and their images to tricks and to kiddy-porn fans.

According to most streetworkers who contributed to this book, hookers on Canada's streets are typically age sixteen to twenty-four. These sources say that most teenagers working in escort services, massage parlours, skin flicks, strip joints, and on street corners today were thirteen to eighteen when they started out. Some started younger; almost all will become discarded merchandise by the time they reach their mid- to late twenties – if a pimp, a trick, drugs, or disease hasn't already killed them. In the business, thirty is over the hill. Most tricks won't pay for has-been bodies.

Many older hookers seem to have been late starters, which means they 'turned out' in their early to mid-twenties. Unlike teens trapped into the trade, older women usually turn to prostitution after other choices and chances have failed – after a long period in which an ex-husband hasn't paid child support, after low wages force single moms onto welfare, and after welfare rates and rules make it necessary for them to supplement their income with illegal earnings. Sole-support mothers in this bind go consciously as free-lances (no pimps) into 'the life,' choosing it over poverty-enforcing alternatives. Among kids, however, there is not even this illusion of choice.

Runaways do not flee their homes, dreaming of a glamorous life of prostitution. None expects to become a hooker. The literature, academic and anecdotal alike, argues that 'no child in prostitution *wants* to be a prostitute.'[2] A cabby who taxied youngsters around the Toronto track was so impressed by their unanimous hatred of hooking that he wrote a convincing exposé. *The Stroll* leaves no room for imagining that young girls, or indeed women, choose prostitution.[3] In the interviews and informal discussions that formed the basis of this book, not one of the girls selling sex said she would choose prostitution if she could make decent money any other way.

Streetworkers across the country say the same thing: given access to an alternative that paid a respectable living wage – not a starvation wage – most girls would give up prostitution. 'I've never met a woman yet who wants to be a hooker,' says Robert Paris, a streetworker at Montreal's Projet d'intervention auprès des mineurs(res) prostitués(ées) (PIMP). 'I've met some boys who say they want to hustle, but even this may be false because it is harder to get boys to open their hearts and express their true feelings.'

What accounts for the traffic in children's bodies? First, our social system. Driven by profit, it lays bare to commerce anything with money-making potential. Human beings, including children, are not exempt. The bottom line reigns. Though socially bankrupt, sexual exploiting of children is bankable. Morality, it appears, derives from economy, not vice versa.

Second, child prostitution thrives because of sexism, a by-product of a society founded on private property and the power it bestows, both primarily male preserves. In reality, few men either own real wealth or possess real power. However, they do inherit crumbs of privilege in the form of superiority over women and children. Sexism in economic, political, and social life plays itself out in microcosm in many significant and subtle ways: pimps owning other human beings they sell, and men buying other human beings they use for sexual pleasure, constitute everyday examples.

Sexist attitudes are deeply entrenched in prostitution. To many, 'tricks' exist only because hookers do, and 'sexual impulses are seen as an understandable form of dalliance which finds expression only because of the existence of hookers. Hookers are sluts, women [and girls] who prey upon the natural desires of ordinarily morally upright men.'[4]

The justice system reflects and reinforces this distorted perspective in many ways. Customers are rarely arrested, whereas prostitutes commonly face charges. In Calgary, for example, 107 hookers and 26 johns were charged over 1986 and 1987.[5] In addition, a Canada-wide study entitled *Street Prostitution: Assessing the Impact of the Law* (referring to Bill C-49, the anti-soliciting law) found that prostitutes, mostly women, are sentenced more severely than are their customers in every city.[6] An international study of child prostitution concluded that judges usually impose light sentences and feel soft-hearted towards tricks. ' "It's the kind of thing that could happen to anyone," said one British judge ... about a man who, when drunk, had sexually abused a girl of ten."[7]

One Canadian organization, Toronto's Metro Action Committee on Public Violence against Women and Children (METRAC), has amassed almost a thousand sentencing reports that show judges often blame victims for provoking sex assaults, downplay the crime's severity, and factor offenders' social status and employment record into lenient sentencing.[8] 'Judges often see real rape as a blameless virgin or older woman at home behind locked doors crocheting a flag who is raped when a man breaks in wearing a balaclava,'[9] says METRAC executive director Patricia Marshall.

Even the language of prostitution expresses the prejudice. Females of all ages are called 'working girls.' It's little wonder hookers are called 'girls' since, as Patsy says, many customers fancy sex with children. A hooker most often refers to her pimp as 'my man,' while a pimp often refers to his hooker as 'my bitch.' Derisive pimp talk designed to demoralize their prey even peppers the language hookers use to describe themselves. 'See that bitch over there?' a fifteen-year-old Winnipeg street veteran said to me, pointing to a skinny youngster in shiny leotards and spike heels. 'She tried to jack me up [rob me].'

Sexism is a boon to the business, as is racism. In Vancouver, a disproportionate number of prostitutes appear to come from native or minority backgrounds. In Winnipeg, aboriginal females appear to be very overrepresented in the sex trade. In Montreal and Halifax, many black girls and women work the stroll, blocked from anything better by the triple jeopardy of being born poor, female, and black. It is little wonder that some, like Della, whom you will meet later in this chapter, quickly become blasé about selling themselves. 'How else can a girl like me [meaning poor, black, and ill-educated] ever make any real money?' she asks.

While capitalism, sexism, and racism undergird commerce in youth abuse, other potent factors also contribute: pimps and tricks. Obviously, juveniles could not sell themselves if no one out there was buying. Besides, without a middleman to initiate and manipulate them, it seems unlikely that many youngsters would stick with the skin trade once they realized its consequences. Surprisingly, many kids seem to possess only a vague notion of what prostitution means when they are first 'turned out.' Some are literally in a trick's car 'giving head' before they understand what 'working the street' for their slick new 'boyfriend' means. The pimp is essential to the mass-marketing of youths.

Exploitation of children by adults takes place in all branches of the trade. As Annie Ample, celebrity stripper and author, describes it, on the club circuit, a manager or agent – a title that often disguises pimping – takes a cut from both the club manager and the dancers, and sells drugs to strippers. In this cosy arrangement, he makes money off them and they make money for him.[10] Ample exposes the so-called adult-entertainment business of the 1980s as an industry where young women, including under-age girls, are forced into acts of extreme self-degradation and are deliberately transformed by managers and club owners into 'coke whores,' 'part-hooker, part-doper.'[11]

The sexploitation of children by adults, whether by the seller or the buyer, further distorts already misshapen lives, robbing kids of all trace of self-respect and making a come-back to a life of dignity all the more complex and unlikely.

FROM RUNAWAY TO PROSTITUTE

No reliable estimate of the number of teenagers engaged in the Canadian sex industry exists. In the United States, an estimated 500,000 juveniles are involved. They each turn on average 300 tricks a year, which adds up to about 150 million incidents of sexual abuse of juveniles.[12]

Canada's uncounted kids are mostly runaways whose parents have not bothered to issue a missing-persons report. Many are transient and difficult to track even if anyone was trying to find them. Those between age sixteen and eighteen who are not wards of the state, that is, in care extended beyond the standard cut-off age of sixteen, have little contact with mainstream agencies that could guess at their life-style. They are statusless individuals, truly missing children, juveniles who do not count.

Child prostitution includes kids exploited in off-street fronts for the trade, such as escort services – listings for such services take up thirty-one pages in Bell Canada's Yellow Pages for Toronto – and massage parlours. They also include part-timers who use the street to supplement welfare, whether general assistance or special-circumstances assistance sometimes granted to teenagers living independently. Taken together, their numbers would shock most Canadians. For example: Street Outreach Services (SOS) in Toronto reported 1,721 'significant' contacts with street hookers aged sixteen to twenty-four in just one month (November 1988).[13] While this number represents conversations rather than individuals – staff may have more than one session with a given individual – it is revealing enough to watch the most visible trade on the main strolls in Toronto or Vancouver. One sees a constant parade of young people imperilled by perverts, paedophiles, and pimps.

Why do many runaways end up in prostitution? While no single explanation covers every case, background patterns among juvenile prostitutes are uniform enough to conclude that practically 'every runaway child who goes into full-time prostitution has a history of continual and profound family conflict.'[14] Over half the street prostitutes interviewed by the Badgley Committee on Sexual Offences against Children and Youth recalled home as a place of continuous squabbles.[15] A 1985 study of forty-two child prostitutes in Vancouver conducted for the solicitor general found that 80 per cent of the girls and 17 per cent of the boys had been sexually abused at home, mostly by men.[16] With only one exception, every female hooker interviewed for this book came from a family that was sexually destructive, physically violent, or mentally cruel.

The exception, whose parents barely spoke English, was expected to follow strick moral and behaviour codes, harsh even by the old-country standards of her parents. This same type of stifling home environment drove Evelyn Lau to spend two years on Vancouver streets when she was fourteen to sixteen, hooked on hooking and drugs.[17]

Kids from similarly inflexible backgrounds, and incest victims, are overrepresented in the street and in prostitution. Though background specifics vary, generally speaking child prostitutes tend to have experienced a deep and damaging divide between themselves and their parent(s) or substitute caregivers. Their family dynamics annihilated the child's self-respect and sowed seeds of self-hatred that would later blossom into self-destruction.

While physical abuse and neglect can precipitate the downward spiral, early sexual trauma may be the most prevalent shared experience among young hookers, especially girls. Prostitutes are twice as likely as typical Canadian adolescents to have had prepubescent sex accompanied by force or threat of force.[18] Early sexual invasions twisted the lives of many of the 'invisible children' (street prostitutes) studied in Britain, West Germany, and the United States.[19] 'The violation of fragile child sexuality, if it is combined with other family tensions or emotional deficiencies – whether in the child or in the family – makes the probability of catastrophe in puberty extremely high.'[20]

That catastrophe includes sleeping with practically everyone street kids meet, even outside prostitution, because physical intimacy is often the only kind of affection they know and the only currency they have with which to buy shelter. 'When they are younger it may be because they have been conditioned to think that this is how to act, and when they are a little older there can be an element of perversity, when the pain and outrage [they feel] lead to behaviour that is deliberately outrageous to others.'[21]

Social class also affects catastrophe potential. Much of the Canadian research confirms what the Elizabeth Fry Society discovered: that street hookers are more likely to come from poorer families than from wealthier ones.[22] But a minority do come from middle- and upper-middle-class backgrounds. Besides incest, which is no respecter of class, outreach workers cite pressures in single-parent and blended families. They also blame families like Mark's, which you will read about later in this chapter, where a parent (or parents) is obsessed with career, making money, living high, and pursuing pleasure. Kids in such families may not be actively abused, but they are actively neglected even amid their excess of material possessions. Like Mark, they feel unloved and unwanted, and seek out love in all the wrong places.

While increasing numbers of better-off adolescents, both female and male, join the street scene, and some prostitute themselves, most street hookers have been raised in devastated, low-income families. Irrespective of social class, however, most victims of violence and incest do not run away and become hookers. Most continue through adolescence, trapped in dangerous families. Testimonies from survivors, few more gut-wrenching than Sylvia Fraser's in *My Father's House*[23] and Elly Danica's in *Don't: A Woman's Word*[24] have become common fare in magazine articles and popular books today.

Those who can't abide the abuse and who feel forced to flee run a great risk of being rescued by a pimp. Family life has prepared them to become a particular kind of victim in a particular subculture. Sex, they have learned, is a ticket to love; their sex the only asset they have to offer.

Feather: Welfare puts us out here

Marie Arrington of Vancouver's Prostitutes and Other Women for Equal Rights (POWER) shared with me the wisdom she had gleaned about hookers beating the street. 'I hope you aren't crediting the system [social services and justice] or streetworkers for getting anyone off. The kids make it on their own tenacity and survival instincts ... All the system ever does is judge them, deny them what it promises, set them up to fail, and reinforce failure when it happens. Most social workers give up on anyone who doesn't turn her life around first or second try.'

Feather, twenty, is seriously trying to turn her life around for the first time right now. She slides into our booth at the Korner Restaurant, POWER's 'second office,' at Helmcken and Seymour, smack on the stroll. Through the chintz curtains, by the light of street lamps, we see the parade of strutting stilettos. Hookers checking out the johns, 'suits' casing the 'hoes.' Feather, her sweater and lipstick both fire-engine red, sidles up to Marie.

'Any common threads in the backgrounds of girls who end up here?' I ask. Marie answers: 'There no mould; they're as individual as their thumb-print, but there's often lots of abuse of some kind, of course.'

Of course.

'I wasn't abused,' Feather volunteers. 'Not all the girls have been abused. Some of them were just rebels like me.' I'm wondering whether her claim is true or just denial when a stunning Asian woman decked out in mohair and leather interrupts. 'I had a bad date,' she says matter-of-factly to Marie, who copies down details for a 'bad-trick sheet.'

If Feather sells herself after our interview tonight, she risks being bought by one of the men or groups of men on the current list, as many are repeaters. They include a guy who rammed a lead pipe up a hooker's rectum after beating her unconscious; another who held a knife to a prostitute's throat and promised to stab her; a man who put a sawed-off shotgun to a woman's head and threatened to kill her. Prostitutes explain that some dates get off sexually with the help of sadism before or during the act, part of the main course of their pleasure. Some prefer a little violence after sex, for dessert.

'Tricks are all pigs and perverts,' offers a plucky young woman who plunks herself down next to me, staring intently into a compact mirror as she brushes generous strokes of blush on her cheeks. 'Of course, we can't say that to their faces because they're our meal tickets, but they are – pigs and perverts.' A woman with a rich fall of dark curls nods agreement as she joins our busy booth and chimes in: 'The more money a trick has, the kinkier he's likely to be. Like, we got one regular, a lawyer who pays $500 a shot to have hairs on his balls burned with cigarettes!' Plucky laughs scornfully. 'That's nothing! I've got one who's into golden showers [being urinated on].'

By now, our booth is achatter with nonchalant young women, late teens and early twenties, on a coffee break, deriding their dates. For all their brashness, they are not going back to a typical work-place with typical risks. They are going out on a street that might kill them tonight, as it has killed at least eight others over 1988 and early 1989.[25] (No arrests were made.)

I quiz the klatch of experts on the local constabulary. On the subject of the police their vitriol is unanimous. They claim cops hold them in contempt, do little to make their lives safer, bust them when they can. Some officers, they say, are not above exchanging favours: a blind eye to their business for 'a free blow job.'

Other strolls around Vancouver, such as the Downtown Eastside and Mt Pleasant strips, attract lower-echelon hookers than the ones chatting with me at the Korner Restaurant. The cream is here, turned out in the best of seductive gear: quality spandex, real wool sweaters with sequins, real fur coats, real Italian shoes. On the east side of town, conspicuously poor girls and women shiver in cheap imitations, working any number of shifts that run around the clock. They stand in hotel doorways along East Hastings in a neighbourhood where welfare is a way of life. Hookers there are more likely to be self-employed, pimpless welfare moms 'sinning for their – or, for their kids' – supper,' as one streetworker put it.

A woman in Tammy Bakker make-up who has worked both classy and déclassé strolls says the difference is only cosmetic. 'You still got to suck off some creep to live.' Warmed by coffee and shop talk, the women in our booth drift back to, as Plucky describes it, 'a shift of blow jobs, hand jobs, lays, half-and-halfs (starts with a blow, ends in a lay), and more imaginative sexual mechanics with strangers. Marie gets busy, spreading the latest bad-trick news to a couple of streetworkers who drop by. Everyone in this friendly all-night café seems to know everyone else. Regulars. Waitresses, young and patient, serve mostly good cheer, never hurrying the coffee-drinkers who occupy tables for hours. Feather and I move to a back booth, the traffic outside increasing as the night grows colder.

'I only lived with my natural family till I was three because my mother drank too much and didn't take care of us, and my father was disabled and couldn't do much for us. My first foster family starved me – I'd often go whole days without food – and beat me with a wooden spoon. My second foster family believed in ice-cold baths for punishments, or in whippings. They'd haul my pants down in front of their family and strap my bum. Sometimes my older sister and I were whipped together since we were placed with the same family,' Feather blurts out in one long breathless rush.

'You said a couple of hours ago that you hadn't been abused,' I interject.

'I meant I wasn't being abused at the time when I became a runaway; I didn't run away because of abuse. Yes, I was abused when I was very young, but I don't think that has anything to do with what I became. Besides, I had it easy compared to my sister. I watched her get raped when she was six and I was three, before we were wards. We were at a baby-sitter's place that was having a party. A boy came into our room and raped her, not that I knew what rape meant, but I remember her screaming and my feeling very scared. When we got home and my mother spotted her soiled panties, my mom demanded to know what *she* had done to make a boy do that to her! Can you believe that? My sister was six years old, for god's sake!'

Feather's family originally came from Calgary, but moved around a lot. When she was six, both she and her sister were placed with a pious Pentecostal family. After that, she never saw her mother again. 'The foster family was very strict. My sister ran away two years before me, when she was thirteen. She got into prostitution and heroin. She tried to get me away from the foster family, but they wouldn't let us see each other.

'When the mother and father split up, I finally got away from there too. All I got in its place, though, was a group home where I met older girls who got me into parties and into boosting [stealing] from the West Edmonton Mall. Eventually we were caught and I ended up in juvey detention. Then I got shipped to another group home for troubled girls. Meanwhile, my natural parents had divorced and my dad – he's French – had married another poor Indian woman like my mom and had had two new kids. I hated visiting them because they were living like pigs on a dirt-poor reserve.

'In my life, nothing was stable and nothing was good. I started running. I'd stay with my sister and her Indian boyfriend, but when she got busted for prostitution, he convinced me I could get her bail by turning some tricks. I'd already spotted for my sister, but I didn't really understand what it was you did in the car. I went out there anyway and just did what the men who picked me up told me to do. I was thirteen.'

Her sister's boyfriend used the money for drugs, not for bail. Then he abandoned Feather and his own fourteen-year-old sister. The girls started selling their bodies for supper and a bed. Occasionally, cops would pick Feather up and drop her back at the group home, from which she would immediately run away. By grade nine, age fourteen, she'd left school. 'There was too much crap in my head for school, plus I couldn't relate to girls my age. How is a kid who is already called a thief, a jailbird, and a whore supposed to get along with girls who are into sleep-overs? I fit in better with an older crowd, though I didn't do drugs myself after I seen the damage it did to my sister.

'I was a wild kid, a rebel, hanging out at the malls during the day, partying at night. And hooking, yes. But not for pimps, not even after I moved to Calgary, which is a pimp-controlled town. The other girls were jealous because the pimps didn't bother me; they even protected me, sort of, because I was so young. When I did eventually choose my first pimp, he went easy on me, didn't make me work every night or put a quota on me, or beat me – strange behaviour for a pimp, don't you think?

'My second pimp wasn't quite so sweet. He dogged me off all the time, you know what I mean – treated me like a punk [a punk is the lowest-status person in the street]. He even had a square bitch [non-street person] he was supporting with the money I made on my quota, which was $400 a night. It took a while, but I started to understand that I was being used. Here I was doing this sickening job, standing out in the cold in high heels, on display, trying to convince a man – who might beat me – to buy me so I could give my money to another asshole who was also beating me. It didn't make sense.

'I paid my pimp his respect though, paid my fine and then chose a mulatto hooker who wanted girls to work for her because she was giving all her money to her man. She had a good scam going. I'd do the work, she'd take all my money, split it in half, give half to her man – claiming she'd earned it – keep half for herself. What did I get? Nothing. A roof over my head. Clothes. At that time, I was making $300 to $500 a night, about $2,000 a week. And I wasn't keeping a cent! Stupid, eh?

'I thought it was time to smarten up, so I split for Vancouver with another ho and her man, but I just ended up handing my money over to him. We lived with his Jamaican mother, a real nice lady. But when his main lady found us in bed together and pulled a scene, he smacked her around so bad that she grabbed her kid and split. Suited me. I figured I finally had a man all to myself. At first, after she left, we were real happy together. He even bought me nice things and treated me good. But when we moved to an apartment of our own, things changed. He got heavy into cocaine and into beating up on me. I started to like tricks better than him! When I got pregnant, he got more violent, accusing me of having someone else's kid. He'd knock me down, kick me black and blue, and put me out on the stroll like that.'

Where did she get the scar above her eye? 'From him, when I was four months pregnant,' she says, touching the nasty gash that even her grainy skin and gobs of make-up can't conceal. 'I wish he'd given me food instead. During my pregnancy, I often went without because it was going up his nose. And I didn't sleep much because of the hunger and the beatings.'

Why did she stay with him? 'I was his only woman and I wanted someone who would be mine alone, all mine, not shared with another lady. Besides, I believed he'd change. After he beat me, he'd always play head games, come on real charming, then turn on the threats. It was so crazy; I though maybe he was just screwed up from the coke ... I can still say I do love him.

'He had me out on the street until a week before I delivered. I was amazed the baby was born healthy after the kind of pregnancy I'd been through. Once she arrived, I knew I had to get away from him but I didn't know how. I was very scared of his threats against me and even against friends who took me in when I first tried to make the break.

'I bounced back and forth a lot. He made me go back out on the stroll while he watched the baby. But the beatings got bad again and I got to a point where I couldn't take it, not with an infant to worry about.' Feather offers a blow-by-blow account of the tedious process of leaving her pimp. Back and forth, back and forth. Always more beatings. Desperate to break free but tied down by poverty and a paralysing sense of worthlessness. Eventually, she managed to get welfare, an apartment for her and the baby, and a restraining order from the court to bar him from her door. Yet, he still comes around, still threatens, still tries to force her back out on the stroll.

How is her life now? 'Bleak. It's impossible to make ends meet on welfare. How can anyone stretch $200 after rent to buy diapers and formula and baby clothes and groceries, just basic necessities? Ask any of the mothers on the street. They'll tell you that welfare forces us out here to sell our bodies to feed our kids. If welfare was tied to the real cost of living, or if we were allowed to work for extra money, some of us could make it. But if we earn legal, they deduct it from our cheques, so we're screwed either way. Hidden work is the only way out. For girls without good educations that means shit work at shit wages – women's work, right? – or hooking, which is shit work for good wages if you don't have to give money to a man.'

Although she is more off the street than on it, Feather is still vulnerable to its main attraction: the lure of making a living if she shakes free from pimps. Does she have any real chance of making a life for her and her baby any other way? I silently wonder.

The Pimp's Art and the Trick's Violence

'When you're fourteen and fifteen, and you can't read and write very well, and have no place to live, and it's cold and you're hungry and you have no marketable skills, you market yourself.'[26] Runaways can be manipulated to sell their bodies for reasons that go beyond the abuse that set them up for sexual exploitation. Underskilled, undereducated, possibly illiterate, disconnected from family and thwarted by deficient public services for kids, they are compelled by economic necessity to do whatever they can to survive. While poverty may not have put them in the street, poverty in the street propels them to enter the trade. As one kid put it, 'You either got to steal, deal, or trick. There ain't no other ways to survive, man.'

Pimps understand the emotional and economic edges on which their targets are teetering. Ferreting out susceptible youngsters at bus terminals, video arcades, fast-food restaurants, and in lonely downtown crowds is their stock-in-trade. If a pimp doesn't perpetrate the swindle himself, he uses his 'wife' or 'main lady,' or maybe his 'wife-in-law,' second in his stable, to nab girls in females-only shelters. Because no one warned them to beware of female strangers, even the most wary of lost kids will respond to a peer. These same recruiters will later become the new girl's guide through her nervous first 'dates' on the stroll. While his top-ranking 'hoes' help him recruit, most seductions into the life are done by the pimp himself.

The pimp 'plays game' on his mark by befriending her, offering 'affection' and generous helpings of the things she needs: food, clothing, shelter, and sympathy. A lot of his conning leverage comes from his natural superiority in her eyes as man the protector. 'She thinks she is nothing without a man.'[27] Except for 'popcorn' pimps, small-time operators who make their current girlfriend work the street and who have no savoir-faire in the manipulation of young minds, these experienced operators, called 'players,' work on eroding any resistance the girl feels. Soon, she will likely sleep at his place, misty-eyed over her good fortune and eager to pay him back, a payment he will exact in bed to try her out and to break her in.

That's what happened to Brenda, a small-town Ontario girl. At fifteen, she fled her savage, alcoholic father, arriving in Toronto by bus, with five dollars in her pocket and a green garbage bag of clothes under her arm. A friendly guy – she thinks he was Italian – picked her up at the terminal, treated her to a hamburger and fries, listened to her woes. Later, after an eye-popping tour of city sights in his plush car, he took her back to his place, where a party was going on. Brenda was wowed by his mirrored ceilings and shag rugs, and impressed with his partying pals – foxy ladies and fancy dudes. 'I thought I was in Hollywood. I figured maybe I'd meet some TV stars.'

In the wee hours, when the party wound down, she was surprised by his demands on her flesh. 'You owe me, baby,' he insisted. Brenda was a virgin, but she figured that if she slept with him, he'd become her boyfriend and protector. He promised her love and fast money. It was all too thrilling. Two nights later, she was 'in love' and on the stroll. She went out almost willingly to help out the 'family' [the stable of girls] the pimp had introduced her to.

That first night, her second date turned out to be a bad trick who roughed her up, raped her, then threatened to toss her off a hotel balcony, before he finally kicked her, half-naked, out of his room. When Brenda fled to her pimp for succour and he pummelled her because she came home with so little cash, she quickly fell out of love and escaped to STOP 86, a hostel. She did not go back into prostitution. (Brenda became a stripper who lived with a series of abusive men. When I met her, she was twenty-six, holed up in a Toronto hostel, hiding with her infant daughter from her husband who had threatened to knife them. Last I heard, she was on welfare, sharing an apartment with another abused single mom she met at the hostel.)

Patsy, desperate for someone to love and someone to love her, in her own mind fashioned her first pimp into a heart-throb. Many girls present these predators as saints and are very reluctant, even after the bloom has been beaten off in a hail of fists, to refer to them as pimps. Feather was black and blue from beatings, out on the stroll a week before she delivered a baby. Yet, she forgave her boyfriend's temper, blaming it on his cocaine habit. Although she lived in terror, in her mind his abuse meant he loved her.

Not all pimps have the finesse or financial freedom to bother with the time-consuming niceties of the seduction. Some simply hustle an unsuspecting kid to the nearest cheap hotel, hit her up with heroin or cocaine, then put her out to work under watchful eyes. The pimp creates a 'hype,' a needle junkie – which many young hookers become, even without strong-arm persuasion – dependent on him for her dope supply.

'My boyfriend taught me a hell of a lesson after I was hooked ... I owed him and he made sure I paid him back every cent for the heroin he fronted me. When I told him I didn't have the money to pay him, he slapped me around and started throwing me around the room. He beat me up and then shot me up. I became his slave and he put me on the street.'[28] A strung-out junkie, however, is not a reliable money-maker, and her time as a hot commodity will be short, so this style of pimping wins little respect.

You hear a lot about respect in the street. Provided she's working for a 'qualified player,' not for some two-bit 'popcorn' pimp whose behaviour may violate established norms, a hooker earns her pimp's respect through faithful service. That means she makes her daily 'quota,' maybe $200 to $300 on week nights and

$400 to $500 on weekend nights. (Rates vary, but are approximately $40 to $100 for oral sex and masturbation, $100 to $200 for intercourse.) She wins respect if she sells her body upward of twelve hours a day, gives her pimp *all* her earnings, never leaves the stroll without his permission, and never, never 'signs' (presses charges) on him or on any pimp. If, however, she does anything considered disloyal, she may suffer serious, disfiguring reprisals.

She may be branded with a hot coathanger or burned with a cigarette; assaulted and raped by the pimp and/or his friends; stripped of clothing and thrown outside; beaten publicly in front of other pimps and/or prostitutes; pushed out of a moving car; or have a hot curling iron shoved into her vagina.[29] From the pimp's point of view, this is not cruel or unusual punishment. It's proof to prostitutes and pimps alike that he deserves respect. Besides, the pimps reason, a girl likes to be slapped around; it reminds her that she's with a real man.

When jailed, pimps are tolerated in the stratified prison world, a macho subculture where sex offenders are sometimes held in protective custody to escape the wrath of other inmates. 'Sex freaks,' when mixed with the population, risk 'shivvings' (knifings) and beatings because 'diddlers' (child molesters), 'rapos' (rapists), and 'skinners' (molesters who attack both girls and boys), as well as other sex criminals, are considered to be warped, worthless scum. By contrast, pimps are regarded as businessmen.

Every time a hooker gets in a car with a customer, she has only her gut instinct to rely on to judge what might happen. Among the more benign range of events, her date may refuse to pay for negotiated sex acts at agreed-upon prices or may abuse her verbally, branding her 'whore' or 'slut' while she does whatever he demands. At the life-endangering end of the range, she may be assaulted, robbed, raped, or threatened with a sadistically imaginative menu of violent acts, including homicide, or she may actually be murdered.

According to the RCMP, eight Vancouver prostitutes were stabbed, beaten, or strangled to death in the fourteen months prior to July 1989.[30] According to some streetworkers, the real count is much higher, hidden by the transient nature of the trade. Marie Arrington at POWER says she personally knew twenty-seven women murdered in Vancouver since February 1985.[31] As of July 1989, no arrests had been made. Neither had any been made in the unsolved murders of ten other prostitutes RCMP believe were murdered between 1985 and 1987.[32] Prostitutes routinely claim that cops view their murders as minor incidents, 'one less ho to hassle,' as a Regina street-walker said.

Because bad tricks are commonplace, outreach organizations across the country pump out daily, weekly, or as-needed alerts. Sheets from coast to coast list the same predominant type: white, and, from their trappings, presumably married, business and professional men in their twenties, thirties, and forties. Otherwise, bad-trick alerts reflect the ethnic mix of particular cities. In Vancouver in 1987, POWER, one of several organizations that issue sheets, recorded 877 bad dates, excluding repeaters.

Violence does not end with tricks either. Prostitutes sometimes attack each other if they suspect co-workers of undercutting competition by lowering prices or of being a 'rat' (police informer). If a girl tries to work another girl's corner, she runs the risk of a thrashing. A hooker might 'jack up' another hooker if she herself has not 'broken' (had dates) that night and is desperate for money. In a group of endangered young women, the bond of community necessary for mutual protection is rent by animosities.

While it is safe to say that most pimps are violent, it is equally safe to say that most tricks are not. Hookers appreciate 'good dates,' especially regulars who aren't into kinky gear and sexual gymnastics, but most consider all their customers contemptible. The only sense of self-worth many hookers salvage comes from looking down on the countless men who use them. Exemplars of ordinariness, many johns are just guys next door, someone's husband, father, brother. Or just lonely men, non-swinging singles. They are titillated to distraction by endless images of women as sex objects and of sex itself as the most worthwhile activity after acquisition of money, power, and expensive toys. They may not have access to the advertised image of a quality life-style, but they do have access to all the sex they can afford.

Mark: Privileged background saves him from 'real lowdown' life

Mark is an exception, and a lucky one to boot. Son of an upper-middle-class family in which both parents are professionals, Mark first hit the street at fourteen, took up residence at fifteen, and quit at nineteen. His background is unusual among kids who last four years. Most moneyed youths who are welcome at home go back fast. Mark could have gone home, but chose not to.

He is also exceptional among street kids because he was not abused – neglected, yes, but not overtly abused. His parents divorced when he was eight. Father kept the two sons in their lavish North Vancouver home; mother moved away from British Columbia with the one daughter. By the time Mark was thirteen, his mother had lost contact with her boys. Although Mark does not judge his father harshly, the parenting he describes dissolved into absence, indifference, and self-indulgence. Mark's brother, older by two years, 'didn't know much more than I did, but he power-tripped on bossing me around, acting like he was the parent.'

Although Mark rebelled against his brother's false authority and his father's absent authority by seeking a family in the street, he went downtown with a suburban map of success scored in his head. That mental map is obvious now. It shows in his comfort with his current surroundings as he sprawls out on overstuffed off-white cushions in his oversize rattan chair. He shares an airy Kitsilano bungalow with two room-mates. Their ferns and rubber trees are lush, their carpets deep, the house a tribute to taste and enthusiastic housekeeping.

Mark, now twenty, is on the short side, with a solid build. His thick ash-blond hair is stylishly shaped to complement clean, good looks. His casual clothes are impeccable. Although he looks and sounds like a confident freshman, he lived outside preppie parameters most of his teenage years. It all started a little innocently – at McDonald's, on Granville Street. (Ironically, some McDonald's and Harvey's outlets, contrary to the family-restaurant image they cultivate, are hang-outs for street kids and hot spots for drug deals.) 'I went to McDonald's with a few kids after a movie one night, met some friends of theirs, toked a joint with their crew in Robson Square, then went home.'

But his friends' friends didn't go home; they stayed in their uptown 'squat.' To Mark, their independent, free-wheeling life – managed through profits from penny-ante drug dealing – was a magnet. He made a point of seeking their company whenever he was uptown. 'They seemed like a really nice, older crowd, seventeen to twentyish, and soon I found myself spending whole days with them: smoking pot, eating in restaurants, roaming in Stanley Park. For a sheltered kid from the 'burbs, it was a lark!'

'My father saw that I was drifting, but he didn't try to pull me back. I think he was tired of me badgering him to spend more time together. He wanted to be free to do his thing: leave home at 6:00 a.m., come back at 6:00 p.m., relax in his bedroom with a beer, and then spend the evening with his girlfriend. He never knew if I was home or not, and he didn't seem to care.'

Mark wanted to be someplace where he mattered. As unusual as it is in street culture, he quickly built a solid circle of friends. While many runaways hope to find a substitute family in the street, most find only fleeting friendships in a loose-knit community bound by common need but riven by distrust. Mark, by contrast, 'ran with a pack of six kids who stuck together over several years, living in everything from one sleazy hotel room to a luxurious West End apartment.' The pack started with one friendship between Mark and Dakota, a black girl who had been adopted into a white family. Dakota, 'trashed by her father,' ran away and had been prostituting since she was twelve. Eventually, their circle expanded to include an older drug dealer, another female hooker, a male hustler, and 'a thug.' 'He was a crazy case from a bad family who did B&Es by the score and would beat up anyone for no real reason. Another guy, a twenty-one-year-old who had high school, was the brains of our operation. He knew some law and became our leader.

'We were all down there for our own reasons, though I could never understand why the graduate left home. He came from a family that was way better off than mine. Two of the kids came from typical suburban homes: their moms baked cookies, and they had cable, that kind of regular. The others had really rough backgrounds.'

The social-class mix in Mark's group typifies West End Vancouver, where the profile of street kids seems less homogeneous than it tends to be in other cities. In Toronto, for example, chances of finding an upper-middle-class kid living on the downtown track for a protracted period are slim. The scene Mark describes is unique in other ways as well, especially with the segregation between vice districts. There are six or seven mini-strolls on the lower mainland, each one relegated to a particular stratum of victims and predators. Mark's Granville-and-Davie turf is top drawer; East Hastings is the dregs. Arguably the most squalid stretch of inner-city real estate in Canada, East Hastings is 'bad, man, real bad. Hookers down there have black eyes, bruised legs, and track-mark arms.'

A desperate poor, bursting-at-the-seams neighbourhood, a bedlam of struggling store-front social services, the downtown Eastside could literally kill kids like Mark. There, male prostitutes, transvestites, and cross-dressers cannot walk safely in the open. It is macho turf where a lethal mix of hard liquor, heavy drugs, and killer violence regularly ignites. Even in daylight, along the wide, gritty sidewalks, the panorama is of debased humanity driven by poverty and despair to an endless party of self-destruction. Young people of indeterminate age and adults old before their time stagger around in a fog, their lives defined by passing out drunk, waking up hung over, and, barely sober, hitting the bottle again. This area bordering Chinatown is a world-class neighbourhood of victims being moulded into predators. On a strip like this, it is commonplace for a mother to be selling herself on the corner opposite her daughter.

Life for many in the McDonald's crowd will not, ultimately, degenerate into the Eastside's degree of rubble and ruin. Tame in comparison with the skids, Granville and Davie – also infamous for transvestites and transsexual hookers – draws many more-tractable kids, like Mark. The lucky ones are just side-tracked suburban runaways awaiting the chance to go home again. Not that Mark was in any hurry.

'I liked the life. We had freedom and money in our pockets and we did a lot of drugs, mostly psychedelics and valium. No T-and-Rs [Talwin and Ritalin, of which Vancouver is considered to be the national capital] or heroin. No needles. Addictions are for downtowners. Kids in my scene were mostly a stay-put type, selling pot by the ounce and acid by the hit. Human vending-machines. No big risks, no big money, getting-by stuff.

'Cops didn't bother me much. The graduate taught us to keep a low profile and to dress like yuppies. When he joined the pack, my wardrobe consisted of bandannas for my long hair and rock T-shirts. He ditched my duds and replaced them with polo shirts. When we lived in cheap hotel rooms, he made sure we avoided joints usually hit by the fuzz. Eventually, he got us into a classy apartment in the West End, hardly an address to draw heat.

'Precautions aside, cops mostly hassle kids who look poor, kids who are in care, or kids whose parents put out missing-persons reports. Worst they ever did to me was pick me up a few times after midnight and take me home. I'd go into the house with my key and go to bed; my room was never touched. Maybe two months would have elapsed since I'd last seen my dad, but if we happened to meet in the morning, he'd say bewildered sorts of things and rush off for work.'

Mark was a fifteen-year-old who'd dropped out of school with a grade-eight education and was living, for all his dad knew, on the street, obviously selling drugs and possibly selling his body to survive. Did he think his father cared? 'After I started hustling, I got busted, only once. I called my dad from the lock-up. He drove down and helped me get released on my own recogniz-ance. When we got into the car – with his girlfriend, who he was about to marry – all he said was "I don't know what you're doing and I don't want to know ... I presume you want to be dropped in front of McDonald's?" He couldn't dump me fast enough. I remember wishing he'd try to reach out, say some-thing, do something. But he didn't, and I went back to my life, which by then was hustling.

'I was almost seventeen when I started. As a young kid at home, I'd always been fascinated by prostitution, not by the act but by the idea that a kid could use his body to make enough money to have control over his life. For my dad, working hard was always about earning big bread to buy nice things. I always dreamed of owning classy toys too. As far back as I can remem-ber, I have craved doing really well at an early age. For me, prostitution represented the chance to achieve that.

'The game was not new to me because I had often spotted for the hookers in our household. A friend fixed my first date. I was terrified, so much so that I made Dakota come with me. She literally held my hand and coaxed me to calm down. The trick, a suit, about fifty, fancy car, the usual, took us to the Château Granville. Dakota watched TV, and I stared at her because I couldn't look at this guy. The gig took fifteen minutes, max. I got eighty dollars just for lying there and letting him get a mouthful. After it was over, I thought to myself, "That wasn't so bad."

'I was young, blond, and new. New has a lot to do with the stroll. I didn't have time for a cigarette between tricks; I'd be picked up that fast. It was such easy, big money that I hustled my way to California and back. AIDS was no threat because I used condoms for everything, including hand jobs. Morally the load was off because I never did lays, which meant I could have sex with men and still be a man. At that point in my life, I didn't know who I was sexually [and at this point he won't discuss his sexuality. 'It's not relevant,' he says] but lays meant assuming a female position, and I couldn't have lived with that.'

While he was hustling, and dealing on the side, Mark lived with his girlfriend, a street prostitute. How did being prostitutes affect their relationship? 'Because we met in the street when we were both hooking, it didn't screw up our personal life. There were no secrets. But, if I had been a straight guy who fell in love with a mysterious woman who turned out to be a hooker, I couldn't have dealt with it. We were both in the life and we understood that hooking has nothing to do with love or sex or anything intimate. It's just making money being a hunk of meat. You don't get off. The only thought in your head is: "How can I get this freak off fast with minimum effort, grab my bucks, and split?" '

If Mark's popularity had held out, he says, he would not have quit. But two things happened to make him rethink his life-style. First, dates started falling off. 'After a while, you became a wallflower.' Second, ratepayer pressure resulted in an injunction that forced prostitutes from the cover of pine-studded residential streets in the West End out into the open commercial streets below Granville. 'I just couldn't stand out there exposed to old friends that passed by.'

So he quit. Just like that. Mark followed his girlfriend's lead by getting on student welfare and going back to school at the Study Centre, an alternative school with self-paced, individualized learning programs for street kids in transition to straight life. Money was tight, and straight life was tough, but Mark only had one 'lapse,' when he was cash-hungry. At the Study Centre, he quickly moved from grade eight to grade ten before quitting to work as a waiter for a year. Now he's on Unemployment Insurance and assessing options for finishing high school so he can qualify for veterinary training.

Compared with the struggle typical street kids face in trying to reclaim a place in straight society, Mark's transition has been smooth. He understands the difference and appreciates his good fortune. 'I was a street kid but never part of the real low-down life that comes with a history of abuse and a heroin habit.' What impact has his experience had on his life? 'Except for the missed education, which I can recoup, it only robbed me of my childhood,' he says glibly, as if childhoods didn't shape lives. 'I've never been fourteen; I was fourteen going on twenty.'

His relationship now with his father? 'It's decent enough. He just gave me these rugs.' He points to two Dhurries in earth tones. 'We can't talk about what's happened to me since I left home, though. A closed subject.' And his mother? 'I'm close to her now. In the years since we've been separated, as a social worker, she's worked with kids, run a rape relief centre, and now she does rehab with female ex-cons. She even tried to help Dakota get off the street.'

What happened to his pack? His girlfriend, from a rural middle-class family, is back in her home town, studying at a nearby business college. The graduate is back home in the family business. The 'thug' from a poor, demoralized family is in jail. And Dakota? Did she beat the street? 'No.' Mark admits with sadness. 'She just can't seem to leave the life. I guess it has to do with the poverty and the violence in her background.'

Hank: Tragic family history repeats itself

Of Cree-German heritage, Hank is the product of North End Winnipeg, a harrowing neighbourhood in a city harsh on native and partly native people. Before Hank was born, his prospects were jinxed by the likelihood of hunger, poverty, childhood illnesses, welfare, family violence, foster homes, and juvenile detention. Chances were that he would have to face substandard education, functional illiteracy, the worst jobs, the meanest wages, slum housing or homelessness, crime, prison, and alcohol and/or drug addiction – perhaps early death. Hank's star was hitched to the ugly constellation of despair that results from racism and genocide.

The streets of Hank's community bear witness to the successes racism and genocide have scored: a hotchpotch of boarded-up buildings, shabby bungalows, broken windows, shattered lives, pawn shops, praise-and-prayer stops, barely subsisting small businesses, cheap hotels, and struggling social services. Streets are crammed with drop-ins, study projects, work projects, recreational projects, self-help projects, housing projects, and crisis projects.

Such is the community that Hank calls home.

It's 10:30 on federal election night, 21 November 1988, a school night, when my guides give me my first tour of Hank's neighbourhood. Knots of youngsters play in the icy streets, hitching a ride on our bumper. Farther along, a klatch of pre- and early teens prop up a frail-looking girl with glazed eyes who limps along like a rag doll. She's spun out on glue or gasoline, probably gas because it's cheaper; a gang of kids can each chip in a few cents to buy a gallon.

The little sniffer and her helpful companions bob in and out of a line of sleazy bars along Main. We do the same. It's early, quiet – except for the bad music that echoes in the cavernous beer halls, like Merchant's and the Savoy. Small groups of teenagers talk quietly over beer, while lonely old drunks brood in shadowy corners. Without rowdy crowds, these dingy dens are more depressing than when they are rocking. The last stop on our tour, the New Occidental Hotel, sports a warning above the entrance: 'No Knives, No Colors.' Gangs unnerve a tough and edgy city, especially in summer, adding to Winnipeg's brutal street life. Two white cops survey the scene, the psychological space between them and the customers light-years apart. Ruby Brass, Beat the Street co-ordinator, apologizes for what looks like a slow night. It's unusual, she points out. 'There's always something going down in here: stabbings, fights, drug deals. The last time I came in, a young girl in the washroom was trying to hit up in her neck but she couldn't find a vein.'

We walk the few blocks around the tenderloin triangle bound by Higgins, Henry, Logan, and Martha streets. I'm shivering in the dampness as snowy swirls gust around our feet. Trying to warm themselves, about a dozen young girls dance from foot to foot in pointed boots, gloveless hands stuffed into pockets of summer jackets, necks scrunched into scarfless collars. It is hard to guess their ages, but heavy make-up doesn't disguise their youth. Recent-model cars driven by Caucasian and Oriental men circle, examining the merchandise. A youngster steps away from the entrance to the Salvation Army and gets into a car. By the time we round the block, she is back at her spot on the stroll.

Across the street, behind the streaked windows of the Mainstreet Project, occasional shelter to Hank, a sea of heads is visible. Outside there's a line-up. A young woman, obviously drunk and desperate, pounds on the door and wails to be let in. The Project – crisis centre, detox, and emergency hostel – sleeps about 3,000 different people a year. Project director John Rogers estimates there are 400 chronically homeless adults in the North End. Estimating the number of kids is more difficult because many have homes they go to during the lulls between parental episodes of drunken despair and abuse.

In the summer, city-core homeless are more likely to sleep in parks notorious for violence, vandalism, and sexual incidents. On the morning after election night, the *Winnipeg Sun* published findings of a leaked report on the state of inner-city parks. The litany runs from knifings and child-molestations to unfed, unsupervised children being left to fend for themselves.[33] The parks, especially the one surrounding the grand colonial-style provincial legislature, are also the turf of young boys for sale.

There is nothing in the North End's grab-bag of indignities that Hank has not tasted. Like many other children, he had to learn to take care of himself. The lessons have been extremely hard, fuelling his fatalism. Hank displays his bitterness in his hard-set mouth. He is sickly thin, very tall, and physically aloof. His

Coke-bottle glasses and the baseball cap pulled low over his high forehead act as barriers to contact. Tattoos run along his corded arms. Lanky and sinewy, he sits with arms tightly crossed and legs splayed, the relaxation in his lower limbs and the occasional tiny softenings of his mouth the only clues to his vulnerability.

'I been through CAS all my life. They're still on my back today,' Hank says. The second of five children, Hank and his older brother were 'snatched' by the CAS while they were still pre-schoolers and placed with two white foster families. Older brother today is doing time for assault, while Hank's next young-est brother is beginning his life on the street.

Like too many of their peers, Hank and his brothers are follow-ing the deep-rutted trail that leads from ruptured native families. City-dwellers, Hank and his siblings were not, like so many other native children, forcibly removed from rural reserves and con-fined to residential schools dedicated to Christianizing native children. None the less, he and his brothers suffer from remnants of the same beliefs that the federal government used to justify the residential-school system. According to that ideology, severing native children from their roots and relatives and relocating them within the dominant culture would elevate these children cul-turally and spiritually. In keeping with this racist philosophy, the state handed over Hank and his brothers to white families ignorant of aboriginal languages and culture.

'I close my eyes today and I can still see the first time they took me. I hid behind my mother, clung to her legs. I begged her not to let them take me. I was crying. It was wet outside, snow and rain mixed. The sound of that car door closing is still in my head.'

Why were the boys removed from their family? 'The alcohol and the violence, I guess. Both my parents are alcoholics. My father's an ex-druggie too, from barbiturates right up to needles ... He scarred my memory with beatings he put on my mother. Knocked her teeth out one time, when she was drunk and brought up a past quarrel over a relationship he had with one of her girlfriends. I got caught in the middle that time, just like the other times. For getting mixed up into their business, I took my share of lickings too. Sometimes he was drunk when he beat us.

Sometimes he was just tired and angry, so frustrated he didn't know no other way of taking out his feelings.'

Hank went through a spate of white foster families and group homes before, between, and after stints in juvenile detention. He rhymes off names of institutions where he did time: Ranch Ehrlo in Regina, even Vision Quest in the United States. His memory of sequence and detail is muddy, but his overall impression of a childhood spent 'bouncing' from one anonymous place to another is vivid. 'Don't you see,' he implores when pressed for details, 'it don't matter; it's all the same. It wasn't home. Even white foster parents and group homes that don't abuse you aren't good places for an Indian kid. They all believe in only three things: rules, punishments, and their cheque.'

As he dispels illusions about the quality of a 'placement' childhood, Hank introduces a theme that will predominate in his narrative: the idea that human closeness is a prescription for pain, that all forms of emotional intimacy sow the seeds of abandonment. After twenty-three years of profound disconnection from the significant people in his life, he knows no words for success.

'You have to live in your own shell. When you let the barriers down, one way or another, you lose. You open up a little to someone – a foster parent, a counsellor, a girl – and they leave you. You get transferred to your next stop, or they betray you. They reject you or they die. My whole life has been like that. Now, I'm such a loner and my emotions are so fucked up, I'll never be able to work them out.'

Despite the loss of all his potentially close ties, he clung to hope of finding love and acceptance in his family. Typical of kids in care, he became a runaway, frequently running back home. 'My mother always wanted to keep me, but my father always sent me back.' By age eight, Hank had gotten the message. Jaded, he found a new place to run to – the streets.

'Before I was ten, I knew every survival trick, from living out of garbage cans to mooching off strangers, to getting every bit of free chow dished out in church basements. I knew all the asshole stunts that street kids play to pass the day, from harassing people to playing cat-and-mouse games with the cops. You get caught sometimes. I've done time at the PSB [Public Safety Building].

Courts and the lock-up are just part of my life – for B&Es, drug dealing, the usual street stuff.

'You do whatever you have to to survive. Because I was so young when I hit the street, there was always a chicken hawk [purveyor of young boys] willing to put a roof over my head. I didn't know what it was about with the first old man that raped me. I was just nine, a little kid. He picked me up in the street, bought me some candy and some kid stuff, then took me to his place.'

Hank claims his sugar-daddy became his pimp, that after a period of being 'broken in,' he was 'turned out' at ten and treated in much the same way female hookers are by their pimps: beaten up when he didn't pay up. He describes their relationship as the same complex configuration of father, friend, lover, purveyor, protector, and abuser that defines the hooker-pimp connection. Like working girls, working boys are also, he says, made to 'do things that are too gross to admit.'

Is Hank gay? 'I don't know. I don't know what I am. I guess I'm bi.' His voice drops, and he mumbles a torrent of conflicting ideas, nodding his head in wonderment about his sexual orientation. Is he still for sale, still tied to his sugar-daddy? 'I'll always be tied to the pimp I got now.' (It is unusual for hustlers in Winnipeg, as elsewhere, to be pimped. In some cities, including Winnipeg, even girls and women are more likely to be free-lances.)

'Sometimes I have a roof over my head; sometimes not. I move all the time. That's what street life is about: constant motion. Like my childhood. Always bouncing around. I can't stay still loo long because, if I stop, slow down even, my problems swarm into my head and knock me under; I get very depressed if I let myself think.'

Thinking is dangerous. Dealing with complex problems is impossible. Better to let dozing demons lie. However, Hank's repressed feelings invariably erupt, usually destructively. They reverberate through all his guarded attempts to make human contact, and they guarantee his failure to connect with other people in ways that work. Foiled attempts at closeness bring more pain, adding to the demon pile.

The most poignant example of this dogged pattern surfaces, not surprisingly, in his relationship with his family. Hank has a wife, and two toddlers fifteen months apart. He married a troubled teenager who already had two kids. Now they have a pending divorce and four imperilled children in CAS care, starting their placement lives. Does he think the CAS should have taken his babies? 'As long as my kids had food and clothes – which they did – it's none of their business what we do at night when the kids are in bed. Someone must have ratted us out for doing drugs.' Hank mounts a weak defence of his parenting abilities and his rights, but ultimately says he wasn't a good father.

His nine-year-old stepson has begun running away from a group home. 'What next will he be into? Probably the same things I'm into. I see myself in him; it's scary. I see what happened to me happening to him and I can do fuck all about it. I can't be a father to him and help him deal with his problems because I can't stop running away from my own. Can't blame the kid – just look at the example he's got in me.'

Hank recalls promising himself his kids would never suffer his fate. He dreamily concocted the perfect family he'd create when he got his chance. He married young, at nineteen, hungry to play house. But he did not have the skills required to reify his fantasy.

Like his father, he tried to flush menacing feelings from his system with alcohol. When it didn't work, or when liquor fired his rage, his emotions spilled out in wife-beatings. Hank is facing assault charges right now. The only time he laughed over the two days of our meetings was during a bravado-laced conversation with another street youth. In it, Hank made threatening references to his 'old lady,' the gist of which was a warning that she had better withdraw charges if she wanted to feel safe from him and his buddies. He admits to the 'flash temper' typical of abused and abusive males.

Underneath the threats, what he really wants, he says, is to reunite with his wife. 'If I don't, it's gonna drive me back onto drugs. I'm off them right now, but it won't take much to get me to stick a needle in my arm. Some people can beat drugs and alcohol in programs like NA [Narcotics Anonymous] and AA. I been through those programs, but they don't work for me. The longest I've ever been sober is a year.

'Let's not kid anyone. I was raised in the street. A life of drugs and crime is not what I want, but it's all I know. The streets are scarred onto my brain ... I admit, a part of me even likes them –

they're my home – but a part of me wants off ... I'm confused, caught between two worlds: the one I've survived in and reality [the straight world].'

He comes back, as he has done so often, to this theme. 'I'm afraid to be in contact with people and have them involved in my life. I can't take the hurt and disappointment anymore.' Besides the psychological knots that bind Hank's life to old patterns, his lack of skills hobble him in his attempts to beat the traps of street life. With a grade-two education, he is illiterate. He frequently talks about the one uplifting force in his life right now: the tutoring he has been getting for almost a year at Beat the Street. He gloats about learning to use a computer.

While it is a relief to see a thread of light in an otherwise gloomy existence, Hank seems destined to wander the darkness. When we say goodbye, I feel about as low as this heart-breaking business ever brings me. Hank yanks his cap down lower on his forehead and lopes away. As he heads for the door, I am suddenly curious about his motivation for having spilled his story to a stranger. 'By the way, how come you agreed to talk to me?' 'I'm trapped in my own little world and maybe I can't do jack-shit for no one, not even my own kids, so maybe this way I can help some other kid.'

The Growing Trade in Young Boys

If new girls on the stroll are hot sellers, fresh 'male meat,' called 'chicken,' is an even hotter commodity among 'chicken hawks,' usually middle-aged men who lust for boys, the younger the better. And since sexism translates on the street into self-employment for males, boys keep their earnings. Raised to control their own lives, most won't relinquish that power to pimps. Pre-pubescent boys, however, are vulnerable to being pimped, and some very young newcomers, like Hank, do fall into the hands of 'sugar-daddies.' Usually these chicken-hawk pimps – some gay, some bisexual – will rape the child to initiate him into his new role on the home front and his night work on the stroll. Like street girls, boys are beaten by bad tricks, plus they risk incurring the rage of 'fag-bashers.' However, most are spared pimp violence.

Although the community of street hustlers is not as homogeneous as that of female hookers, parallels exist. Many boys run away for the same reasons girls do: to escape fathers who rape and families that fight. Once on their own, males are propelled into prostitution by the same economic necessity that females face. Like the girls, they lack education, skills, and contacts to better their choices. Like their female counterparts, they are loath to turn to a child-protection system they may already distrust. Even if they have not yet been through foster or group homes, they are not likely to seek out agencies and adults they view as authoritative and officious.

Some boys get ostracized by their families because of confused sexual orientation or overt homosexuality. They get called 'fags' and failures, often by the father or father-surrogate who sodomizes them. On the street, the more sexually mixed-up boys usually profess heterosexuality and either have or claim to have a girlfriend. These 'straight hustlers' say they are 'in the game' to make a buck. They allow tricks to use them as objects, usually for oral sex and masturbation, but not for anal sex. Likewise, they are willing to perform sex acts on tricks with one proviso – no penetration. The relatively few older adolescents one meets on the stroll tend to be gay and no longer use prostitution as a way to sort out their sexual confusion. They stay in the sex trade for the main reason they started: to make a living.

AIDS and Drugs

AIDS does not seem to threaten the street population to the same extent that it does the rest of society. Life-threatening disease is just one more risk in a dangerous life. While many street prostitutes are not compulsively concerned about contracting disease, the real professionals never voluntarily have unsafe sex. Even before AIDS, they were afraid of getting STDs (sexually transmitted diseases) or of being impregnated by tricks. Besides, on the street, condoms are the real and symbolic divide between doing business and making love.

Today, some pros even 'double bag' (use two condoms) and some use latex gloves for masturbation. Certainly, roving street-workers who dispense information and condoms are raising awareness among novices and non-professionals of the need for protection. But self-protection is an unreliable motivation among kids with bargain-basement self-esteem. Youth Horizons street-workers in Montreal have found that most child prostitutes and their clients do not use condoms.[34] Kids are out there to make money. For the bottom echelons, that means selling themselves to the highest bidder on any terms, including no-condom inter-course.

Believe it or not, that's what some johns want. 'If they wanted safe sex, do you think they would [look for it on the street]? They want fantasies ... Condoms aren't part of fantasies.' In any case, the choice of using condoms is not always the hooker's or hus-tler's to make. As one prostitute pointed out, 'You know how it is on the street; you get raped a lot.'[36]

Sleeping around to survive may not be the highest-risk factor in spreading AIDS among street kids. Needles may be. Intravenous drug-users are at very high risk of contracting AIDS; a sick junkie doesn't think about clean needles, only about jabbing the next hit into any vein in the arm, neck, or thigh that is not too calloused from overuse.

While many street kids somehow cling to the glimmer of hope it takes to prefer life over death, and while some do what they can to protect themselves, looking from the bottom of society up, AIDS does not look the same as it does looking from the top (or middle) down.

Della: What else can I do when I'm no longer fit for the stroll?

Despite their tough-talking street-cockiness, many young hookers tend to be emotionally frail and profoundly naïve and immature – and, more than anything else, self-deprecating, definitely not in charge. Della, by contrast, seems poised and self-confident. She is well-spoken, smiles easily, makes eye contact comfortably, and generally comes across as a smart young woman.

At twenty-two she is exquisitely beautiful, the legacy of Span-ish, African, and European genes. 'Many people think I'm Medi-terranean rather than Bahamian,' she explains. It's easy to see why, with her thick auburn waves, black almond eyes, and flawless olive complexion. Petite, dressed for work in black leather and spike heels, sitting she easily hides her six-month-pregnant belly.

Della has been on the Halifax stroll for four years, one of forty or so female regulars, besides transients and part-timers supplementing their welfare income. Young hookers lean on the iron fence along Hollis Street around the provincial legislature and behind the lieutenant-governor's official residence. In the heart of the business and banking district, with icy steel and stone towering over them, prostitutes wander among the homeless who also stray in this area. After dark, they are invisible to everyone but customers prowling for girls and trolling for boys in the 'pink triangle,' adjacent to picturesque Citadel Hill.

Della's seniority affords her a desirable spot – though not the most desirable, at Cornwallis Park. Rookies and has-beens are banished to darker, more dangerous corners, on Lower Water Street. Others are assigned less-prestigious lamp-posts and laneways in the poor North End of town. There, in a neighbourhood in flux, where tenements are razed for townhouses, hookers sell themselves to men staggering out of taverns. As they stand their turf, the women watch the lights flicker down by the harbour, that other world of the chic Historic Properties, where the tourists and moneyed mingle.

Unlike most street prostitutes in Canada, Della claims she now makes enough money to be part of that world, though she says fat wads of cash 'just slip through my fingers.' But, four years ago, she was not making $100,000 tax-free, much of it from bookings in Thunder Bay, Alaska, and other stops on a northern circuit she travels when Halifax business is slow. If she makes and keeps that kind of money now – as she claims she does – she is in a minority among street prostitutes, even among those who aren't paying a pimp. (There's more money in classier off-street prostitution; the street is the bottom of the barrel, in every respect.)

Della's first sexual experience, at seventeen, produced a child. Much to her shock, her previously inflexible mother, a devout Jehovah's Witness, did not abandon her. 'My mother was a widow who was relieved when my father died because it ended the alcoholic cruelty he inflicted on her.' Nor was she abandoned by her older brother and sister; or by her younger brother, now nineteen and serving time for car theft. Her mother, scraping by on social assistance in public housing, helped as best she could.

After the baby's birth, Della was at first determined to get a job that paid enough to support her and the baby and to pay for childcare. With no high-school diploma, no work experience, and no special skills, she soon discovered that her goal was unattainable. Given the history of racism in Nova Scotia, being black was probably another mark against her on the job market. Eventually she gave up her search and her hopes and ended up like her mom, on 'pogey.'

A man entered her life. 'From a typical black Nova Scotian family – poor and always struggling – he played a head game on me about how I could get off the dole and get ahead if I worked the streets.' He also 'encouraged' her with beatings to do what he wanted. 'I kept a diary. After his beatings I'd often write "If this is love, I don't need it," but then, after having run away, I'd go back to him.' Sometimes she went back, eyes still black, face still swollen, ribs still broken, or broken jaw still healing.

At first, the idea of prostitution shocked her. 'I wasn't rejected or unloved by my family the way most of the girls are; I didn't need, as they say, to look for love in all the wrong places. I still don't understand why I agreed, or why I'm still out there ... except I did love him a lot, and I did need the money. How else can a black girl without high school ever make any?

'He got me into a family which was running escort services, which is where I broke into the business. I've been back and forth between the services and the streets ever since. I prefer the services because they're classier – classier clients, better pay, better benefits. Instead of standing on a street corner, you wait in a house for calls. Macho types who get off on degrading us and calling us "you whore" while getting their rocks off, pick you up in the street. Men who use escorts are usually professionals, like lawyers from the South-West End who are afraid of being seen picking up girls in public places.

'Buying sex isn't beneath them, they're just choosy about how it's done. Sometimes they don't even want sex. Sometimes they just want the company of a pretty lady for dinner and talk. I get to dress classy, not trashy, and I get a better feeling about myself from men who pay for my time even without sex.' (Della's distinction between tricks is not one I heard from anyone else. In general, hookers say that street johns come in all shapes, sizes, and perversions, ranging from working class to upper class, with a preponderance of 'suits,' meaning business and professional types. If Della's experience is true for other Halifax hookers working both services and streets, anonymity may account for the difference. It's easier to go unnoticed in downtown Toronto or Vancouver than in smaller, gossipier towns.)

When she first started on the stroll, Della 'felt terrible' about what she was doing. 'But the other girls help you block out the misgivings. You eventually get it into your head that it's just a service, a blow job here, a lay there. Nothing personal.'

It's especially important to believe there's nothing wrong when you feel there's nothing else you're fit for, when you have a hungry child, a hungry landlord, and a voracious pimp. And it's the safest thing to believe when you have a brutal man controlling your mind, your movements, and your money. 'I felt he had complete control over me; I had no control whatsoever over my own life.'

Throughout the interview, Della refers to her pimp as her man, boyfriend, or lover, and several times when I refer to him as her pimp, she denies he is one. 'Well, I guess you could say he had a pimp side to him, the side I hated. My first two years, he wouldn't let me leave the stroll, not even for a coffee break. Eventually he figured out that you don't have to beat women to death to make them work – a belief he came by from having pimp friends, even though he wasn't one himself. But when the beatings stopped, the mental control began. He'd try to drive me crazy by refusing to talk to me for days on end. He switched from bruising me outside to hurting me inside.'

Her pimp was not the only one hurting her, though by street standards, she's been lucky. 'One jerk pulled a knife; another one tied me to a bed and raped me; but at least neither of them killed me! Both incidents happened when I was desperate for cash and accepted the kind of dates I wouldn't take if I was in the money. Luck and a reliable gut for bad tricks have saved me from the real horrors that can happen. I've never even had any of the lovely diseases, and I've been tested for AIDS and don't have that either.'

Luck and intuition did not, however, save her from a pregnancy last year. 'It might have been a trick baby because I worked in a house with a no-condoms policy for a while, so I had an abortion.' (Using birth-control methods didn't occur to her.) The baby she is carrying now was fathered by her boyfriend, who has given up his 'pimp side,' she says. He has a straight job, doesn't take her money, and no longer beats or emotionally abuses her, she claims. 'Things have changed between us. I know he really cares about me. He'd take care of me now, too, if I wanted, but once you're used to having real money, your own, it's hard to give it up. I'm out there now because I want to be, not because he's forcing me. He doesn't care if I work; it's up to me. I've gotten to a place in my mind where hooking doesn't mean anything, so why not?'

Della's biggest fear is imagining what awaits her four-year-old in the playground. What if another kid announces that his mother is a 'whore'? 'All the mothers on the stroll worry about that day. But what else can we do? I've learned never to depend on a man; they're here one day and gone the next. I have to be able to support myself and my kids. But what on earth can I do when I'm no longer fit for the stroll? This is a small town. Everyone knows I'm a hooker. Who'd hire me, even if I had skills? And who'd pay me a living wage? Only the street.'

Trapped

If prostitution is so grim, why don't kids just quit? Because most can't; entangling forces trap them where they are. First, as long as a girl's body still sells, her pimp will not be inclined to let her go. A prostitute is as disposable as a paper diaper, but only when her pimp decides she is ready for the trash bin. If she observes certain conventions of the trade, a reluctant pimp might grant her freedom. Girls can choose to work for another pimp or, as they get older and more street-wise, for themselves. Such a move requires the pimp's permission and, once that is granted, usually involves a heavy fine of perhaps thousands of dollars. But, not unlike slaves of yore, the girl is stuck with the pimp until she pays her passage. If the pimp does not want to let her go, he sets the price high enough to sabotage her ability to negotiate a release from bondage; such was often the case when slaves wanted to buy their freedom.

Feather, for example, says that, at one point in her attempt to dump her pimp, she 'paid him his respect by telling him I wanted my freedom and was willing to buy it. He said "Fine, bitch, but first you got to pay me $2,500." Now where was I going to get that kind of money after I paid my quota?'

The prostitute may be desperate enough to get away that she will allow another pimp to bail her out, after which she becomes his property. Pimps also sell girls like chattels, without their permission, to other pimps, as Patsy's first owner did.

A hooker can try running away, which some do. Unless she is willing to press charges against her pimp, however, she cannot turn to the police. She has likely been excommunicated from family and lost touch with old friends, and she won't resort to the CAS because she hates child-welfare authorities and can't imagine a return to foster or group homes, from which she may have already fled. So, she escapes to another city, one, she hopes, beyond the reach of her pimp. Except, in the next city, her poverty, poor education, and limited skills close in, forcing her to survive in the only way she knows how – by selling herself. The cycle begins anew.

Let's suppose she's inordinately brave and decides, instead of skipping town, to charge her pimp. The moment she betrays him, the word goes out on the street: it's open season on her safety. As they gain more street savvy, many youngsters privately express the urge to turn their pimps in. 'I want to testify against that bastard ... but I'm scared that I might get beat up.'[37] Among those who pluck up the courage, many don't attend court proceedings when the case comes up months later, presumably having been terrorized into silence. A tiny minority of street hookers do sign, testify, and get their pimps jailed.[38]

By the time a teenager has been on the street for a couple of years, she will be cut off from straight society and will have a niche in her renegade community. Although a competitive and fragile place, it offers among its rewards camaraderie against the outside world, a protective shield for 'bad' girls and boys from sneering judgments and rejection by family and 'good' citizens. Even though the street is an intolerant place, it will accept a hooker, a doper (which she may be – yet another major obstacle to quitting), and an outlaw. Here, on society's margins, she feels at least a glimmer of that sense of belonging we all crave, a sense of place she may never find in the mainstream. The wall between her side and the other side seems like an iron curtain. Crossing back becomes prohibitively difficult with time.

Perhaps the most insurmountable obstacle to leaving prostitution is low self-esteem. Evelyn Lau used to ask herself 'Why is there that remembered feeling of worthlessness when [tricks] move closer, when their eyes don't register your face, much less your thoughts?'[39] As ex-hooker Trudee Able-Peterson says, whatever self-worth a child brings to the street gets banged out of her by so many men she loses count. Call a girl a whore long enough and she will come to believe she's not worth more than the $40 she gets for a blow job. Able-Peterson also believes that the more debased the tricks' desires, the lower the girl sinks in her appreciation of herself, thinking she must be the dirtiest thing on earth. 'Was it true, as pimps used to say to me, "Baby, the only people ever gonna love you is a pimp and a trick"?'[40] Even older hookers stew in self-contempt, convinced they 'could never get respectable in a million years. It was as if [you] carried an old sign that said [you were] a whore, even though the sign was inside where the scars were.'[41]

The streets are mined with booby-traps for any kid who tries to escape. Nevertheless, some kids do break through the wall. There are no magic wands, no miracle formulas, usually just brazen acts of individual will at crucial moments: after a life-threatening episode with a bad trick or pimp, after the birth of a baby, after the accidental appearance of a caring person in a hurt person's life, after a drug overdoes that almost kills. Some kids seize their lives in time, before the street claims them irretrievably.

JUSTICE AND SOCIAL-SERVICE SYSTEMS

Many front-line workers in contact with street kids would agree with ex-hooker Christine Femia-Wiseman, past director of Toronto's SOS for street prostitutes, who says that 'the legal system pimps kids to death.'[42] She explains how kids get fines they can pay only by selling themselves, and how each successive bust earns them harsher fines, court appearances, and jail sentences. To earn up-front money for non–legal aid lawyers, they are again forced back to the street to sell themselves. 'If you want to know who's really pimping these kids, it's the [justice] system.'[43]

Technically, prostitution has never been a crime in Canada, but virtually every activity associated with it – like pimping and soliciting – is outlawed, making prostitution illegal in practice. Bill C-49, an anti-soliciting law, has been almost universally condemned for effectively criminalizing prostitutes. By so doing, the law further entrenched prostitutes' need for pimps, because, as the law became more repressive, women needed more protection and more bail money. It also compounded the dangers for juveniles by increasing a pimp's motivation to hide them away in rooming-houses and cheap hotels where they would be less accessible to arresting officers – and to outreach workers who might help them beat the street.

C-49 was motivated by the same interests that usually account for upheavals in life on the stroll: home-owners of newly gentrified inner-city boarding-houses. When property-owners understandably howl about used condoms littering their lawns and laneways, and about the noisy parade of hookers and honking cars shattering their tranquillity, something usually changes. In 1985, C-49 was the answer to residential pressure.

C-49 may have appeased some home-owners. The law also led to more arrests, fines, and jail sentences for tricks, who normally get off scot-free while prostitutes pay the fines, do the time, and live with the records. However, it also led to more women being saddled with criminal records. The consensus among such organizations as Elizabeth Fry who work with street prostitutes is that the law did more harm than good. Like its predecessors, C-49 has done nothing to solve the problem of sexually exploited children.

The justice system has always treated prostitution as a victimless crime, never as a crime against women and children. Prostitutes have always borne the brunt of law enforcement related to the sex trade. The law's subtext, however, seems to suggest that if any victims exist in the relationship between sex seller and buyer, it is the johns. Prostitutes end up in the guise of criminals, whereas their tricks appear as little more than public nuisances at worst.

Even people who might easily agree that prostitution constitutes a crime against children would not necessarily condemn
it as a crime against women. In fact, some feminists and prostitutes, along with some of their organizations, contend that
outdated morality is the real culprit. Spokespeople inside and
outside of the trade ask: why shouldn't prostitution be seen as a
social service and its practitioners accorded the dignity that work
bestows?[44]

They do not oppose prostitution; they oppose the conditions of
its practice. They lobby to legalize the trade, eliminate pimp
power, increase prostitutes' control over the business, reduce the
risk of violence, and boost health protection. In the name of
emancipating women, they fight not for an end to conditions that
force a woman to sell her body but for better conditions within
her enslavement. They seem to accept the dictum that prostitution will always be with us and conclude that sisterhood consists
in lightening the burden of female fate.

No amount of progressive-sounding language, however, can
mask the fact that prostitution stands as capitalism's ultimate
form of exploitation wherein human flesh serves as a commodity.

Yet, some hookers and their advocates also argue that prostitution empowers otherwise powerless women. 'I like the power
that I have with men. I like making them do whatever I want
them to do ... [I like] the power thing in making them pay for
[sex] and in deciding whether or not I'm going to date them. If I
want to be nice to them, that's my choice, and if I want to be a
straight up bitch, I can do that too.'[45] Evelyn Lau derived the only
sense of personal power in her life as an 'orifice for abuse' from
the fact that men found her attractive enough to 'pull bills out of
their wallets before pulling down their zippers.'[46]

One street prostitute in her twenties interviewed for this book
said, 'It's sad, eh, when the only power a girl's got in this world
is between her legs.' Another one, also a veteran over twenty,
warned, 'Don't let the girls fool you. Even if we've figured out a
way to live with what we're doing, deep down we all hate it. We
got no choices, it's that simple.'

Almost without exception, prostitutes, ex-hookers, streetworkers, and ordinary women who contributed to this book expressed
the belief that women's power to command cold cash for cold sex
does not in any way ameliorate female powerlessness in society.

Rather, most concur that poverty, sexism, and male violence, more than other factors, fuel the global factory that produces prostitution.

Devastating childhood experiences condition children for the eviscerating violence of street life and for the pimp's hypnotic grip. For many kids at risk for a life of ruin, the child-protection system seems incapable of diverting their descent or buffering their fall. Without this public ballast, prostitution will continue to lure endangered kids.

Homeless and Hungry

For many Canadians, wretched multitudes of children in Asia, Africa, and Latin America may seem remote, part of a far-away world very different from our own. A 'them' issue that doesn't touch 'us.' Misery for children in Canada may not seem comparable to that in, say, Calcutta. Yet, the most striking images in *Salaam Bombay*, the acclaimed 1988 film about India's street gamines, apply internationally. Except for culturally distinct references, such as street children working as tea vendors, the story parallels that of throwaway kids in European and North American cities.

Canada's cast-offs, like India's, sleep in back alleys; serve time in detention centres for petty crimes they commit to survive; exist on meagre rations of scraps; and risk the perils of street life, particularly violence, drugs, and disease. Employers exploit them, pimps corral them into prostitution, and street-wise veterans drag them down into the base morality of the street. Like the street-urchin hero of *Salaam Bombay*, many make valiant efforts to pull themselves up, but end up buried in the rubble of their own lives, as if the whole weight of society were bent on keeping them down.

The quality of life urban nomads endure world-wide is increasingly homogeneous. In *Down and Out: Orwell's Paris and London Revisited*,[1] two writers who retraced Orwell's journey through the cities' underbelly found life for 'dossers' little changed except for 'an additional fifty years of grime and dilapidation' added onto the hostels, which, they discovered, are not much more civilized than were their poorhouse and workhouse antecedents.

These contemporary writers found one thing Orwell didn't find: a mass of young people, including families, reduced to dire circumstances traditionally associated with hoboes. Anecdotal accounts they recorded from drifters, young and old, bedding down in British 'spikes' parallel those Canadian's hostel-dwellers recount.

U.N. figures indicate that, globally, one in four people is either homeless or living on the brink of homelessness.[2] A quarter of the world's population – over one billion people, a number too vast to comprehend – have no secure place, with minimum health and sanitation standards, to call home. Of them, 100 million have no shelter whatsoever.[3] Estimates of the number of street children around the world vary widely, ranging from 10 million to 100 million.[4] The U.N. calculates that as many as 100 million children are homeless.[5]

In the United States, the Coalition for the Homeless estimates that 3 to 4 million people – 500,000 of them children – live in the streets. An additional 14 million children live in poverty. An estimated 10 million families hover on the brink of homelessness.[6] In Canada, our homeless population stood at about one million in 1987.[7] About one in four Canadian children – a staggering 1,121,000 – live in poverty touched by hunger and/or homelessness.[8] A disturbing number of youngsters – possibly as many as 200,000 – have no fixed address other than Main Street.

What does homelessness mean? Definitions vary. A baseline set of factors that characterize homelessness emerged from the U.N. General Assembly's 1987 International Year of Shelter for the Homeless, a year that produced many conferences but few new affordable-housing starts.

Homeless people include those forced to live in dwellings that violate health and building codes. The Canadian Council on Social Development estimates that half a million renters – mostly elderly people and single women with children – live in such conditions.[9] Poverty and the shortage of affordable housing force people into overcrowded and makeshift arrangements. Hundreds of thousands of families and individuals in Canada live constantly with the fear of eviction from their inadequate domiciles, some in boarding homes threatened by up-market renovations, and others in basement bachelors, often declared 'illegal' during municipal crack-downs. In Vancouver, about 26,000 apartments violate zoning laws; in Toronto, an estimated 100,000 people now live in unregulated units.[10] Like illegal refugees, they await with dread the knock on the door. 'Living underground has taken on new meaning; it is just as likely to involve single mothers and their children as it is criminals.'[11] Many other people living within and outside zoning laws double up in residences far too cramped for their occupants.

Those forced to spend so much on rent that they cannot afford other necessities, particularly food, are also considered homeless. The Canada Mortgage and Housing Corporation (CMHC) estimates that one million families are in 'core need,' meaning that more than 30 per cent of their gross income goes towards rent. The Ottawa-based Co-operative Housing Foundation of Canada puts the national core need at an 'absolute minimum' of 1.5 million.[12]

'The lack of a secure home is perhaps the greatest obstacle to participating in our society ... It is remarkable the extent to which a place of residence is a condition of citizenship, and "no fixed abode" a label which consigns people to wholly inferior status.'[13] This inferior status diminishes people to faceless throngs, making them refugees in their own land. 'Homelessness is more than a lack of shelter: it is powerlessness and lack of control over one's life.'[14]

What kind of people are homeless? The majority do not conform to the old stereotype of the muttering derelict living in his own demented little hell. They are no loner single older men who have failed at and been failed by life, or ne'er-do-wells and non-conformists relegated to society's fringes because that is the only place they fit in.

Even though the number of these familiar vagrant types is increasing, they are becoming less conspicuous in the changing street bazaar. A new breed is usurping inner-city street corners, back alleys, dumps, dingy doorways, bus shelters, park benches, heating vents, church basements, greasy spoons, soup kitchens, flop houses, and roach-ridden rooms. Much younger and more aggressive, they squeeze weaker squatters from their home patches of pavement. Anxious to keep themselves and be left alone, the mumblers decamp to working-class and lower-middle-class neighbourhoods, where most people will treat them kindly or ignore them. Even the most befuddled of them know better than to invade neighbourhoods where people have real money. But, in ordinary neighbourhoods of large cities, it is common these days to recognize resident bag ladies, polite derelicts, and apologetic beggars.

The population shift is much more conspicuous in the inner-cityscape where young people with abject posture and eyes to the ground line up at shelters and soup kitchens, and embarrassed young couples queue up at food banks. In every line for hand-outs and hand-me-downs, young mothers calm crying toddlers and proud adolescents shrink from eye contact, humiliated by having to live second-hand lives. At every place where the homeless huddle, edgy teenagers seethe with the frustration of doing nothing and going nowhere. Many employable people populate the line-ups and street corners, and, straying among them, a new, less-employable group: people labelled mentally ill who have been released from institutions and left to fend for themselves with little or no community supports.

Although reliable demographic data on the street population Canada-wide is scarce, anecdotal evidence suggests that, until a decade ago, the hard-core bulk was male, over thirty, alcohol-addicted and/or mentally unstable, and not work-ready. Fifteen years ago, such single men were predominant among Toronto's homeless population.[15] These men shuffled around downtown and depended on a circuit of church missions for food and lodging. Among them, whole families, single women, male and female young unemployables, and kids were once so scarce as to be almost invisible. Today, in Toronto, these groups make up 58 per cent of the homeless population, and most are age eighteen to twenty-five.[16] The same mid-teen to mid-twenties trend, including a surprising number of girls and women, is evident across the country.

These young people hope their bereft state will prove to be nothing more than a temporary detour en route to a better life. For many, however, their lessons in humiliation – in bread lines and in line-ups for lodging – give way to little better than more of the same, a shattered life from which escape seems impossible. That's what happened to Jane.

At age seventeen, after a much-gossiped-about rape, she fled her Northern Ontario mining town for Toronto. 'I left after my family decided not to take my case to court because the boy that raped me came from a big-shot family. We were just poor, plain folks that figured we wouldn't have a chance in court up against a big-whig lawyer and a judge the boy's father plays golf with.'

Depressed and penniless, Jane spent her first night in the city in STOP 86, a women's shelter. That was eleven years ago. Since then, in a generally luckless life marked by one disaster after another, Jane has lived on and marginally off the street, often staying in shelters. Petite, plain-looking, and plain-spoken, she hates hostels.

'Some relief you get from the street by being in those places overnight! You get to sleep in a sardine can, people practically piled on top of each other. You're surrounded by women coughing and crying and acting crazy from the lives we're all living. Everyone grubbing for themselves. Everyone scraping for the same scarce things. Women scrapping – women can be dirty fighters, you know – for beds and food and clothes. You got to sleep wearing your clothes, or on top of all your possessions, or they get stolen.

'It's the kind of place where tempers flare up. Hostels taught me to fight at the hint of attack. There's no such thing as trust. You can't trust the staff – even though some of them are really nice people – because as a street person you know that all authority is your enemy. And the women can't trust each other because we're all so hurt and needy. We've got everything in common, but the situation pits us against each other.

'I don't mean that the street is any better for sleeping. Sometimes, it can be worse. You've got the constant threats. The threat of rape. Muggings. The threat of police harassment ... It's all the same, really, the street and the hostels, all part of the same life.'

Although housing is a basic need, the Canadian government has never treated it as a basic right. While no policy-maker would publicly argue against the idea that every resident is entitled to shelter, in practice those with power to guarantee basic necessities allow housing to be treated as a commodity. Like all commodities, it is regulated by profit margins, not by social needs, thereby leaving a minority of Canadians out in the cold.

To offset the caprice of the market-place, from the mid-1940s to the early 1980s, the federal government helped house some people who could not afford the cost of shelter. Government built subsidized units that absorbed neediest renters. While accommodating a portion of the poor, these projects also ghettoized and stigmatized lowest-income people, particularly women and their children, seniors, national minorities, and people with disabilities. For decades, housing activists have been needling government to force developers to integrate subsidized and otherwise affordable units into new residential subdivisions. Such integration of housing has not occurred on a wide scale, and even the socially outmoded types of housing projects have not kept pace with the need.

Social housing activist Grant Wanzel explains that the Tory government dismantled even the limited housing programs previous Liberal governments introduced, preferring 'policies of malign neglect in favour of smash-and-grab capitalism ... The present federal government has willed this dilemma: by systematically reducing social-welfare expenditures and encouraging well-meaning if sentimental volunteerism in their place; by withdrawing from its lead role in housing in general and by "targeting" its miserly support for social and public housing in particular,'[17] the federal government never delivered on its 1986 pledge to build 5,000 co-ops a year. In 1989, after the budget was announced, many were further disappointed when the office of the federal minister of state for housing admitted that Ottawa would be cutting back its financial aid for co-ops even more, to its 1986 level of support. In actual housing terms, that meant a maximum of 1,800 dwellings might be built across the country in 1989.

The 1990 federal budget brought more frightening news to people desperate for housing. Government slashed a whopping $50 million over two years from planned housing programs, which added up to a 15 per cent cut-back in social-housing spending. By 1990, the Tories were devoting a mere 0.0014 per cent of the country's budget to housing.[18] By then, the private market was supplying more than 96 per cent of the country's housing – a situation with damning repercussions for neediest renters.[19]

As housing demand escalated in the 1980s, publicly sponsored productions of all kinds of housing declined, exacerbating the shortage in the private sector. Declining household size has also worsened the shortfall. Statistics Canada reported that 2.81 people constituted the national average household in 1986, down from 3.21 in 1976 and 4.0 in 1961. The growth of one- and two-person households added to competition for the declining stock of affordable housing. In these market conditions, landlords, who are generally choosy anyway, can bar all but those tenants they consider most desirable.

A combination of forces continues to drive homelessness up, especially among those on its visible edge: young, employable street paupers. That is not to suggest that homelessness is something new in this country. Adequate, affordable housing has never been guaranteed; scores of poor people have always lived on the fringe, in shabby, substandard, insecure shelter. Until the 1980s, however, with the exception of the Depression era, the homeless have, for the most part, stayed hidden in their ramshackle rooms. Now, even those rooms are scarce.

Gentrification

Speculation and gentrification – what used to be called 'urban renewal' – argued about but ultimately blessed by municipal governments, have catapulted developers' profits and pitched the poor deeper into poverty. Given their enormous contributions to municipal elections – in Toronto, for example, the development industry contributes an average of 75 per cent to election funds reported by municipal politicians[20] – it is hardly surprising that developers' interests dominate city politics.

While developers may believe that converting multiple-occupancy dwellings into single-family units expunges squalor and reclaims cities for the respectable classes,[21] lodgers do not view their evictions in the same light. They express their reactions in graffiti smeared on the hoardings of boarded-up rooming-houses waiting for the wrecker's ball. One building in downtown Toronto was plastered with the slogan 'Gentrification = Homelessness.' One in Vancouver where kids were 'squatting' was spray-painted 'Condemned Building for Condemned People.'

Indeed, inner-city renewal has hit major centres throughout the industrialized world. This trend has displaced scores of single boarders and doubled-up families to accommodate a relatively small number of professionals with few or no children. Boarding-houses that rented rooms for $300 have been transformed into row houses that sell for $300,000 and more. Ironically, the dislodged tenants often have no place to go other than emergency shelters only blocks away from where they once lived.

Homelessness can splinter families. Because of the short supply of family shelters, displaced families are broken up and scattered among separate accommodation, often great distances apart.

Some parents whose families are thus torn apart confess to child-protection authorities that they cannot cope with the terrible instability, and that fraying tempers and open conflicts erupting between them and their children frighten them. It appears that more parents nowadays voluntarily place their kids in the care of child-protection authorities. Toronto's Catholic Children's Aid took in 100 child victims of the housing crisis in 1986–7.[22] Both Metro and Catholic CAS officials believe that the housing crisis is partly responsible for dramatic increases in child abuse that both organizations recorded between 1985 and 1988.[23]

Real-estate speculation and luxury renovations most often uproot those already least privileged: the working poor, welfare-dependent, single mothers, elderly, mentally unstable, disabled, and recent refugees. Against the combined power of city hall and the development industry, their protests are largely impotent. Housing and legal advocates for the poor have been complaining for years about how few rights vulnerable renters have in law, and how ill-equipped they are in any case to fight the unfettered power of landlords intent on evicting them.

Community legal workers in Parkdale, a Toronto neighbourhood with scores of slummy rental rooms, report that landlords commonly harass, intimidate, and violently interfere with tenants in order to discourage them from taking political action and from opposing evictions. Advocates have worked with boarders whose belongings have been confiscated, and who have been underfed by boarding-house keepers. The legal workers have recorded incidents where landlords have collected tenants' welfare cheques and then presented them for endorsement face down so recipients would not see the full amount of their cheque. Some of these landlords have kept more than the rent money.[24]

Runaways often hide out in condemned buildings slated for demolition. Like Gilette and his 'doom rockers' (chapter 2), they create a 'squat' where hordes of hard-pressed kids 'crash.' Skinheads and punkers of various ideological bents are well known for camping out in this way. Slumlords who are trying to evict resistant tenants in order to meet a developer's conditions for buying a building may deliberately rent rooms to malevolent-looking kids whose noisy, irreverent life-style disturbs more sedate tenants.

Despite uncertain tenure and maltreatment, roomers and apartment renters at the bottom end of the housing market have few, if any, choices. Most are desperate to hang on to what they've got. In the major cities, their chances are not good. In Vancouver, the Downtown Eastside Residents Association (DERA) estimates that 3,700 affordable units were lost between 1978 and 1986. DERA contends that hotels, each containing 30 to 40 units, are being demolished at the rate of one a month.

Between 1978 and 1987, Winnipeg lost 4,145 housing units.[25] In Edmonton, over 70 per cent of remaining rooming-houses have less than six years of structural life left.[26] Based on information from Ottawa's community development and zoning departments, boarding-house stock appears to have plummeted by 65 per cent between 1976 and 1987. In that period, 450 rooming-houses were reduced to 192.[27]

In Toronto, worst off in the country for affordable housing, between 1978 and 1985, total net stock – the difference between gains and losses – diminished by 10,940 units, according to data published by the city's Planning Department. Licensed boarding-houses, which leased approximately 5,000 rooms in 1980, had only 1,500 left by 1988.[28] The city's Social Planning Council reported that 2,128 affordable apartments disappeared between 1985 and 1989. A quarter were demolished. The rest were lost in conversions from multiple- to single-family units. One 1987 study estimated that 26 or 27 affordable units a day were being lost across Ontario to gentrification.[29] The picture does not improve in Montreal where ex-mayor Jean Drapeau's costly inner-city clean-up has apparently made rooming-houses almost extinct and swept hundreds of people into the street.

While squalid buildings that housed the poor are being razed, comfortable homes for the luckier are being built. The cost of home ownership at the beginning of 1989 across the country averaged 44 per cent of median income before taxes.[30] Financial institutions usually allow buyers to contribute a maximum of 35 per cent of their income to home buying. In Toronto, the Royal Bank of Canada reported that housing prices were so high in 1989 that four out of five households could not afford a down payment on an average-priced, single-story bungalow selling for $264,000.[31] To afford a small house, a buyer needs an annual income of $82,000.[32]

Even if most low- or moderate-income families could afford a modest home in major cities, many would be out of luck because most construction has been aimed at pricey new-home and condo buyers and at up-scale renters. For those most in need, new construction has not lessened the burden. Even the low vacancy rates regularly reported in the press – about 2.5 on average in major cities, 0.5 in Vancouver and 0.2 in Toronto – mask the severity of the competition. If rents for adequate housing strain the resources of yuppies with kids and so-called DINKs (double-income, no kids), they are completely beyond the budgets of people on low or fixed incomes. Consequently, the majority of people living on a shoestring and many on middling incomes cannot secure adequate housing.

Homeless Women and Children

Despite the economic and other gains more privileged women have achieved over the past twenty years, gender inequality has remained a constant feature of our society. According to the National Council of Welfare, single women run twice the risk that single men do of living below the poverty line.[33] Whether welfare-dependent or working, women are likely to be poor. Since they typically earn less than 65 per cent of what men earn in comparable jobs, most women who work outside their homes are wage-poor.

The threat of instant poverty discourages battered wives from leaving their homes, especially if they have children. This is not to suggest that all women who flee abusive men face impoverishment. Some have money. Some have options. A married woman – but not a cohabiting one – may even win possession of the family home through the courts. Staying in the family residence, however, is risky because violent men often stalk their former victims and even intensify their beatings in order to punish women for leaving them. One study found that two-thirds of women divorced for six to ten years were still being battered by their ex-husbands.[34]

Despite the risks, more and more women are living without men. Fewer are marrying, more are divorcing, and more are keeping babies born out of wedlock. Given a mother's poverty, and dependent kids to whom many landlords object, in a market with little affordable housing, women find themselves in an even weaker position than poor men. Consequently, women on their own or with children constitute over 85 per cent of tenants in public, non-profit, and co-op housing.[35] Many, however, are not lucky enough to secure space in these settings.

Some women fleeing abusive husbands with their children cannot even get into temporary shelters, let alone subsidized apartments. The severe shortage of 'second stage' accommodations – temporary, assisted bridge housing between emergency shelters and independent living – forces some victims to return to batterers. The equally severe shortfall in affordable permanent housing prevents women who are admitted to shelters from moving out. For them, a temporary shelter can become a semi-permanent address where they live under the pressure of making way for the next wave of beaten women with their children.

The housing crisis, traditional welfare-sponsored female and child poverty, low wages with eroding purchasing power, and the increasing numbers of women raising children on their own have led to increases in homelessness and hunger among women and children.

Dumping Institutional Inmates

Deinstitutionalization has also boosted homelessness in this country. The idea of closing down psychiatric hospitals (and some chronic-care facilities for physically handicapped people), of integrating people with unusual needs into the mainstream, was, and still is, hailed by champions of human rights and dignity. Advocates of deinstitutionalization and 'normalization' insist that everyone deserves to live in the community, that no one should be banished to warehouses for people with challenging needs. They oppose exclusion on the basis of any disability. They argue that people do not 'get better' or live quality lives in sprawling institutions run on a medical model that emphasizes ritualized care and drug management. They say that all disabled people, no matter what the diagnosis or degree of disability, want and need the same things as anyone does: to be part of some type of family unit, to be loved and accepted as they are. A rich community, they say, is a diverse one that appreciates the

varied gifts of its members and accommodates itself to the whole spectrum of human needs.

Governments, usually slow to embrace radical new ideas, glommed on to deinstitutionalization in the 1960s. Publicly, they suggested that new psychotropic drugs made it feasible to put hitherto 'crazy' people back into the community.[36] Although they couched their phase-out and shut-down plans in the noble rhetoric of social progress, they glossed over a critical plank in the integrationists' platform: the necessity for community-based supports and resources to help patients relocate and reintegrate.

Advocates claim that, in practice, deinstitutionalization amounted to nothing more than cost-cutting at a time when increasing unionization of mental-health workers and physical deterioration of turn-of-the-century mental asylums were making the psychiatric status quo too costly.[37] Instead of agreeing to union wage demands and restoring old buildings, government opted to close the institutions.

After a lifetime inside, some patients were so profoundly institutionalized in their thinking that they had become what street kids call 'institution junkies' – that is, they were terrified of living outside walls. Other patients had families who vociferously resisted any change. Government reacted to the backlash by rehousing a handful of recalcitrant former patients in contracted private facilities that paid lower wages to caregivers than the state had paid to institutional employees. Most other formerly institutionalized people were left to their own devices in transferring to the community.

In 1960, Canada had 47,600 psychiatric beds. By 1987, only 1,000 remained.[38] Psychiatric hospitals decreased by one-third between 1970 and 1978, as did the length of in-patient stays for emotional and psychotic illnesses. In 1960, 50 per cent of the 75,000 Canadians in mental institutions had been hospitalized for more than seven years. Today, nine out of ten patients stay less than a month.[39]

Manitoba's practices typified what happened to vulnerable people who had been confined in chronic-care hospitals. From 1950 to 1986, Manitoba's institutionalized population plummeted from 2,700 to 727. Although a caseload of 20 post-psychiatric patients per worker is considered realistic, 20 community mental-health workers inherited a deinstitutionalized caseload of 85 patients each. Of their 1,697 patients in 1986, only 25 per cent had been rehoused in residential group homes.[40] While many people, including lots of former inmates, were cheering the close of outdated and what they considered inhumane holding tanks, others were mourning the way in which government had orchestrated the demise.

In *Forgotten Millions*,[41] author/psychologist David Cohen argues that the humane vision of community care was bastardized into wholesale neglect. Tens of thousands of patients, many of them long removed from the community and long abandoned by family and friends, were literally sent off into the streets. Today, ex–psychiatric residents constitute 20 to 40 per cent of Canada's street population.[42] Many live revolving-door lives, in and out of hospitals, in and out of seedy rented rooms.

Maria: Pregnant panhandling teen, living in hostels

On a balmy Sunday night during Ottawa's May tulip festival, a very pregnant young woman stands dejectedly at the corner of Laurier and Bank, begging change from the smattering of passers-by.

'Excuse me,' she says as we approach, 'but could you help me out? I need three dollars to pay my way into a hostel tonight ... There aren't many people around; it's the first really warm weekend and everyone's gone to the cottage.' She apologizes for panhandling: 'If I weren't so pregnant, I could be working at McDonald's and I'd be able to pay my own way into the hostel.'

We give her some money and have a long chat. I ask whether she'd be willing to be interviewed. She thinks it over, studies me. 'I've only got fifteen minutes to curfew at the Y, but I can talk to you tomorrow if you'd like.'

She goes to her hostel, and we go to our hotel but I can't sleep. I'm chilled by the image of this child, large with child, roaming the streets. She can't be more than sixteen years old. Falling prey momentarily to the notion that intelligence determines destiny, I lie awake baffled about how such an apparently bright girl could end up on the street. Street kids, on the whole, seem no sharper or duller than the general population, but this teenager was different. Her speech, her insights, her self-confidence – all impressed me as unusually developed for someone so young.

Next day, Maria confirms my initial impression. She is intellectually superior and articulate, but she comes from a crippling background. Maria says her natural intelligence hasn't mattered a whit in shaping her life. What has mattered, she says, has been her family and the child-protection system. 'They put me where I am today – on the streets.'

Today she is tired and pale and can't eat a whole meal at a sitting because the poverty of the street has trained her stomach for small, infrequent snacks, mostly of coffee and junk food. She is covered with dry, itchy eczema, and her straight blond hair, which needs cutting, falls into her eyes. Maria is a dead-ringer for Jodie Foster made up as a street urchin.

She pushes a few greasy strands off her small baby face and complains how hard it is to nourish the eighth-month baby she is carrying. 'I'm living in hostels and eating hand-outs, which means sleepless nights and almost no fresh food. My own nutrition and health care are pathetic, and the baby's living off my body, so what can it be getting?' She talks fast, in a squeaky, high-edged voice. Her pitch rises and her brow furrows every time we touch what she calls 'the traps' – welfare and the CAS.

Unlike most street youths I've met, Maria will probably read this book. She likes reading. In fact, she took me to a bookstore down the street from the Lucerne Restaurant, where we talked a day away, insisting that I read two books on street life that she had found insightful. One I'd read; the other was new to me. As we browsed through the bookstore, she gave me a lecture on the politics of hunger and homelessness.

It just doesn't look good to have hungry, dirty people in the street in the nation's capital. That's why the government makes sure the riff-raff are swept off the pavement during the daytime when good citizens and VIPs might catch a glimpse of the truth about our so-called welfare state. Their big PR concern with hiding us actually works to our advantage because it means that it's easier to get into Futures and other youth-diversion programs here than in other cities.

Night-time, however, it's a different story. Brian [Mulroney] doesn't worry about us then because the good people are in their nice homes and hotels – and we can rot as far as the politicians are concerned.

There are plenty of us rotting, believe me. It's an older crowd, mostly men, hard-core types like winos and old geezers screwed up on turpentine, or psych patients ping-ponging in and out of hospitals. Daytime, they hang out in government and church drop-ins.

But, after dark, there's no place to go. There are only about 3,500 hostel beds in the city, very few of them for women. Not that there are that many women in the streets here – although lots more than the number of beds. There are almost no juvey hookers. Most working girls are older and work for themselves, not for pimps. Luckily, it's not too dangerous here; you hardly ever see anyone get rolled. Some men stay on the street overnight by choice because the hostels really stink. I've been inside them, so I can understand why a guy would prefer a dose of stomach bitters and a doorway.

There's a chance they'll get beaten up by punkers or skinheads. Haven't you seen their graffiti around Parliament Hill? [I had seen spray-painted racist slogans, particularly against Pakistanis and Jews and in support of apartheid.]

There's still a few tumble-down boarding-houses – although they're disappearing pretty fast – where street kids can rent or squat. Some dump with a dozen kids is not a whole lot better than actually living in the street, but it's a roof. I rarely pan enough money to both eat and chip in for rent, so I have to stay in hostels. Some of them charge a token fee. If it's warm enough these next six weeks till the baby comes, I'll sleep out in a park most nights.

I can't get any type of financial assistance because I fall through the cracks in the system. That means you're sixteen to eighteen years old, aren't a ward of the state or in school: exactly my situation. You can't get welfare so you have to get a job. Except, you need a place in order to get a job because you need a shower and decent clothes before you can go job-hunting. Obviously – just look at me – you can't stay clean or look decent living in the street. Or you need a place to get a home visit to maybe get kiddie welfare – which is almost impossible to get if you're not in school – but you need a deposit to get a promise of address to get a home visit to get a first cheque. Get the picture? What it all boils down to is that you can't get assistance and you can't earn a first and last month's rent to get a place and get on your feet. It's a trap for sixteen- to eighteen-year-olds.

So, why didn't I get my CAS wardship extended so I could get help through this pregnancy? Because they think I'm a lost cause and they refused to help me. I had a baby when I was fifteen and still in care. In order to take him for me – I refused to give him up voluntarily – they terminated my wardship. That meant I lost my allowance, lost my subsidized room, and was forced back on the street, where they could claim, and rightly so, that I couldn't be a fit mother.

In other words, they deliberately destabilized my situation in order to take my baby away from me. At the time, things had actually been going quite good. I was with Dan, my boyfriend and the baby's father, and by the time I delivered, we had a rented room. I know we were young and poor, but we both wanted the baby. I didn't let him go easily; I fought back. I didn't crumple when they came after me. CAS records are like prison records; even if you change cities, workers manage to get your file and find out about your past misdemeanours. I'm paying for mine now by being forced to spend this pregnancy in the street, panhandling. I'll be on some street corner when I go into labour.

My mother is a hooker and a heroin addict; my father is a bisexual I never met. But I did meet my stepfather. I lived with him and my mother once, for six months, when I was twelve. That's when the CAS apprehended me and stuck me in a foster family. It's also when I began running away.

Stepdaddy is a real doll, an Italian sign painter who fancies himself a regular Michelangelo. His paintings are like his personality – demented. But since he prides himself on doing eight hits of acid a day, it's no wonder. He also beats my mother. He likes his women docile and dependent, so he approves of her addiction. From time to time, she has tried to kick her habit, but he'll leave a rig [needle] or a hit of heroin around to tempt her. When I was twelve and staying with them, he kept me locked in a bedroom with a cakepan to piss in and a pizza box to shit in – literally, no exaggeration. His idea of kindness was giving me marijuana when he let me out. When he allowed me to eat, I was given warmed-over spaghetti that had been moulding on the stove in the same pot for about a week.

That was the worst six months of my life, not that the rest of growing up was any picnic. I don't know where I was before age two, but I know that my grandparents adopted me then. They're old-fashioned Italians. They were so scared I'd follow in my mother's footsteps that they sheltered me from life. As a child, my world was their basement. I had a plastic swimmingpool down there, a swing set, even a little roller-skating rink. When I was let out, which wasn't often, I wasn't allowed off the back porch.

My grandparents couldn't have coped with a normal kid, but to make matters worse, I wasn't normal. I was extremely hyper and very bright; in fact, from grades three to six, I went to a special school for gifted kids. In that school they had a class for brainy brats with behaviour problems – that was me. Looking back, I can understand why I was such a little hellion at school; I needed to have some freedom after the heavy discipline. All us 'behaviour problems' were drugged out of our minds. I was on Ritalin [a mood-altering prescription drug widely used on children considered hyperactive].

My grandparents never told me about my mother. As far as I knew, they were my real parents, and my aunts and uncles, who were much older than me, were my brothers and sisters. It was always a little confusing because I was repeatedly warned against this mysterious 'sister' who might try to spirit me away from the school-yard. 'If anyone tells you they're your mother and tries to take you away from the school, don't go with them.' I heard this warning often but never understood what it was about.

Until one day someone slipped. My real mother, who I thought was a cousin or a distant relative, was on one of her rare visits to the house when an aunt referred to her as 'Maria's mother.' Maria's mother? Could she be my mother? Somehow, I couldn't let go of the idea that she might be my mother, and for weeks after, I hounded my aunt. By the time she admitted the truth, I had become obsessed with finding out.

After that incident, I was sent to live with one of my uncles and his wife. He was wonderful to me, really wonderful, the first person ever to be sensitive or understanding. She was a bitch, insanely jealous of his affection for me. The arrangement didn't last. That's when I was shunted to my mother's, and you know what happened there – the cakepan-and-pizza-box routine.

Next, the CAS stepped in and I started my year-long merry-go-round of foster and group homes. You knew none of them wanted you, that you were just a meal ticket. Foster kids never get what natural kids get. Running away seemed the only out to me. I'd run; the police would find me and take me back. As soon as the cruiser disappeared, so would I.

I never ran home, though, like so many other kids do. I'd run to the street. I'd certainly never run back to my grandparents' house, and I couldn't go to my mother while she was living with that creep, which as far as I know, she still does. Last time we saw each other was in a fleabag hotel in Toronto, over two years ago. I didn't have enough cash to cover rent for the room and food. She disappeared in a car with a guy and came back with a sixty-dollar 'loan.' Two weeks later, she took my last dollar, supposedly to repay the loan. She probably bought heroin with it. I haven't seen her since.

Basically, I was a full-time street kid from age twelve and a half. Before I was thirteen, I knew more than you'd ever want to know about the street. I had smoked a joint of [hashish] oil and fallen asleep, I guess, behind the Eaton Centre. Next thing I remember, but only vaguely, is some guy shaking me to wake up ... Even when I think about it now, it's like a bad dream you know was real. Then I was asleep on a bench set in a basement but I don't remember how I got there ... The guy who tried to wake me must have carried me. I do remember what happened next, though. Vividly. I woke up because something was penetrating my bum. The pain was unbelievable. Then some guys were holding me down and shooting semen into my mouth. I must have passed out from the fear, or maybe I'm just blocking some of the memory, but next thing I remember is being awakened in an alley by cops who took me to the CAS.

The Eaton Centre is full of bad memories for me. That's where I was hanging out when Blondie, a runner for a skinhead pimp named Chicano, recruited me. Chicano, incidentally, is now doing time, I heard, for holding a gun to the head of a twelve-year-old who refused to work for him. Soon after Blondie picked me up, I was in and out of cars, having sex for money.

From age thirteen to fifteen screwing men for money was my whole life. The bit of cash Blondie let me keep was my survival. The work was dangerous and dirty – lots of johns won't use rubbers, you know – but it was still better than CAS foster homes. No way was I going back to them or to a Section 16 school [specially mandated schools in Ontario for group-home and institutionalized kids] where the teachers look down their noses at you and make you do simple, repetitive drills, no matter how smart you are. I got my grade eight, but I certainly didn't learn anything.

I was just a little girl and I looked it; in some ways, that helped me in the streets because older girls protected me. They never hassled me about stealing their turf or their tricks. None of the sleaze bags running the trick pads cared that I was underage; they only cared about the twenty-five dollars they got from the johns for the rooms. You should see these rooms – holes, that's all they are – in the kind of cribs with broken neon signs flashing 'Rooms for Rent.'

The other girls were great, but the pimps weren't. They beat you, threaten you, and control you. Don't think you can just walk away like that if you want to, which I did want by the time I was fifteen. You can't imagine the kind of tortures they threaten you with if they sus-pect you'll try to quit.

Sometimes, the threats are enough to keep a girl in line a long time. Like what they did to me. I was forced to witness a brutal beating of a hooker who had a contract on her because she was trying to get off the street. She was a big money-maker and her pimp wasn't prepared to let her go.

A creep by the name of Yogi – everyone's got street names – was my pimp at that time. I was standing near the corner of George and Dun-das, just back from a date. Yogi came up to me.

'Got any Sheiks?' he asked.

'No, all out.'

'Take a coffee break at Pioneer Donuts. No tricks till I come back; I'll grab you some rubbers from Ford's.'

While I was in the donut shop, a date came up to me. 'Want to go out?' he asked.

'Can't. I'm waiting for my man to come back with some condoms.'

'Don't worry, baby, I don't want sex, I just want company.'

'All right, but if my pimp sees me going with you, you'll have to give me forty dollars.'

'No problem.'

Everything seemed fine. We get to his room, which was nearby, and he makes me tea, of all things, which I take with a couple of speed bennies. We smoke a joint and watch TV. It was nice, actually, a real nice change from the humpers. Next thing I know, he's pinning me to a bed and I'm screaming. He was choking me with one hand and hitting me with the other, hollering 'Shut up, bitch! Shut up!' I re-member seeing colours and feeling his fist punching me, punching me, punching me in the face. I could taste my blood. I have no idea what his trip was; he probably just likes beating up on women. Lots of men get their kicks from that.

I came to on a fire-escape, covered in blood, my blouse drenched. I could barely call loud enough to attract someone from the street below.

A guy scrambled up the fire-escape and, when he saw me like that, he called for help. That was the first time I ever fell willingly into a cop's arms! I was crying. 'I'm only fourteen. I'm only fourteen. My pimp's going to be looking for me. He'll kill me.'

I couldn't get off the street alone, but I wanted off. A young guy in a Texaco uniform – not exactly a knight in shining armour, but he was good enough for me – helped me get away from my pimp. Dan became the only real friend I've ever had. He also became the father of my first baby. He was sixteen; I was pushing fifteen. He had occasional work, a little bread, and sometimes a rented room, which meant he was better off than me. Dan introduced me to panhandling and a new neighbourhood and a new crowd.

We clung to each other. We were both so needy that even when Dan didn't have enough money for a room, we wouldn't split up at night in order to sleep in separate hostels. One night we almost froze sleeping in a kid's tree-house in a bitter wind. Dan kept whispering 'I want to go to sleep,' and I kept begging him to say awake. 'If we go to sleep, we may never wake up.'

You already know what happened to our baby. Even though we lost him, we still had each other and we tried very hard to stick together. Life in the street forces couples apart. You can barely take care of yourself – get enough to eat, a bed for a night – let alone take care of another person. But we were together as much as our circumstances allowed. In fact, we hitch-hiked to Ottawa together, but by then we weren't a couple anymore, just friends. I was on my own again, living hand to mouth, surviving day to day.

Because Ottawa is a laid-back small town compared to Toronto, there's less push-push here, even on street people. But that doesn't make the streets seem any warmer on a cold night. When you don't have a cent, you don't have a place to sleep, it's 3:00 a.m. and you're shivering, you accept any bed you're offered. Sex is a small price to pay for a warm place to lay your head. I knew the guy I went home with the night I got pregnant; I really didn't think he'd make me sleep with him. I thought he was just being kind because he's helped me out in the past. But I was wrong – and here I am eight months gone.

Pregnant is just one more thing to knock you down when you're always struggling but never able to get up. In the streets, it seems that something always pushes you back when you manage to take one small step up. Getting ahead is just a dream; it's never real. I know, because I've taken small steps before. Even having a room of your own is progress. But the landlord evicts you because he's found a sucker he can soak for more rent, or the slummy boarding-house gets torn down ... Something always kicks you in the face.

You just have to keep trying, I guess. After the baby is born, I'm going to give it another shot. Incidentally, the baby is being adopted out through a doctor. He told me about several couples who wanted a kid. I picked the parents myself, a biochemist with a PhD and his lawyer wife. This kid's going to get a crack at a decent life. Afterwards, my social worker is going to help me get a job and get into night school.

Can you believe that I've got a social worker who really wants to help me? Professionals have been around me since I can remember. They're forever claiming to understand, but they don't. How can they? They haven't been screwed by umpteen men and passed around like a piece of meat. Street kids, if they trust anyone, which most don't, are more likely to trust streetworkers, especially the ones who have been on the streets themselves.

My social worker can't do much for me right now. There's no place in the system for a pregnant seventeen-year-old who's been blacklisted by the CAS. So, I have to stick it out in the street for the next month and a half. Take the digs from upstanding citizens who are cursing me under their breath for being pregnant – as if it's different from when their teenagers get knocked up. In the meantime, I have to live on the charity from people who are more sympathetic. Most people you pan-handle don't have a clue how kids end up where I am. From conversations I've had with the few friendly ones, I don't think it ever occurs to them that I didn't choose this life.

But I know it's not my fault that I ended up in the street. Yet, I often feel that I'm being cornered into a lifetime of punishment for things others people did to me. Nobody deserves that ...

God, I want more than this!

The Public Bed and Kitchen

Tonight he is trying the spike and, despite the miserable wrinkled old man who shares the shower with him and tells him repeatedly how lucky he is, it is his worst experience yet.

He receives his bed ticket, goes to the dining room where he is given some grisly stew, some bread and hard cheese, and tea. He hardly notices that he is eating. A jolly, high-spirited, yet gentle drunk takes a liking to him and decides to show him the ropes. He leads him to the blanket room, and from there to his dormitory; even helps him make the bed and scrounges a clean pillow. After this, he takes himself to the television room. At nine-thirty, too tired for anything else, he goes back to his dormitory and falls asleep.

Half an hour later he is woken roughly. It is dark. There are shouts and curses from all around the dormitory. There is a fight going on in one corner, but he doesn't worry about that. He has been woken by someone trying to get into his bed. He lashes out feebly. Luckily, the intruder is worse off than he is and falls onto the floor, where he lies gently moaning.

He stays awake for the next two hours. Gradually the shouts and curses die down, the sporadic fighting stops. The intruder ceases moaning, seems to slide further away under someone else's bunk. By this time, he needs to go to the toilet. He decides to risk it and leaves his bed.

He finds the toilet covered in ordure. The smell, the sight and his misery combine and he retches in a corner ... He smells his own sick among the competing smells of piss, shit, alcohol, stale sweat and cigarettes. He feels ashamed.[43]

To cushion the fall from family grace, from institutions and from the bottom of the housing market into the street, municipal governments, churches, and private agencies offer 'emergency' hostels for 'temporary' shelter. In every major Canadian city, they are overflowing, unable to accommodate more than a fraction of distraught adolescents, beaten women and their children, displaced renters (some, entire young families), and ex–psychiatric patients. Aside from shelters open exclusively to battered women with their children, and a few open only to kids, most do not specialize. Everyone of the right sex is eligible for a bed – if one is available and if the applicant can stand the indignities and the dirt.

This means that a healthy teenager earning minimum wage washing dishes who can't find an affordable room has to sleep with drunks, drifters, and miscreants in an environment like that of the British spike described above. It means that child victims of family violence in need of safety and succour must bunk in a barracks-like environment with desperate adults.

The humiliation of the public bed is compounded by the abysmal condition of most of them. Some smaller refuges for women and youths offer private, dignified, even comfortable surroundings. Their staff have time for residents, time to hold a woman while she weeps, time to rock a confused and scared child to sleep. Even these 'good' shelters, however, as one study found, tend to reinforce women's traditional domesticity and dependence rather than helping them build independent, self-reliant lifestyles.[44]

On the whole, hostels are decrepit storehouses of misery. At one level, they provide relief from distress. At another level, they serve as a penalty for failure. Like America's welfare hotels that emerge in all their ugliness in *Rachel and Her Children*,[45] Canada's betray the tacit condemnation of the homeless as the undeserving poor. The message, however, is not lost on the people who use hostels; they understand all too well their status as outcasts in the social order. It is hard to miss the point when one's survival is reduced to a circuit of hand-outs and hang-outs, when the concept of choice, sacred even if elusive for many in North American life, is totally unattainable. The homeless get what they are given and go where they are sent, or they get nothing and stay on the street.

In fact, many homeless people of all ages exercise their one choice, as Maria points out, by avoiding hostels altogether. In *Street People Speak*, homeless males voice their objections:

I don't use hostels ... The places are too dirty, real hell holes, and too many drunk people.

... I'd rather sleep outside. You get sick in hostels; there is a concentration of sick people. People vomit and wet on beds, have colds and other bugs. Some get in fights. I'd rather buy my own food than eat their white bread.

Hostels are only a flophouse. They don't really help you.[46]

Homelessness has given rise to what has been called the 'homelessness industry,'[47] to the spectrum of mostly private agencies – especially hostels, food banks, and soup kitchens – that sprouted up in the 1980s after the first food bank opened in Edmonton in 1981. Most commentators on and even directors of these new-age charities admit that agencies that were supposedly set up to deal with a specific emergency have become institutionalized fixtures of the welfare system. In protest over government's failure to feed people who cannot feed themselves, and in a bid to force the state to assume its responsibility, various food banks have deliberately closed, while others have announced their intention to close. The Metro Food Bank Service in Halifax, for example, which now provides food to about 5,000 people a month, proclaimed that it will shut its doors permanently on 1 January 1994.[48] Other food banks, dependent on the already overtaxed generosity of volunteer staff and private-citizen donations, cannot keep abreast of soaring hunger. By the summer of 1990, Metro Toronto's hunger-relief system, which feeds more than 80,000 people a month, found itself close to collapse.[49]

It is little wonder that the system has been strained to the breaking-point. According to Canada-wide data accumulated by the Canadian Association of Food Banks (CAFB), the number of centralized, regional food distribution clearing-houses across the country has climbed to 159.[50] Each clearing-house distributes foodstuffs to member agencies in its own area. These outlets, in turn, directly provide meals or groceries to Canada's hungry. The CAFB estimates that almost 400,000 people (not including repeat users) across the country are now fed each month. Forty per cent are children.[51]

Across Canada, the working poor comprise 6 per cent of food-bank users; in Metro Toronto, 17 per cent of people dependent on emergency food have jobs.[52] The city's Daily Bread Food Bank has documented that customer families living in private rental housing have an average of $23 a week to live on after rent.

In Canada's biggest, richest City of the Dome, 84,000 people could not afford to feed themselves in 1989.[53] The known numbers of hungry people, however, only hint at the real extent of need, because many proud people go without any food or without regular meals for days, even weeks, before resorting to the public display that charity entails. More than half the people who show up at Toronto food depots haven't eaten for a day or more.[54] In a study of runaways conducted by the Social Planning Council of Winnipeg, most of 127 respondents reported that, out of pride or out of fear of being caught by police, they never asked for food.

Nor do numbers say anything about the nutritional insult of meals eaten by food-bank and soup-kitchen dependents. Charity food is poor food. Heavy on starches and sugars from tinned, processed, and packaged foods, and light on protein, minerals, and vitamins from fresh produce, the public soup makes a mockery of Canada's food guide.

Numbers say nothing about the consequences of hunger and the search for food. The Physician Task Force on Hunger in America found that 'the shame experienced over the inability to provide for one's family can become a serious psychological burden with corresponding physiological consequences ... The reported misery and depression are risk factors for disease.'[55] Hunger and the search for food can make people sick in mind and body, just as hostel life can actually precipitate mental illness, especially deep depression.[56]

Street kids avoid hostels and food banks if they can, relying on park benches and 'burger runs,' referring to the cold, desiccated hamburgers they rescue from dumpsters behind McDonald's and similar chains that discard food after it has staled under heat lamps. Try though street kids do to live rough and to feed themselves – which most often means eating rarely and poorly – cold and hunger eventually force most homeless kids into public beds and public kitchens.

Homelessness and hunger are foisted on runaways by the same forces that thwart adults struggling to house and feed their families: affordable-housing shortages; below-subsistence welfare and minimum-wage rates; social-service gaps and cut-backs; so-called urban renewal; institution closures without back-up community supports; and the grinding poverty that daunts women, whether they collect wages or welfare. Squeezed out of failing families, kids fall through gaping holes in the state's rescue net into the snafu of street life.

5

The Crime Traps: Poverty and Illiteracy

Poverty, curtailed during the boom years of the early 1970s, made a stunning come-back in the 1980s. Journalists, statisticians, social scientists, and especially watch-dogs, such as the National Anti-Poverty Organization, recorded the grim trends. By the late 1980s, misery had reached levels unprecedented in the history of this country, with the exception of the Dirty Thirties. Unemployment vaulted, wage value plummeted, and the social net shrank, causing some Canadians to question their belief that our government provides the buffer that ensures basics for all. With the proliferation of poor people, the growth industries of despair – hostels and food banks – prospered.

The phrase 'feminization of poverty' entered our lexicon in an era in which traditional female-specific economic problems reached crisis proportions. Women's share of poverty increased radically between 1973 and 1986. Poor households, mainly young families headed by single mothers, jumped from 366,000 to 1.8 million.[1] Women head 86 per cent of low-income, single-parent families.[2] Fifty-six per cent of these sole-support families live below poverty lines. About 50,000 young families of this kind are added each year to the welfare rolls, which already include one million households across the country. An additional million Canadians, a disproportionate number of them female, depend on short-term jobs and Unemployment Insurance. Yet another two million, many of them women, work at or near minimum wage.[3]

Young mothers are as likely to be watering the baby's milk as women age sixty-five and older are to be subsisting on toast and tea. More than half the women over age sixty-five who live alone are poor. Women constitute 73 per cent of the elderly poor.[4]

Despite advances some women have achieved for themselves over the past twenty years, in general women continue to slam up against gross wage disparities. Research done by the Canadian Advisory Council on the Status of Women has repeatedly confirmed that the underpaid drudgery of the service sector traps most work-place women. 'The women who moved into the bottom rung of the labour market ten years ago are still in the bottom rungs,' says Advisory Council executive member Sylvia Farrant.[5] 'Women's work' tends to be non-unionized and insecure, part-time, temporary, on-call, or in shifts. Statistics

Canada reports that 72 per cent of women work part-time, although half of them would prefer a full-time job.

The Advisory Council on the Status of Women says that women constituted 60 per cent of 2.8 million adults defined as poor in 1986, and almost half of these impoverished women worked full- or part-time. Between 1971 and 1986, the number of working women living below the poverty line increased by five times more than that of men.[6] Women's worsening situation is hardly surprising, given that females earn, according to Statistics Canada, about 65 cents on the male dollar. (This average, skewed upwards by the high incomes earned by the small number of female professionals, prettifies an even wider gender-based wage gap.)

Women, especially single mothers, are caught between the pincers of financial need and domestic demands. Many have work schedules that conflict with their children's routines. With work hours they cannot control and wages that rule out suitable childcare, some mothers are forced to leave 'latchkey' kids inadequately attended or on their own. Left to care for themselves, some of these children end up in trouble and on the street. Typically, their mothers, who struggle against impossible odds to raise their kids well, are blamed. By scrapping indefinitely a promised $4 billion national childcare strategy for 200,000 new daycare spaces, the 1989 federal budget further tightened the vice around young mothers.

Poor women and their advocates write angry, impassioned exposés of their plight. One, identified as 'Diana, a white woman in her late twenties,' spilled out her anguish in *No Way to Live: Poor Women Speak Out*: 'poverty kills women,' she wrote, and 'poverty kills children. Women in the community I work in [downtown Eastside Vancouver where 75 per cent of women have incomes under $8,000][7] die twenty-two years younger than the national average ... Poverty over a long period of time is like a slow form of death ... You are robbed slowly of your self esteem ... There's too many people who have died as a result of the kind of repression that poverty brings. For me, it's really personal. My mother committed suicide, and I really feel there was a direct correlation between the fact that she was totally impoverished and her simply giving up.'[8]

Working Poor

In the boom days of the mid-1970s, social-policy bureaucrats bandied about heady schemes for a guaranteed annual income for all Canadians. Far from delivering it, by 1989 government had allowed the value of the wage to fall by 22 per cent, preventing working people, let alone welfare recipients, from earning an adequate income.[9] According to the National Council of Welfare, more than one in seven Canadians in 1987 did not earn enough to cover necessities. At that time, the council reported that typical welfare rates fell anywhere from 16 to 78 per cent below the poverty line.[10]

Many Canadians believe that working full-time and earning a livelihood, perhaps meagre but at least enough to scrape by, go hand in hand. In 1975, that assumption would have been accurate to the extent that minimum-wage earnings then put a two-income couple with two children 6 per cent above the poverty line. This is no longer the case. By 1989, that same family needed an 18 per cent wage boost, just to reach the poverty line.[11]

Poverty now is as much a consequence of low-wage work as it is of welfare dependence. In 1988, according to Statistics Canada, 48.9 per cent of the heads of low-income families were in the work-force.[12] They were not lolly-gagging on the public purse. In 1989, after paying federal and provincial income tax, Canada Pension Plan contributions, and Unemployment Insurance premiums, the minimum-wage worker who grossed $9,360 at a $4.50-per-hour wage, took home $8,305, or $160 a week.[13] That year, the CCSD's poverty line for a single person in a city with a population over 500,000 was $12,037 ($24,481 for a family of four and $28,526 for a family of five).[14] Generally speaking, wage earners working full-time for legal minimums take home 20 to 30 per cent below the government-defined cost of subsistence.

Given paltry minimum wage for hard, disagreeable work, it is quite remarkable that so many people cleave to the work ethic. And yet they do – a fact lost on those who perpetuate enduring myths about poor people as lay-about schemers who breed like rabbits and want something for nothing.

Writers who interviewed men, mostly in their thirties, living on Toronto streets – presumably, the most demoralized of workers –

were assailed by their subjects' frustrations at seeking work and being rebuffed day after day. Many of the men they polled, rather than shiftless, were relentless in their trudge from one low-paying prospect to the next.[15] Despite poor discipline that evolves naturally from their topsy-turvy street lives, despite their dirty and dishevelled appearance, despite their paucity of skills, most of the youngsters interviewed for this book periodically look for jobs and work for wages that cannot both feed and house them. Most poor people do not lack the work ethic so much as the access to work that pays a living wage.

For those who can't work or who can't find work, getting off welfare is a lot tougher than getting on it. The disincentives are legend. Single mothers lose housing and day-care subsidies as well as their drug cards, things that, given the kind of incomes most can expect to earn, they cannot afford to relinquish. If kids aren't in daycare, mothers can't work. If they take minimum-wage jobs, they can't afford to pay for daycare, even if they are able to find spaces for their children.

Among their limited range of options for supporting their families, welfare poverty may be safer than working poverty. 'At least I could fill the prescriptions when the kids were sick, instead of leaving the doctor's office knowing I couldn't afford to buy the drugs,' Carole, a single mother of four told me. For years, Carole has wrestled with the typical dilemmas that trap women on welfare. 'If I work part-time and declare more than the few dollars I'm allowed to earn, they cut my cheque. It's a no-win situation.'

Assault on Social Spending

Between 1984 and 1988, the Tories whittled more than $100 million from statutory social programs, according to the National Council of Welfare, a government advisory group.[16] In the same period, the council says, low-income Canadians were burdened with a 44 per cent tax hike, predicted to jump to 60 per cent by 1991. Middle-income Canadians paid 10 per cent more on their way to a 17 per cent increase by 1991. By contrast, rich taxpayers enjoyed a 6 per cent decline in taxes by 1988 and will pay 6.4 per cent less in 1991.[17] The Pro-Canada Network compiled figures that reveal the same trend. Between 1984 and 1989, the government lowered the basic tax rate for the rich so that families earning in excess of $117,000 paid $3,750 less. Meanwhile, families earning $35,000 paid $840 more.[18]

Statistics Canada figures reveal that 93,400 corporations with profits that tallied $27 billion in 1987 paid no tax whatsoever.[19] While tax 'reforms' that favour highest earners were put in place, social programs were dislodged. Despite mounting public cynicism, even rage, the government persisted in a broadsword attack on social spending. By introducing pension and baby-bonus 'claw-backs,' the state erased the principle of universality from Canadian social programs, thereby undermining other cornerstones of the country's social security. In 1989, the government also announced its plan to opt out of the unemployment-insurance business in 1990 and to shift the burden for premiums onto workers and employers. Most employers were expected to pass their new costs onto the consumer, while workers would pay their contributions in wage losses. The Conservatives estimated that the $1.3 billion cut from Unemployment Insurance, along with more stringent eligibility criteria, would put 30,000 claimants at risk of disqualification. Others insisted the population at risk was much higher, more like 130,000 people, over one-fifth of all 1988 claimants.[20] At the same time, opponents of free trade warned of unemployment consequences they feared would follow in the deal's turbulent wake.

In response to the assaultive 1989 federal budget, an already restive population was aroused to resistance. A so-called crabgrass coalition from points east and west made its way across the country to Ottawa to protest the cut-backs. In public hearings staged by the government after announcing its plan to slash unemployment insurance, politicians were bombarded with opposition from virtually every corner except chambers of commerce. Consumer, advocacy, labour, and women's groups blasted the government, cataloguing the dire consequences they expected the cuts to bring. The National Anti-Poverty Organization's predictions were typical of fears expressed by many presenters: the spectre of more employable people, especially vulnerable female workers and their children, being forced onto welfare, into food banks, into hostels.

Besides tinkering with benefits, the government paved the way to introduce a 9 per cent goods and services tax in 1991. Opposition to this inherently regressive tax (the poor pay more) was swift, vocal, and near-unanimous; even members of the government were forced to publicly express doubts and distance from their leadership over the issue. International trade minister John Crosbie was quoted in the press as having said, 'It's just a case of how much we can get from the public to pay the debts we're incurring, without having them rise up against us? ... If the government insists on going ahead, I'm going to support the government and hope they don't rise up against us.'[21]

In general, the mid- to late 1980s set new standards for losses in social programs and for rising costs to consumers for basic services and goods. These losses and rising costs, felt most keenly by ordinary families, carried some over the dividing line between coping and collapsing.

One and a Half Million Poor Kids

Canada has the second-poorest children in the industrialized world, according to a report from the U.S. Urban Institute.[22] One in five children across this country are growing up in poverty. Since the generally accepted figure of one million impoverished children under age sixteen derives from 1986 census data, it is fair to suggest that numbers today are much higher. Senator David Croll, in his eighteenth annual update of his poverty report, calculated that 1.5 million kids in 1988 were blighted from birth by poverty.[23] No matter what the numbers, studies have proved that childhood poverty carries with it debilitating, life-long consequences for each of its victims.

Even before they are born, the babies of the poor are gravely disadvantaged by inadequate nutrition. Many poor mothers are well aware of the risks their newborns face: premature birth, low birth weights, infections. The health gap in Canada between rich and poor babies is startling. Roughly twice as many poor infants and children die as do their wealthier counterparts.[24]

Teens across the country who are at once mothers and street kids often bemoan the built-in tragedy of their situation. Maria, whom you met in chapter 4, was seventeen, eight months pregnant, living on the streets, and subsisting on coffee, cigarettes, and snacks. She hadn't had three square meals a day in years. Gaunt and hollow-eyed, she looked ill and readily admitted that her foetus was not getting the nourishment it needed. Feather was living under the tyranny of a violent, cocaine-addicted pimp when her baby was born. Her pimp was tooting cocaine with the grocery money and forcing Feather to work the street pregnant and hungry before coming home to brutal beatings. She was amazed her baby was born apparently healthy, though one wonders what's down the road for this child.

Nutrition is a potent factor in life chances. Poor people cannot afford to follow Canada's food guide. They cannot chase all over town in cars they do not have, to scavenge for bulk bargains they cannot afford, to store in deep freezers they don't own. Economical shopping requires a cash flow. The poor nutrition that characterizes the diets of most impoverished people is often attributed to ignorance; rarely is it seen for what it mostly is: the inability to afford a balanced diet. People who subsist on starch, fillers, and refined sugars do so for a reason: because Kraft Dinner, Wonder Bread, and Kool-Aid fill them up and provide an energy rush at prices they can afford.

Poor food in the critical first five formative years retards every aspect of child development. Numerous studies have linked school failure with bad diets. One from Harvard Medical School concluded that 'subnormal nutrition was associated with under-achievement, lassitude and irritability ... many of the academic failures prevailing in high school students may have their roots in nutritionally associated learning problems.'[25]

The foremost mental-health concern in Canada, according to Dr Dan Offord, head of child epidemiology at the Chedoke-McMaster hospitals in Hamilton, is the children of the urban poor. A survey he conducted among 3,000 children concluded that poverty impacts heavily on psychological development and that welfare puts kids at risk of emotional problems. He found that 40 per cent of boys age six to eleven and 40 per cent of girls age twelve to sixteen in welfare families suffered psychological disorders, compared with 13.9 per cent of boys and 17.3 per cent of girls in non-welfare families.[26] Their diminished life circumstances erode their belief in their own capacities, a self-regulating message confirmed by the standard catalogue of labels schools typically impose on poor kids. The innumerable stresses of poverty eat away at self-esteem: hunger, poor nutrition, inadequate housing, frequent moves, little recreational and cultural stimulation, negative stereotyping, little positive reinforcement.

Offord says these kids, far more than their privileged peers, need enriching experiences to soften the cruel edges of their alienation. In Canada, in the 1990s, slashes in education and social spending mean that the children who need the most will likely continue to get the least.

One in Five Cannot Read and Write

In 1990 Canada served as a host country for International Literacy Year, an ironic honour considering our record. As the 1987 Southam News study *Broken Words* reported, one in five citizens over age fifteen cannot read this statement.[27] In other words, about five million Canadians have literacy and numeracy skills below what they need just to skim by in everyday life.

The demographics of functional illiteracy in Canada have been among the country's better-kept secrets. Many people are still incredulous at the facts. According to *Broken Words*, British Columbia has the lowest rate of illiteracy, at 17 per cent, while Newfoundland has the highest, at 44 per cent. The national average stands at 24 per cent. Contrary to the notion that recent immigrants predominate among non-readers and non-writers, more than 70 per cent are Canadian-born.

Even the shockingly high illiteracy count of one in five underestimates the problem as it does not include street kids and other transients; natives on reserves; armed forces personnel; immigrants who speak neither English nor French; those living north of the sixtieth parallel; or people residing in psychiatric institutions, nursing homes, and prisons. *Broken Words* calculates that a half-million from these groups are illiterate as well. Since an estimated 60 to 70 per cent of prison inmates in Canada can't read or write competently, the half-million stands as yet another conservative estimate. Recorded and hidden functional illiteracy then affects well over 20 per cent of the population.

Nationally, about 30 per cent of students drop out before completing high school.[28] In Ontario, according to the Radwanski Report, 79 per cent drop out from basic education and 62 per cent from general education – the two streams with the greatest numbers of poor, working-class and minority youths. Twelve per cent drop out from advanced education where socially privileged, college-bound Caucasian students predominate.[29]

An exhaustive American study of streaming – called 'tracking' there – concluded that 'tracking separates students along socio-economic lines, separating rich from poor, whites from non-whites. The end result is that poor and minority children are found far more often than others in the bottom tracks.'[30]

Tracking also imposes costly consequences on girls. A report form the Canadian Advisory Council on the Status of Women suggests that working-class girls are slotted into non-academic streams that dead-end their future prospects.[31] In her study of teenage girls in Canada, Myrna Kostash found that typical composite high schools with general, business, and matriculation streams 'are as neatly divided between the social classes as are the arts and sciences between the sexes.'[32]

School works for 60 to 70 per cent of kids to the extent that they graduate. Diplomas, however, are no guarantee of functional literacy. The Southam survey discovered that one-third of functional illiterates graduate from high school. Reaching grade nine, a popular drop-out level, does not bode well for reading competence either. In Canada, 2.4 million students who had completed grade nine tested functionally illiterate.[33] Even 8 per cent of contemporary university graduates read and write incompetently.[34]

On the racial front, our education record is dismal. Aboriginal students, although by no means the only educationally cheated group, have suffered the brunt of race discrimination in education. Until 1988, the government-sanctioned and often church-run residential-school system uprooted native children from their families and cultures and forcibly detained them in English-speaking, ideologically Christian schools reviled by many natives.

During the spring 1989 face-off between the Indian Affairs ministry and native students over the government's attempt to 'cap' post-secondary spending – seen by natives and their supporters as disguised cut-backs – newspapers reported the long-ignored realities. By the 1960s, only 3.4 per cent of aboriginal students were even finishing high school, and almost none were going on to university. With the mid-1970s advent of the Post-Secondary Student Assistance Program, more natives gained access to higher education. But even by the late 1980s, in the program's highest spending years, only 4 per cent of natives were entering colleges and universities, compared with 27 per cent of Canadians as a whole (about half of whom complete their program of study).[35] The skirmish over capping also brought to light the disheartening news about high-school education among aboriginal youth. By the late 1980s, only 20 per cent nation-wide were finishing high school.[36]

While these data on aboriginal education, along with the illiteracy data, indict the myth that Canadians enjoy universal adequate education, they cannot be dismissed as aberrant and exceptional. Rather, the state of native education appears to be the most extreme distortion on a continuum weighted against viable education for a large minority of Canadians.

To be fair to teachers, this bleak picture is not their fault. As is the case with most professions, teaching sees a broad range of competence and dedication among its practitioners, from inspired to indifferent. Excellent or poor, however, teachers work in a system that is not set up to encourage all students, independent of their social class, race, gender, creed, and challenging need, to approximate, let alone achieve, their best.

From a cultured, humanistic standpoint, and from the perspective of the country's small population, great ability, and wealth, Canada's low level of educational attainment appears baffling. Viewed in an economic context, however, an otherwise mystifying reality begins to make sense. Historically, our economy has been geared to selling natural resources while remaining relatively backward in manufacturing. Until the recent technological explosion, therefore, the education system meshed well with a market-place that mainly required relatively unskilled, low-cost labour.

But business needs have been changing according to a study by the Business Task Force on Literacy.[37] By the early 1990s, technology is expected to alter about 40 per cent of jobs. Consequently, basic skill demands for entry-level positions have been rising. Now, almost all large enterprises require high-school diplomas and about 70 per cent of occupations require workers able to read at grade-nine to grade-twelve proficiency levels. In 1986, in the fifteen-to-twenty-four age group, 50 per cent of prospective workers would have fallen short of these minimum standards. The study drives home the message that Canadian commerce can no longer afford to let a significant percentage of students fall through cracks in the education system.

For ninety years, Frontier College, Canada's oldest adult literacy organization, had been publicizing the education crisis and pressing government to fund a campaign to obliterate illiteracy. Its appeals, along with a chorus of pleas from voluntary adult-education programs across the country, fell on deaf ears until 1988. Then the Business Task Force on Literacy, studded with such corporate names as Abitibi-Price, Petro-Canada, and Mac-lean-Hunter, published its report.[38] In it, the task force focused on the business costs and losses resulting directly from illiteracy: lost markets, lost productivity, low morale, training costs, and industrial accidents, among others. The task force claimed that illiteracy costs business more than $4 billion a year. In addition, indirect costs to society as a whole through public assistance, prison per diems, and social programs add up to an estimated $10 billion annually.[39] After the study was released, the federal government pledged $110 million to combat the problem. It was the first time in Canada's history that any lump sum worth notice has ever been promised. Some literacy groups hailed the announcement but pointed out that $110 million would barely make a dent in the massive task of educating 20 to 30 per cent of the population. On a more cynical note, they also pointed out how business interests prevail in the provision of education.

What happens to teenagers when they leave school poorly educated? They end up out there competing with readers in a job market characterized by high youth-unemployment rates – 12.1 per cent by the end of 1988 – and low minimum wages, even lower for adolescents than for adults. In the least-competitive position, even for go-nowhere jobs, illiterate people wind up poorer than their reading-and-writing peers. Southam found that they are twice as likely to suffer long-term unemployment and, when employed, to earn 13 to 44 per cent less than readers.[40] Likely to be daunted by poverty, illiterate parents face additional indignities from a society and school system that perceive them as failures and are likely to label their kids as non-achievers.

Illiteracy, among many other handicaps, cripples street kids in their struggle to cobble together a dignified life. As profiles in this book attest, teens who end up on the street rarely leave behind them stellar academic careers. Rather, most regard 'school' as a dirty word, and 'special classes' as the most profane epithet of all.

Deeply troubled kids who roam around the inner city have usually graduated from the outs at school after being labelled trouble-makers and consigned to back-row isolation or to stigmatizing separate classes. Today, in Ontario public schools, 6,000 children are segregated in what are called 'behaviour classes.'[41] Nearly 3,000 elementary pupils spend half of every day in such classes.[42] Most are poor. Many are among the estimated 10,000 children stalled in the backlog awaiting psychiatric intervention,[43] as if mental-health treatment might solve the social problems likely driving their disturbed behaviour.

They act out, then wait for help that may not come in time or may not work; then they drop out. Studies have shown that many drop-outs are ineligible for government-funded trades training, and that many among those who do qualify drop out because their literacy and numeracy skills are too weak for the academic work required.[44] In addition, today's literacy initiatives tend to focus on young beginning learners and on adults who are easiest to retrain, what *Broken Words* author Peter Calamai has dubbed a 'train-the-best-and-forget-the-rest' approach. Unless they can manage to improve their basic skills, however, many teenagers will be left with only one niche from which to cull a living – somewhere in the subterranean economy of crime.

DANGERS AND INDIGNITIES

The fact that many people cannot read and write at passable levels does not say anything about their intelligence. Studies have shown that literacy and intelligence are not related. In fact, non-readers and non-writers are known for their ingenuity in masking their terrible handicap and getting by undetected. It is a game of bluff and fakery that only the clever can play.

At its worst, day-to-day life for non-readers is an obstacle course of potential disasters: for example, choosing a medication for their children or guessing at safe doses. In a world of written prescriptions and proscriptions, navigating the petty passages of everyday life can be terrifying.

The Southam study found that 20 per cent of adult Canadians could not decipher dosage directions on a bottle of cough syrup; 20 per cent could not glean a fact from a newspaper; 29 per cent could not single out long-distance charges on a phone bill; 33 per cent could not calculate the change owed to them for snacks under $3, and 50 per cent could not find their way in the Yellow Pages.[45]

If illiteracy is dangerous at worst, at best it is deeply embarrassing. In a lettered world, illiteracy carries great shame and constant fear of exposure. Non-readers typically blame themselves for their inadequacies and channel their abilities into hiding their secret. Stories of adults who fool even their own spouses are common. Tracy Lequyere, ex-con, ex–street kid, co-founder of Beat the Street, kept everyone, including employers and his wife, in the dark for years. Then, one day, his wife saw him pour antifreeze into the oil tank of their car. 'What's the matter with you, can't you read?' she quipped with off-handed impatience. 'No, I can't,' Tracy finally confessed.

'See, everybody assumes that everyone else can read and write,' Tracy explains. 'If you screw up because you can't, the last thing that occurs to the guy next to you is that you can't read. In a way that makes it easier to cover up. You devise tricks for getting by. When I needed to read a document, I'd fake bad eyesight and forgotten glasses and get some stranger to read for me. When I needed to write anything, maybe fill out an application on the spot, I'd whip out my trusty bandage and grow a sprained hand. When I had to order in a restaurant, I'd stick with my few favourites.'

Even with all his tricks, Tracy had to steer away from situations that threatened to expose his problem. An employer eventually caught on and sent him to Frontier College for tutoring. Tracy, who survived into his twenties on exemplary con artist talents of verve and verb, became a 'born-again reader and writer' in 1984 at age thirty-three. 'I'm still no miracle of speed and accuracy but at least I'm out of the blind alleys that illiteracy leads you into. Illiteracy is like a personal tyranny that rules your life.'

Because he found an avenue in which to develop the skills society had denied him, Tracy is an exception. The majority of illiterate Canadians are not so lucky. Bent on burying their shame, dead-set against going back into regular schools that humiliated them as children, they tread carefully through the mine-field of marginalized lives, ever mindful of their fragile position at work and in society.

BEAT THE STREET: HOOKERS TUTOR HOOKERS

Because street kids generally have had devastating experiences in the education system, efforts to lure them into any program that even hints at school as they know it are bound to fail. Most runaways and throwaways have been, as Beat the Street co-founder Rick Parsons says, 'labelled into ignorance. The major problem for most of our students is not letters, it's labels.'

Eminent Canadian reading and writing theorist Frank Smith echoes Beat the Street's disdain for disabling labels. He contends that 'once you're persuaded that you can't learn something, then in fact it's very, very difficult for you to learn something. All your study habits go wrong and your attitude goes wrong and your motivation goes wrong and especially what goes wrong is that the people who try to teach you do it in a different way. They treat you like an idiot.'[46]

That's what happened to Tracy. When he first exhibited difficulty reading, in the early grades, the school labelled him a 'slow learner' and shunted him off to vocational school, where he couldn't keep up with the work. As he became increasingly confused, embarrassed, and restless, the system still didn't offer individualized attention to help him catch up. Tracy became a 'trouble-maker.' Then, after being humiliated in front of his class during a spelling bee, by which time everyone expected him to behave like an 'idiot,' he didn't disappoint them. He dropped out of school and became an outlaw.

Tracy claims that 'it's the most liberating thing in the world for a street kid to have someone they respect tell them, "It's not your fault that you have problems reading and writing. You needed help that no one ever gave you. You didn't fail, the system failed you." If you want to see a spark return to the dead eyes of some punched-out kid, try that line on him!'

Beat the Street, a school for street kids in Toronto, Winnipeg, and Regina, runs on a peer-tutoring model where hookers tutor hookers and skinheads tutor skinheads. The idea that a tutor may be only slightly more literate than his or her student is foreign to traditional approaches to schooling. Yet, Frank Smith claims that peers, not qualified teachers, instruct kids best. 'And not the good readers but the mediocre ones, because the good readers will come on too strong and act like teachers and pick up all the mistakes. You don't need someone who is a brilliant reader, you just need someone who is a little better than you.'[47]

While most street kids can't be lured into schools, they can be enticed into alternative education that builds on their strengths and emphasizes their needs and interests. Lessons can take place anywhere kids congregate. In arcades, for example, a savvy street worker/tutor from Beat the Street can convert an electronic game into a math lesson. Lessons that start in this unorthodox fashion build relationships between street kids and staff. Eventually, kids wander into the downtown learning centres and hook up with a peer tutor, a match-making process orchestrated by staff, some of whom are reformed street youths themselves. Participants can study and tutor at the same time, perhaps helping someone with their writing while being helped with math. When students reach the level of their tutor's competence, they move on to another, more suitable tutor. Being a tutor empowers young people who've been drilled into believing themselves failures. Being a student – a successful student, because all students are successful at Beat the Street – can boost self-esteem. In fact, the program is as much about building self-esteem as it is about reading and writing.

Beat the Street is not a tidy little school operating smoothly or according to any discernible schedule. Kids drop in and out of the learning centres as suits the vagaries of their existence. With staff and peer support, some slowly pull their lives together: get a job or student welfare, get a room, get off drugs, make a stab at a new beginning. At best, they gradually opt into more formal lessons with one or two tutors outside the learning centre. Some eventually work with straight tutors, including volunteer teachers from school-boards who help kids plough through correspondence courses.

Self-paced, individualized learning has earned credibility as the most effective approach to adult basic education. While Beat the Street offers its own peculiar brand, it is by no means the only school for street youths practising these principles. The Study Centre in Vancouver, for example, staffed by board-of-education teachers, offers a more structured version for kids who are a few steps removed from street life. But the handful of alternative-education programs across the country capable of attracting the most disenfranchised youth can reach out to only a fraction of those who need them. Barring a drastic reversal in education policy, most young non-readers will, throughout their lives, experience the world as an intimidating jumble of numbers and letters.

Louis: A struggle to beat the odds

The Manitoba Métis Federation has long maintained that the Métis are a desperate people living out the legacy of genocide committed by successive Canadian governments. The grim conditions the federation ascribes to Métis life parallel those natives across the province endure. According to the Assembly of Manitoba Chiefs, two-thirds of Indians over age fifteen have an annual income under $5,000. Indians account for 22 per cent of penitentiary inmates, although they make up only 5 per cent of the province's population.[48] (Legion racism in the justice system led to the 1988–90 provincial Aboriginal Justice Inquiry.)

Louis, of Sioux-French extraction, knows all about the legacies of genocide and racism. Until recently his life has been a quick study in their consequences – a debacle of despair and destruction. Now, from the ruins and against the odds, he is struggling to rise. Talking to me, a stranger and one outside a life and culture defined by defeat, is part of the work. For Louis, every word is effort-full, every sentence a small lien against returning to familiar habits: self-hatred, drugs, alcohol, violent crime, prison.

With obvious difficulty, Louis looks me straight in the eye: 'I'm talking to my counsellors [at Alcoholics Anonymous and Narcotics Anonymous], to you, to anyone that wants to listen. I used to have a fuck-you-mind-your-own-business attitude. I was mean and tough; that was my image. I couldn't stand nice people. Nice was a disease; it made me want to puke. It's still hard to be around nice people, and it's a real shock to find I got some of that niceness in me. I can't believe that the person I'm becoming today was inside me all the time. Neither can my old partners [in crime]. I meet them in the street and they think I've flipped out.'

I understand their problem, even though I didn't know him as a street ruffian, bar brawler, and armed robber. Louis exudes a vulnerability that does not fit underworld moulds. It is hard to envision him brandishing weapons and bashing-in heads. However, he rendered two men unconscious, sending them into hospitals to fight for their lives, the last one a fifty-four-year-old passer-by who tried to stop Louis from breaking into a car to steal it.

By the time this incident occurred, Louis was caught up in the cyclical life of the law-breaker: commit a crime, do some time. If he had stayed in 'the game' much longer, he feels he was bound to kill someone, bound to fall over that semi-conscious divide between sparing your victim his life and not caring if you kill him. 'If I don't get a grasp on myself now, I'll end up killing someone, I know I will. There is just too much anger driving me. I was too hurt and I ended up hurting other people, trying to get back I guess. It got out of hand; sometimes I have no control.'

He comes by his fury honestly. His father was the kind of man 'that didn't open doors, he just kicked them off their hinges.' Louis grew up as one of five besieged kids in the poor family of a raging drunk. The only light-haired child in a dark-complexioned family, he was singled out for special mistreatment by his father who would boozily claim that Louis was another man's son. From his first six years of life, Louis remembers only violent incidents, variations on a theme, his drunken marauding father pummelling everyone in sight, especially his mother and himself.

'My mother was very screwed up by his beatings. She had several nervous breakdowns. In fact, even though she finally left him, to this day she's still in and out of hospitals, getting shock treatments. I blame him for her depressed state of mind. He terrorized her; he terrorized all of us.'

Why didn't his mother grab the kids and run? 'She did, many times. We were always in hiding, on welfare, always moving, always living out of boxes. He'd find us and the cycle would start all over again. She could never manage to shake him off. My mother's a good woman, educated [grade eleven], from a real nice family. She deserved better. I could never figure out why she married him. I guess she did it because he got her pregnant. I always wished she'd get away from him and find someone who'd really care about her.'

Every time Louis mentions his mother, his broad face saddens. Every time he mentions his father, his face contorts: he tightens his thinly moustached upper lip across his top teeth and juts out his jaw, and a small mirthless laugh catches in his throat. Yet, for all the anger he harbours for his father, he forgives him a little bit too. 'He had it very hard, growing up in a rough, drinking family with an alcoholic father. He was only a kid himself when he got shipped off to the Second World War as a commando. He used to boast about the way he murdered guys. His idea of horsing around was to put us kids into holds he used to kill German soldiers. Scared the hell out of us ... I think his childhood, the war, and the booze made him crazy.'

Except it was Louis's mother who went to a mental institution when the boy was six. When his mother was put away, the CAS scattered the kids among a roster of white foster families. Louis was eight when his foster father first abused him. 'He made me play with him and he played with me. He said that if I ever told anyone, I'd never see my mother again. Since the only thing I wanted in the world was to go home to my mom, I kept my mouth shut.' He couldn't turn to his foster mother because 'she was one cold animal.'

Soon after the abuse started, Louis 'spun out, had fits,' for which he was committed to a psychiatric ward. Once there, he went 'completely berserk, lost my memory, didn't recognize anyone. I was terrified of people. I guess I was that scared because of the sex abuse and the fear that I'd let the truth slip out and that I'd lose my mother because of it.' He didn't confide the abuse to his psychiatrist. 'Who could I trust?'

After the 'nuthouse,' Louis went home. Nothing had changed except that his mother, who within her limited capacities had tried to help her kids stay in school and on a straight path, was completely burnt out. Louis and some of his brothers were big enough by then to try to protect their mother from their father's fearsome temper. When they jumped him or threw themselves between their parents, the kids caught the pounding instead. They tried calling for help from the police. 'The cops would take my father to the cooler overnight and my mother to the hospital to get patched up. Next day, he'd walk in the door: Wham!' Louis slams a fist into his open palm. His face twists into a scowl.

Home was hopeless, and school was heart-breaking. There, Louis was labelled and 'dumped in a class with isolation cubicles for hyperactive retardos.' His father junked medication Louis brought home from the psychiatric hospital 'because no kid of his was a loony, right.' At school he got into more glue than books and started hanging our with 'bad' kids. Although he went home less and less often, he started yelling at his mother more and more. 'I still can't believe that I even threatened to hit her – though I never did actually touch her. Without realizing what I was doing, I had picked up threatening my mother from that bastard. I was eighteen before I understood that I was following in his footsteps.'

By the time Louis saw the path he was on, he didn't know how to go anywhere else. He'd been in and out of 'hell-holes' for as long as he could remember, including, from age twelve, the usual round of juvenile correctional facilities where he had sharpened his street skills and criminal cunning. He had not, however, gotten an education. Whenever he was in school for short stints, he found himself in classes for 'slow learners, dyslexics, retards, and dummies – in other words, for kids from poor and broken-down families.' He connected with one teacher, the first person other than his mother he ever trusted. 'The teacher was murdered by another student.'

When Louis wasn't in custody for shoplifting, drug dealing, B&Es – 'I was a real little criminal, eh?' – he lived in an abandoned garage and stole food. 'I ate a lot better there than at home.' Other kids in his pick-up street gang 'were going through the same shit I was. Who else you gonna find on Main Street with gas-soaked rags hanging in plastic bags from their noses at two in the morning other than a kid whose old man is beating up on his old lady or drinking himself into a rage or screwing his daughter? Or an eight- or nine-year-old on the run from a boys' home?'

Police would pick Louis and his pals up and deliver them back to their last address on the institutional circuit. In one of these anonymous places, Louis met the second adult he trusted, a counsellor who befriended him and helped him break his glue habit. Weekends, the counsellor sometimes took Louis home and welcomed the boy into his family. 'I remember the word the big boss used to try to say that, by taking a personal interest in me, my counsellor was out of line. They said he was acting "inappropriate." ' The inappropriate professional also started Louis thinking about his future and about the need for an education. 'He showed me that maybe not everyone will hurt me. I started coming out of my shell, started to get along with people.' When the counsellor was transferred, Louis was crushed. He felt abandoned, betrayed by another adult.

It was all downhill from there. Age fifteen: into a facility for more unmanageable juveniles, and into heavy drugs, shooting up coke. 'It's a breeze to score drugs in detention. Someone brings it back from a run. You run away, steal, fence the loot, get some cash, score some coke, smuggle it back in. In my crowd, that was the cool thing to do.'

Sometimes he was stoned or smashed when he attended the community school near the institution. 'I was pretty violent by then.' Angry enough to pack a pellet gun: 'I didn't shoot anyone, but I really wanted to. If I hadn't got caught, I probably would have.'

Violent enough for the next step up the ladder of justice: provincial jails for 'pulling down' stores (armed robbery) and dealing heavy drugs. On and off, from age eighteen to his current twenty-eight, the lock-up became his home away from the street. It also became the site for three suicide attempts, one in earnest that resulted in a death's-door rescue, and another two that amounted to desperate pleas for help. 'Over the last ten years, I done about six and a half years' time. I'm on probation now and I still got an assault rap over me. I'll be back in court and I may have to go back to the bucket [provincial jail], but I'll never do big time [federal penitentiaries for sentences longer than two years]. My life of crime is over, and my time for doing time is almost done.'

For the past five months, Louis says, he has been clean. No drugs, no alcohol, no crime – the first time he has quit doing any of these. He's been doing a different kind of time: hours upon hours of AA and NA meetings; private sessions with counsellors; and long, hard-working days at Beat the Street, learning to read and write. Louise figures his academic level is about grade three. The turning-point was the man he nearly killed. 'I was drunk and on acid; I could have killed him without meaning to. When I read about myself in the paper and realized what I'd done, I freaked. I knew I had to get some control over my life before I kill someone.' (According to *The Last Dance: Murder in Canada*,[49] men like Louis are the perfect candidates to commit murder. His life is an amalgam of themes common among men who kill.)

His phobia about doing the hard time he felt was fast approaching triggered his turn-around decision. Luckily, he had the support of his straight girlfriend, who has stuck with him, to his amazement, over five tumultuous years. 'She's a high-school graduate, she doesn't drink or do drugs; she works and saves money. I don't know what she's doing with me after all I put her through. Don't get me wrong, I've never laid a hand on her – I could never hit a woman after seeing my father destroy my mother – but it's rough being a bandit's broad, especially when you don't agree with the life.

'Now that I'm living on her side of the street, I thank my lucky stars everyday for this woman. I never understood before how blessed I was to have her; I took her for granted. Now I can love her for the first time because I'm starting to like myself. To tell you the truth, it's a relief not having to be a gangster anymore.'

Louis admits that this kind of radical shift is not easy. It's a hard daily grind – hard staying away from his old gang; hard convincing ex-partners that he's not joining their next scam; hard keeping a low profile in a neighbourhood where everyone knows him as a thug; hard living on the wages of welfare after the big scores of robbery; hard staying off the bottle and off the needle; hard allowing himself to be sipping tea with a 'nice lady' and talking over his feelings, rather than thrashing them out on someone's skull.

But, at this moment, he is doing it, all of it. Louis says he wants to discover the 'good me,' the real person buried under the weight of a down-trodden people, a demoralized family, and a devastating child-welfare and juvenile-justice system. His wanting is palpable. 'When I look back now, I feel cheated. I was just a kid. Shouldn't someone have helped me and my family, or protected my mom and us kids from my father instead of putting my mother in a mental hospital and me and my brothers in foster homes and jails? Do you have any idea how many professionals knew what was going down in our home? Lady, you can't imagine how much "help" has marched through my life, and how useless most of it has been. How can that happen? Can you answer that?'

Injustice for Juveniles

The juvenile-justice system has a long history of taking in petty offenders like Louis and churning out career criminals like Louis almost became (and may still become). Although Section 38 of the 1908 Juvenile Delinquents Act (JDA) promised to treat the young law-breaker 'not as criminal, but as a misdirected and misguided child ... needing aid, encouragement, help and assistance,'[50] Canada's first attempt to create a justice system specifically for juveniles did not produce a benevolent parent for wayward children. JDA detractors pressed for reforms when evidence mounted that too many youngsters were becoming enmeshed in the system because of trivial offences. Rather than deterring juveniles from crime, contact with the system increased the likelihood of deeper criminal involvement.[51]

In 1984, the Young Offenders Act (YOA) replaced the JDA. It promised to protect the public and to rehabilitate young offenders whenever possible. If, indeed, the YOA was earnestly dedicated to helping young law-breakers steer clear of a criminal path, very few kids charged with property and petty offences would be subject to traditional, intrusive punishments such as incarceration. Yet, under the YOA, more youths across the country are being placed in custody than was the case under the JDA.[52] Far from coddling juveniles, the act has proved harsher than its predecessor. For example, despite a 13 per cent drop in the number of teenagers in Ontario in the past decade, numbers of sixteen- and seventeen-year-olds held in 'secure custody' – effectively jail – have climbed steadily, from 1,042 in 1985–6 to 1,554 in 1987–8.[53] What's more, according to the Ontario Ministry of Correctional Services, the average time served by sixteen- and seventeen-year-olds has been rising. In 1988, kids served an average of 132 days, compared with 91.3 days before the YOA. Even more significant, by contrast, adults in 1988 served an average of 74 days.[54]

When kids are found guilty, judges assign consequences from a range of options that typically include, in increasing order of severity: absolute discharge, in which a child receives a criminal record but no conviction; community service; victim restitution or compensation; probation (the most popular disposition); monetary penalties; open custody, such as a group home; or secure custody, such as a correctional facility or treatment program.[55] In most provinces, for first-time offenders who qualify, the Alternative Measures Program offers an opportunity to acknowledge guilt and to bypass the courts. The child agrees to a resolution, usually worked out with his parents, the victim, and a social worker or probation officer.

As for the YOA's effectiveness in deterring crime, Ontario's London Family Court Clinic recorded the city's youth recidivism rate before and after the YOA. Numbers of repeat offenders jumped from 27.5 per cent in 1981–2 to 65 per cent in 1986–7.[56]

While the non-violent majority of young offenders have fared worse under the YOA, the violent minority have been better off under the legislation because it restricts maximum sentences, even for major crimes, to three years. Statistics Canada data for 1988 show that property offences account for 60 per cent of youth crime, while violent, major crimes – murder, manslaughter, aggravated assault, sexual assault, and armed robbery – account for 13 per cent.[57] According to justice ministry data, in the 1987–8 fiscal year, only 0.05 per cent of 34,896 charges laid in youth court were for murder.[58]

Although violent crimes committed by juveniles have risen sharply in the past few years, at 13 per cent they are still relatively rare. None the less, the media tend to concentrate on savage and exceptional crimes, thereby creating the impression that young psychopaths pose a major threat to society. Reasonable

concern with readmitting kids who have committed bizarre and heinous crimes to the mainstream is so exaggerated as to make young offenders seem a demonic lot.

The pressing question of how to deal with dangerous, deeply disturbed kids will probably result in changes to the YOA, requiring adult court and adult penalties for teenage murderers and long maximum sentences for major crimes prosecuted under the act. However, by focusing on major crime in their discussion of youth, the media have diverted attention from a far more pressing problem: the thousands of youngsters languishing in detention, waiting months for court appearances on minor offences. During this 'dead time,' kids learn new tricks of the criminal trade. Even though this situation doesn't make sensational news copy, it constitutes a far greater and far more prevalent social problem than the putative rash of murders by maniacal young people.

YOA critics have lambasted the act for enshrining a teenager's right to refuse psychological and other forms of court-ordered treatment. Certainly the public is bewildered about how an order from a judge can require the consent of a child. Some corrections officers complain that a law allowing a child to override a judge by rejecting treatment is toothless and undermines the rehabilitative potential of their institutions.

The objection seems to be based on the belief that if kids were forced to undergo therapy, they might be 'cured' before release. Appealing as this notion sounds, it defies evidence that real personal change requires the subject to participate voluntarily in his or her own reform. Little proof exists, in any case, that incarcerated kids 'get better' with therapy and don't without it, even if they participate ostensibly as volunteers. Gordon Hogg, director of Willingdon Youth Detention Centre, in Burnaby, BC, points to studies that show that the kind of youths incarcerated at his facility – a fairly representative sample of institutionalized youths across the country, except that it includes a higher proportion of natives – are less amenable to psychiatric treatment than they are to an 'opportunities model' that stresses realistic education, job training, or job-finding goals upon release.[59] Hogg admits that many children who receive psychiatric treatment, just like those who don't, end up back in Willingdon as recidivists.

Even those who believe institutionalized youngsters benefit significantly from rehabilitative programs with a psychological bent generally agree that very hurt and damaged children need long-term support. Therapy in institutions tends to be short-term and spotty. Youths who are spun through the typical chain of revolving doors – group homes, detention centres, and treatment programs – rarely have the opportunity to build a trusting relationship with one steady counsellor that might exert a positive influence in their lives.

PUNISHING POOR KIDS

In the *Myth of Delinquency*, a landmark study of East Coast training-school inmates, anthropologist Elliott Leyton reported scientifically what is anecdotally evident in custodial settings across the country. The overwhelming majority of locked-up kids are poor kids. In Leyton's study, all but three of the inmates came from the working class. Seventy per cent were from the hopeless, 'stagnant bottom' of society, from the 'permanent underemployed who are chained for eternity to the degrading trough of welfare.'[60]

Although social class seems to have little bearing on whether a teenager vandalizes and steals property or terrorizes people, poor kids face a higher risk of detection, prosecution, and incarceration than do rich kids, many of whom engage in delinquent acts with impunity.[61] Children of privilege know that police, social workers, and 'snoops' in general invest more time and resources tracking disadvantaged kids. They know that, if they get caught, their parents can hire a clever lawyer. They know their respectable families carry more clout with judges than do beleaguered families from the housing projects.

Any street kid will tell you that there is a rich man's law and a poor man's law, and that all are equal only in theory, but not in the back seat of a cruiser or in the front of a court room. They know the jails are full of kids like them: poor kids, native kids, black kids, abused kids, and all the others who begin with few choices and who grow up watching their options disappear.

Leyton argues that delinquency is not driven by deficiencies in individual children. Rather it is driven by a deficient social system that humiliates the family. In turn, the disabled family spurns the child. He sees the child's acts as 'merely one of the alternative metaphors communicating rage and inconsolable grief.' Delinquents 'grasp only too fully the reality of their own lives, that they have been denied a place in the familial order without just cause, and they will undoubtedly spend their lives outside the social order or at the bottom, burying their mourning in opiates and disorder, and reproducing themselves in the next generation.'[62]

Leyton explains how their grief explodes in rage against themselves. (Slashing and suicide attempts are legion in detention centres.) It explodes in rage against their parents, often manifest as fracas at home, or in rage against symbols of family and society, which becomes the 'nihilistic assaults on persons and property' associated with classic delinquency.[63]

Leyton's familial-rage theory aside, not all juvenile law-breakers are vandals. Survivors rather than iconoclasts, many engage in drug-dealing, prostitution, B&E, and other illicit street trades not primarily as a metaphor for pent-up fury but as a literal attempt to survive. Those who are excommunicated from the family order jockey for position in the social order of outcasts. Society, by failing to toss them a life-line, sends them to the street, and it is only the most hypocritical of on-lookers who can express shock when these kids resort, as many inevitably do, to crime.

THE LURE OF GANGS

Puberty's roiling hormones often set off recklessness in otherwise 'normal' kids. Society used to regard the cavalier disdain for socially accepted attitudes and behaviour some teenagers flaunt as little more than 'growing pains.' In a more positive light, many people thought of 'crazy' teenagers as spunky, spirited, and spontaneous, passing through a tricky phase that would give way to more sober personalities. But this measured patience with immaturity has been severely tested by the rotting values evident in much of contemporary pop culture and commerce.

The mass-marketing of amorality designed to sell veneer as values delivers the message that a leather jacket is a more worthy attribute than a social conscience. Sophisticated advertising campaigns that target the fragile self-image of adolescents and wrap it in expensive trappings bilk young people of allowances, part-time earnings, and every penny they can beg from besieged parents.

Culture sold to kids often espouses values that are vapid, violent, or decadent. Nihilism, hedonism, and materialism are easy to pitch to a generation that fears ecological if not nuclear destruction. In this spiritual wasteland, violence, canonized in rock videos, films, and TV programs, becomes a type of survival norm, a way of doing things and getting things, a way of protecting oneself, a way of venting the confusion that implodes in truculent kids.

The swell of teenage gangs and quasi gangs along with the new violence they savour can be seen as indicators of the contemporary moral vacuum. These days, particularly in Montreal and Toronto, kids sometimes 'swarm' their victims to filch fashionable boots and jackets. Goods in hand, they ruthlessly beat victims – for the fun of it, they claim – before scattering.

Many people feel at a loss to understand these bullies who'd sooner commit moral crimes than fashion crimes. Popular explanations often revert to inadequate child- and family-blaming formulas. Some people cite more adequate explanations of the poverty wall that blocks legal access to cherished commodities and builds rage. Others attribute escalating street violence to the anger felt by some recent immigrant and national-minority youth. Like poor kids in general, they feel pilloried: targeted by schools and alienated by the mainstream. For some kids, gangs present themselves as the only portal to a special place in society.

Occasionally a commentator offers a broader view linking developments in the economic and social system with mayhem mirrored in the street. After witnessing a 'swarming,' writer/broadcaster/film-maker Kevin McMahon wrote:

The cavalier greed that inspires swarming is constantly demonstrated by the monopolistic corporate practices of what is euphemistically and reverentially known as The Private Sector. They have not the slightest compunction about using the muscle of their accumulated capital to forcibly pocket the assets of any weaker company, to rape natural resources, to boot into office politicians who will shamelessly deliver the policies they demand or to pummel the public with marketing which is competitive only in its insider rivalry to set new standards of insidiousness.[64]

Given a climate of frenzied corporate acquisitions in a society that markets materialism as a civil religion, McMahon wonders how anyone can be mystified by a little street violence to grab a leather jacket and a jolt of power.

Young people drawn to these activities come from different well-springs of trouble. Many of them are still in school and still at home and have money in their pockets and designer labels on their backs. Coveys of 'weekend warriors,' drawn by the magnet of glittering lights, pour into 'the city,' slumming really, in search of exotic sensations. Some of these sensations, derived from drugs and alcohol and mixed with the anonymity of a group, embolden them to go beyond the limit, to rob and to assault.

Other kids who are still in school and at home don't have money in their pockets, but they want designer labels on their backs. They want to be 'in,' but they and their families cannot afford the price of admission. These kids have grasped the advertising message that image equals substance. They are desperate for the expensive uniforms and accessories vaunted by their more affluent high-school peers.

Among street kids expelled from family life altogether, gang membership solves psychological and practical problems. Being part of one means they can finally fit in somewhere, enjoy the kind of protection their families never offered, and count on collaborators for their struggle to survive in the competitive street economy. In general, gangs and street cliques attract kids who feel unwelcome in the world; they offer an accepting place, plus a base for lashing out and hitting back.

Among the loose amalgams of street kids, punkers and skinheads are most visible. Clone-like in their carefully ripped stovepipe jeans or army pants with suspenders, clanking around downtown in their ubiquitous black boots, they actually have very little in common and splinter into a maze of subgroupings. As menacing as they want to appear and as rowdy as they seem strutting on street corners, most are pure street: all image, little content – just lost souls. Many of these kids aren't even aware of the racist undercurrent of their movement.

Some of them, such as those who sport racist emblems like a red circle divided into four quadrants, symbolizing racial division, do know. They have definite ideas, all of them repugnant, and are drawn to neo-Nazi blowhards, primarily from Britain and the United States. Racists and fascists conscript followers and goons from this small flock. These kids serve as marshals and bodyguards at meetings that provide ultra-rightists with public platforms.

The extent to which gangs and poseurs are a real threat to other kids and to the populace in general is unclear. The media's insatiable appetite for sensation may be exaggerating a relatively minor trend. Whatever the breakdown between empirical reality and perceived threat, flash-and-flee street violence committed by youths is clearly on the rise. And since, under the YOA, kids younger than twelve are not prosecuted – police usually warn them sternly and deliver them home – hoodlums use pre-teens as 'mules' to carry drugs and messages, indoctrinating them at a very early age in the wiles and violence of the street. These fresh-faced law-breakers are at very grave risk. If the street doesn't destroy them, chances are that they will harm themselves.

An Orgy of Self-Harm

According to the National Task Force on Suicide in Canada, suicide is second only to accidents as a killer of teenagers in North America. Young males age fifteen to twenty-four are five to seven times more likely to kill themselves than are young females. Boys choose more deadly methods – guns primarily – while girls prefer less-violent methods – drug overdoses primarily.[65]

The task force found suicide attempts more common among kids who feel emotionally distant from parents; who fail in school and other activities that involve public exposure; or who suffer major family disruptions such as death, separation, or divorce. While scores of average kids experience some of these set-backs, most street kids experience all of them. More telling, the task force identified the most potent triggers for suicide as a history of stealing, truancy, and running away from home; drug and alcohol abuse; and social isolation. In light of the prevalence of these risk factors among them, street kids are prime candidates for suicide.

If down-and-out and delinquent kids don't court death while they live free, those locked-up in grim places like the Willingdon Youth Detention Centre often do. A sprawling complex of low buildings in a green, park-like setting make up Willingdon. At first glance, from the outside, the chain-link fence is the only clue that Willingdon is not a school. Inside, there is no mistaking that it is a penal institution. Cells show no signs of personal decoration – none of the typical teenage rock-music-poster wallpaper, no colourful sweats and runners strewn around. Each cell is as anonymous as the next bare cubicle with a bunk.

Kids kick around disconsolately in regulation greys, herded in little groups from one drab setting to the next. In common areas, plastic chairs of the type used by restaurant chains are ripped from their moorings, their steel stubs testimony to the frustration festering inside the inmates. Flying fists have pock-marked the greasy beige walls.

Willingdon is 'the most damaging place to send kids because they get no rehabilitation, just interaction with other juvenile delinquents who do nothing but sit around talking about what they did to get in there,' according to John Kirkbride who served time in the facility on and off from age twelve to eighteen.[66] Kirkbride claims that even 'advanced jails' can't help troubled kids turn around.

Lumped together with other low-status youths, they understand the social message built into cells and steel doors. Obviously, they are little better than the cockroaches that keep them company. In this environment, only their crimes confer credit. Jailed juveniles, therefore, have an exaggerated stake in presenting an image of themselves as the toughest, meanest little criminal. Consequently, they like to sit around, embellishing details of their bandit escapades and boastfully dropping names of relatives and friends serving time in penitentiaries for major crimes. To be seen as a somebody and to feel important in a group of 'bad' boys and girls, they compete for position as the 'baddest of the bad.'

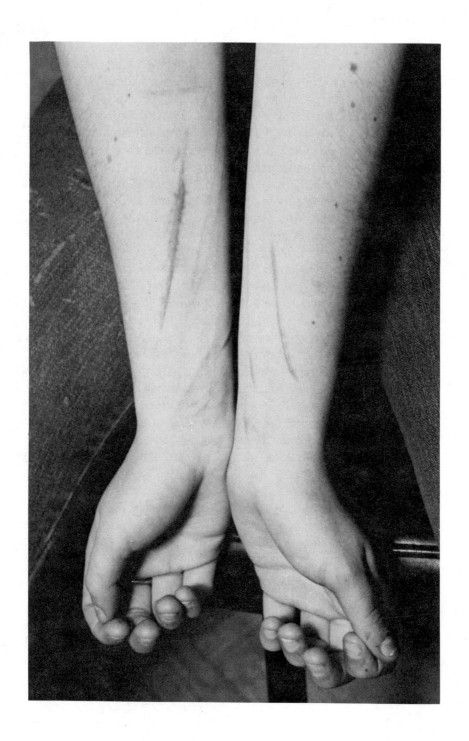

In 1984, the institution compiled a profile of its young charges. Like the youths in Leyton's East Cost sample, these incarcerated West Coast kids are economically and educationally deprived, and have suffered neglect or abuse. The institution describes them as depressed, impulsive, hostile, and aggressive.[67] The majority serve time or wait for court dates on property offences. In short, they typify locked-up kids across the country.

The most exhaustive North American study of self-harm, done by a former BC ombudsman, focused on Willingdon's population from 1979 to 1987.[68] It uncovered 203 incidents. Dr Robert Menzies, who conducted the study, says that these kids have been abused and degraded so regularly that 'self-harm is almost a rational response.'[69] During 1984–5, slashing up and suicide attempts hit an all-time peak. The ombudsman found 90 incidents of self-mutilation in less than a year. Willingdon officials claim that no one has died from suicide while in their care. They do admit that 6 per cent of inmates attempt suicide and that four or five serious incidents occur each month (on average, one a week).

In *Inside Out: An Autobiography by a Native Canadian*, ex-offender James Tyman describes the brutish backgrounds from which many young inmates hail, and the brooding torment of young lives blockaded behind bars. Self-mutilation, he says, is commonplace. 'Inmates mutilate themselves with razors, or with nails smuggled from the carpentry shop, or just by banging their heads against the wall till either they're dead or they've knocked themselves unconscious.'[70]

Kids don't attempt suicide only because they are desperate to get out of this world or to get some attention in it. They also cut open their veins to get respect. The logic may elude regular citizens, but to kids in institutions, scarred wrists and arms are badges of courage, part of the proof that they are 'baddest of the bad.'

For most of these children, juvenile detention will substitute for primary school; provincial jail for high school; and penitentiary for post-secondary education. Most begin with minor crimes and graduate into more serious ones. They start out young, and presumably somewhat tractable; after they have been through the justice system, however, many will become intractable, some violent beyond taming.

If it was, in fact, a revelation that the justice system – far from reforming and deterring most young law-breakers – more often hones petty delinquents into professional criminals, one might understand the system's stubborn resistance to radical reform. But the evidence that traditional approaches, particularly incarceration, tend to harden inmates into antisocial outlaws rather than to help them turn their lives around is by now a stale old truism. Yet, the corrections bureaucracy soldiers on, a seeming conspiracy of denial couched in the language of deceit. As long as punitive law enforcement, targeting predominantly poor, native, national-minority, abused, and disadvantaged juveniles, masquerades as justice and rehabilitation, troubled and trouble-making youngsters cannot expect a real second chance. Nor can the rest of us expect a reprieve from the rising spectre of youth alienation and violence.

Drugs:
Killing the Pain

Crystal: From illiterate 'junkie whore' to college grad

'Hello, my name is Crystal ... I'm just a junkie whore' began the audio tape. I'd put the word out to my network that I wanted to meet street kids who were struggling to get their lives together. Crystal was eager enough to tape an introduction and deliver it to me through a mutual streetworker friend. She began by talking about her family.

Crystal's brother is dead. Stoned insensible, he dropped a lit cigarette on a couch and was incinerated. 'My brother had no drug of preference; he preferred anything he could get,' Crystal says. Her other brother, addicted to alcohol and drugs, still uses everyday, and her sister – the most 'normal' of four kids – is 'nuts,' from life in the shadow-land between mental hospitals and the street and from years of psychotropic drugs.

Crystal herself almost died from gutter life and seventeen years of heroin addiction. A close encounter with death finally pushed her to choose life, though the struggle to finally live drug-free was harrowing. When we met in her sunny co-op apartment in Regina in autumn 1988, she looked surprisingly youthful for a thirty-two-year-old reclaimed from the skids. At that time, she was two years off junk and two credits away from a university degree.

Everything about her apartment and her appearance says 1960s: long, unstyled hair; sweeping caftan; rows of Mason jars full of grits and grains; well-tended hanging plants; and earthy pottery styled by her own hand. 'Yeah, I know, I'm caught in a time-warp,' she admits, smiling with effort.

I heard it on her tape and confirm it in her presence: the flat affect typical of people who've known too much hurt. Crystal claims she can't cry, 'not since the CAS took my first child from me, a heroin-addicted baby I gave birth to when I was seventeen. Now I yearn to feel a full range of emotions, but I'm still emotionally handicapped. For now, I have to settle for my private Greek chorus.' She means her Narcotics Anonymous sponsor, a sympathetic woman who sometimes weeps over Crystal's pain. It is almost, she says, as if her sponsor is expressing the anguish Crystal can't yet release herself.

Crystal was born in small-town Saskatchewan into a severely dysfunctional family. Her father is poor and alcoholic; her mother is a 'martyr' from an upper-class family that 'owned a factory and a private plane – that kind of rich.' The wealthy in-laws provided Crystal's family with a home in 'the kind of neighbourhood where the living-rooms are like ballrooms.' A once-prominent federal politician lived on her block.

'Here we were, poor as church mice, barely enough to eat, living with the upper crust. We couldn't hide our poverty because my dad drank away what little cash we had. I can still remember the embarrassment of showing up at school in Sally Ann rags, sitting next to the best-dressed kids in town.'

Crystal identified with the handful of native kids bussed to her school. 'Even though I wasn't Indian, I may as well have been because my life was as bad as theirs. Teachers and kids didn't distinguish too much between "poor white trash" and Indians. Everyone took for granted that we couldn't amount to anything, so we were pushed to the back of the class and ignored.'

In spite of the negative attention, Crystal learned to read. She did not, however, learn to write, an apparent contradiction that none the less dogs many youngsters. Like other kids in this book who were actually failing in school, Crystal was given passing grades. Although she would advance to high school before dropping out, no one would even attempt to teach her to write. 'The teachers called me "dyslexic." As far as I'm concerned, that label excused them from teaching. After all, if a kid's "dyslexic," which implies that she can't learn, no one has to bother trying to teach the kids, right?'

She was fourteen, and in grade nine, when she left school. By then Crystal was already using psychedelic drugs, which her late brother had introduced her to. 'Remember, we lived in a small town where hash, grass, and acid were viewed as remote big-city evils. My brother was the first person in our area busted for possession of street drugs. The open-line shows went wild: rednecks screaming that he should be shot, news headlines, the works. My brother was sent to detention. A psychiatrist was sent into our home to straighten us out.

'A lot of good family therapy did.' Her sister had a 'nervous breakdown,' lost weight, developed tremors, and began her perpetual junket between psych ward and shattered home. Around that time Crystal was gang-raped 'by six guys from respectable families. I didn't tell anyone, not one person. Who would have believed me? I was a nobody from a family with a notorious alcoholic father and a famous druggie brother.'

Crystal did what many lower-class girls in her position do – she left town. 'I was fourteen when I moved onto Vancouver's skid row. It wasn't a long slide from my family life and my drug experiments to selling myself for the price of a hit. I wasn't a good hooker. I was just a druggie hooking to get by. I'm ashamed to say it, but I'd fuck anyone for a fix. If your only passion in life is jabbing junk into your arm every day, then you whore, deal, or commit other crimes. Women usually sell themselves while men steal, and sell women.'

Like all street prostitutes, Crystal is no stranger to violence and murder. Her best friend, a sixteen-year-old hooker, was beaten to death with chains during a drug deal. 'I went to identify her at the morgue but I didn't recognize her. She was IDed through dental records. Another close girlfriend was stabbed to death over a deal. The list is pretty long: I've probably known a dozen girls who've died from drug violence or suicide.

'Skid row is a war zone where early death is a normal part of life, especially among junkies. Every time you hit up, you don't know if it's a hot cap or Draino. Maybe a friend will die today; maybe this time it will be your turn. Any way you cut it, street life is about self-destruction, so it's no surprise when lives are destroyed.'

Death may not be surprising, but, oddly enough, pregnancy usually is. Street kids typically either are ignorant about conception and birth or imagine themselves immune to the risk of pregnancy. If they are prostituting and have a pimp, they may use condoms, unless a customer forces them to have sex without one. If, like Crystal, they are young, work for themselves, and are not real pros, they will have sex on any terms, as long as the buyer pays.

Homeless, heroin-addicted, and ill with her first of three bouts of serum hepatitis, Crystal discovered she was carrying a baby. 'I couldn't believe it. I figured if you didn't get knocked up the first time you had sex, it meant you were sterile or had something wrong with you that would prevent pregnancy! Until I went to pre-natal classes, I thought babies were delivered through their mother's stomach – it just opened up and the kid popped out!'

In the months preceding and following the baby's birth, and whenever she was too sick to sell herself, Crystal scammed welfare. She learned that the quickest, most reliable way to get on the dole was to get on welfare workers' nerves. 'You have to make them feel desperate to get rid of you; that way, they'll cut through the bullshit and the red tape and get you a cheque. One of my tricks was borrowing a friend's baby, waiting till the kid had a smelly diaper and was crying from hunger. Then I'd go, babe in arms, to the office. It usually worked.

'I've had lots of experience with social workers over the years, especially since I started my long haul to getting clean. Provided you come on powerless and remember your place, ask for help they think is "appropriate" – their favourite word – then they will help you get money and training to stay within your social class. They'll agree, for example, that secretarial training would be "appropriate" for someone like me. But, get uppity ideas about controlling your own life or getting a university education and see how much they'll help you then!

'Most of the social workers I've encountered have been upper-middle-class white women who think they are the world's saviours, but they have no idea how the world thinks – or suffers. They are simply agents of social control.'

Ironically, Crystal is headed for social work herself, 'but not the kind that's been done to me.' She plans to become an addictions counsellor, believing that peer therapy works best with people motivated to change their lives.

Crystal is now, after eleven years of part-time university studies without being able to write, two credits away from a Bachelor of Arts. She has scoured the social sciences. Sociology, anthropology, psychology, economics, and history texts cram her book shelves. Her reading, and the gut instincts she learned from life at the bottom of society, have given her an astringent worldview.

It's been a long trek to the brink of graduation, beginning with small steps forward and interrupted by giant steps back. The idea of cleaning up came to her after she gave up her first baby for adoption. Heart-broken, she overdosed badly and suffered a stroke that killed some feeling in her left side, caused her face to sag and one eye to cross, destroyed her depth perception, and left her weighing eighty-five pounds. She bottomed out. Then, a small inner voice whispered that it was not too late to rehabilitate.

'Initially I went back to my home town, but I couldn't stay in a one-hospital town with no support or sympathy. After I survived withdrawal at the hospital and went to my family home to recuperate, the cops came by, three days running. They forced me to sit in the back of their cruiser while they busted some guys. By the second day of this charade, every rounder in town figured me for a stoolie. I had to leave, which is exactly what the cops had in mind. Once a junkie, always a junkie, right – even if you're only eighteen!'

For the next two years, Crystal was in and out of methadone clinics – 'just another addiction, only it's legal' – and treatment centres in Regina and Saskatoon. Once outside, without any supports or opportunities, she'd relapse. She even developed a new addiction – to a man who tortured her. A 'MDA freak' and 'poly-drug glutton,' he lost his reliable drug supply when the couple moved to Red Deer, Alberta, so he drank instead. 'The tortures would start with him calling me a whore and go through a twenty-four hour cycle of beratings, beatings, and threats to kill me. He'd strangle me, while promising, "This time you'll die, you whore." I'd scream and beg, and eventually pass out. His rage would fizzle out in about a day. I'd run away from him; he'd find me and then the whole honeymoon cycle would begin again, with his crying and apologizing and pleading.

'I stayed with him four years altogether. I was twenty and weighed ninety-five pounds when I found myself pregnant with his baby. By then we were back on Vancouver's skid row. I had stopped putting holes in my veins. Instead, I was doing MDA, smoking dope, and popping prescription pills. In my ignorance at that time, I considered myself clean just because I wasn't hitting up! To my mind, an addict was someone who used needles.'

Crystal's son, now twelve, with her to this day, is epileptic. 'Maybe the epilepsy resulted from my drug use, maybe not. He was a very sickly baby. I didn't get him inoculated. He had whooping cough and pneumonia and used to turn blue all the time. The seizures started after the illnesses and the blue episodes.'

Six months after he was born, Crystal, who, in a gesture to responsible motherhood had laid off everything except hash and grass during her third trimester, was back on prescription and street drugs. 'It's a cinch to score drugs from doctors.' She did Percodan, Talwin, and Dilaudid or 'drugstore heroin.' The real thing was too expensive for a welfare mom; pharmaceuticals were more economical. Because of her love for her baby, she often thought about and made frustrated attempts to clean up. Her son was a year and a half old when she finally managed to stay off needles for a while.

'There were two things I knew how to do in life: take drugs and communicate. To make something of my life, how could I put those to use? It was obvious: become an addictions counsellor.' Like mother, like daughter? Crystal's mother, married to a lifelong alcoholic and mother to four drug abusers, is also an addictions counsellor who has worked in detox centres and prisons. 'She has an addiction too – to martyrdom. My mother is the typical spouse of an alcoholic. Her life is an obsession with my father's behaviour, a desperate need to believe he can't live without her. Yet, she's a strong feminist and union organizer! Figure that one out.'

No matter how far Crystal looks back in the family tree, no matter where she searches the extended family now, she finds addicts, or people married to addicts, 'which is the same thing.' The family norm, however, does not include beating addictions. It took Crystal a very long time to make family history.

Using her strong communication skills, she got herself admitted to the University of Regina. She is articulate, reads a lot, has a remarkable memory, communicates well, and generally sounds like an intellectual – a perfect example of a person you'd least expect to be illiterate. No one suspected she couldn't write. But the inevitability of being found out caught up with her. 'Exam time. All my usual methods of fooling the professor and beating the system failed. Faced with an in-class, written test, I couldn't rely on tape-recording essays for someone else to type, or on the sympathy of fellow students I'd confided my problem to, in order to get their help. I was caught.'

Crystal panicked, and dashed out of the exam room. She

dropped out and sank back into her familiar drug quagmire. But it was a temporary lapse. Still dependent on her old tricks and her usual drugs, she enrolled again and pulled off a 75 per cent average. 'I scammed my way around the exam problem by choosing courses with take-home assignments instead of monitored exams.' Academically, her dodge may have carried her straight through to a degree, but her body gave out. Kidney disease, renal failure. She had to leave university and appeal to her mother to nurse her and take care of her son. Crystal spent close to two years in bed in her family's house.

'The only thing that kept me going was my love for my son. Nothing else could have saved me from dying a junkie.' When she was back on her feet and off drugs, Crystal enrolled once more in university and picked up where she left off in her studies, still unable to write but still able to maintain an 80 per cent average. 'I knew I was safe from discovery as long as I stayed in university, but the closer I came to graduation, the more worried I got about carrying my deception into the work world.'

That worry drove her to admit – finally – to someone who could help, that she couldn't write. She phoned a community-based upgrading program, told them the truth, and asked for instruction. They turned her down, saying she had too much education. She tried another work-preparation program and got the same response. She was 'overeducated,' they said.

'The closer graduation came, the more urgent the need I felt to stop living a phoney life. Here I was in many ways living a socially acceptable life – clean, a student, a responsible mother – but trapped in the poverty of welfare and knowing I could never make it in the world without writing. Except no one wanted to teach me.'

Crystal heard on TV about Beat the Street's plan to start up in Regina. 'I was practically waiting on the doorstep when they opened. At that time I could write my name and a scattering of words but not whole sentences; that was about it.' Since her first one-on-one tutorial, she has progressed to the point of writing essays that need only touch-ups. But writing is still a major challenge. She remains awed by classmates able to take copious notes during lectures in her favourite course, 'The History of Christian Social Justice' taught from a Marxist viewpoint.

For Crystal, every day is a precarious struggle to stay in the straight world. But it is also an adventure, the 'magic' of ordinary things an addict never knows. Waking up feeling well. Liking yourself, sometimes. Going on a date. I met Crystal soon after she started dating a straight man with no knowledge of her past. He wonders why she's so committed to mysterious meetings more important to her than getting together with him. Soon she will tell him about Narcotics Anonymous where she gets the sustenance to live one drug-free day at a time. She will tell him about her worrisome health: the constant pain from bone degeneration, the daily pills to regulate a malfunctioning adrenal gland, the heart murmur, the renal problems, the herpes, the fear that her past will destroy her future.

Meantime, her life goes on, full with the work of being a student and her joy in being a mother. It is a far cry from the full year after her son's birth when she carried a needle around in her purse in case the urge to give up overcame her and she could inject an air bubble to end it all. 'I thought about that fit [needle] in my purse first thing I got up every morning and last thing every night. It was my insurance against too much pain.'

That year seems a distant memory to Crystal as we sit in her cosy kitchen, sipping rosehip tea and talking about social justice. As her son bounces in for lunch, the first easy smile washes over her face.

Several months after we met, I received a letter from Crystal. She wrote:

My son and I are doing well. My boyfriend and I are doing moderate. He is straight. Straight people are very boring. It is very hard to cope with someone who doesn't beat you, that is dependable, that doesn't sleep with other women, that won't even sleep with me because he says it is to soon (what a bazarre concept).

... After you came over to interview me, I did quite a bit of thinking about what you asked me. You asked why I was interested in being interviewed. I aganized over this! I asked myself over and over, what was my motivation. Was it some kind of worped ego thing about my past? Was I bragging about how fucked up I was or was I really trying to show that there is hope for the future. Was I really trying to sped the message of recovery? I came to a positive conclusion. I decided that what I was really doing is trying to participate as much as I can in life. I honestly se myself as being reborn. Everything is new to me. I am like a small child in a lot of way. I am learning so many new things. How to be productive, how to be happy, how to be honest, how to be giving, how to love myself, on and on and on. The things that most people learn in there youth I am learning now. The things that most people experience in there youth I am experiencing now. I went so many year with tombstones in my eyes that I want to get the most out of life that I can. Everything that I experience is like an adventure to me. Nothing is boring. Even bad times are an adventure. How many people in this world get to be in a book? I am really happy that I got the opportunity to do it.

Crystal graduated in spring 1989. She is working as an additions counsellor.

Cocaine and the Pandemic of Drugs

About two million Canadians regularly shoot up, smoke, swallow, or snort illegal drugs, for which they shell out about $10 billion a year.[1] Illegal drugs are everywhere, from the school playgrounds in trendy neighbourhoods to housing-project hallways in tough ones. Often to support their own habits, penny-ante pushers cruise the parks, pinball arcades, poolrooms, shopping malls, high-school and college corridors, locker rooms, bars, and boardrooms.

To the uninitiated outsider who, at most daring, has purchased pot for a party, buying cocaine may seem clandestine and dangerous. In fact, the risk of police detection is minuscule. The pusher, contrary to the stereotypes of tattooed ex-cons or pimps weighed down by gold chains, could be the clean-cut college boy next door or the pin-striped businessman snorting white powder in the next cubicle in the men's room. As Victor Malarek's *Merchants of Misery* shows, the business transaction between small-time peddler and individual user is last in a corporate chain controlled by huge international cartels.[2]

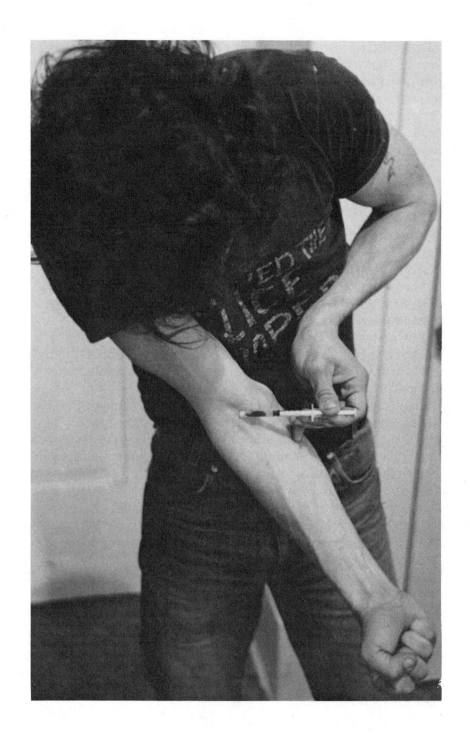

Drug lords wield financial and political clout equal to, perhaps greater than, that of the biggest multinational companies. The prosperity of Colombia's drug barons, for example, whose annual sales are valued at $110 billion, rivals that of General Motors. If cocaine profits had been repatriated to Colombia in 1988, cocaine could have outstripped coffee as that country's largest earner of foreign exchange. Leaders of Colombia's two drug cartels at one time offered to pay off the country's entire foreign debt of approximately $15 billion.[3] In 1989, Khun Sa, undisputed opium king of the Golden Triangle in Southeast Asia, offered U.S. president George Bush a deal. Khun Sa would sell his entire poppy crop to the American government for $48 million a year for the next five years, if the U.S. government would train hill-tribe peasants to grow other crops and would build roads to get their produce to market.[4]

Given the extraordinary margins between original production costs in poor countries and market values in rich countries, it is little wonder that drugs have such a fierce and enduring grip. Next to armaments-producing merchants of death, drug-producing 'merchants of misery' sit astride the most profitable industry in the world.

They prey on impoverished peasants in developing countries whose agriculture and domestic markets are destroyed by government-subsidized food imports from whichever developed country – usually the United States or EEC members – that subjugates their region. To spare themselves life in urban slums or a rural subsistence, farmers grow the only cash crops that offer them a living: opium poppies; cannabis; and coca leaves, the base for cocaine. Developing countries, whose devastated economies are stunted by dependence on industrialized 'backers' and crushed under debt loads to foreign powers, have made the masses dependent on illicit sectors.

The RCMP estimates that, world-wide, income from street-drug sales may be as high as $1 trillion annually.[5] It's a breath-taking business subject to remarkably little effective interference. Despite media hoopla over major drug busts, the impression that law enforcement significantly stems drug-trafficking is false. In 1988 Canada Customs seized only about 5 per cent of drugs entering the country.[6] Since Canada Customs accounts for 80 per cent of all drugs seized across the country,[7] it is fair to say that distributors are almost unimpeded in their trade.

According to the RCMP, most cocaine habituées come from lower and middle socio-economic groups, but the drug is attracting a growing number of upper-middle-class, professional males age nineteen to thirty-five.[8] Statistics Canada reported that in 1988 cocaine offences jumped 36.3 per cent over the previous year.[9] While crack, a cocaine derivative, tops the narcotics popularity list in Toronto, the menu of favourite substances across the country is still broad. In 1987, an estimated one million Canadians age eighteen to twenty-nine smoked marijuana; 100,000 swallowed tranquillizers; 250,000 ingested various stimulants, excluding alcohol; 700,000 snorted or injected cocaine, doubling the use reported in 1984.[10] Until the competition from crack cocaine, addicts traditionally preferred heroin, a powerful sedative for psychic and physical pain. There are 20,000 known heroin addicts in Canada.[11] Despite cocaine's current favour among addicts, heroin has been making a come-back among some users wary of needles.[12] They prefer smoking brown heroin, a practice known as 'chasing the dragon.'

Many people, including an incalculable number of 'soft drug' enthusiasts, dabble in drugs, but their experiments do not deliver them into the unmerciful clutches of dependency. Addiction rates are growing, however, and the trend can only accelerate, given cheap and available narcotics such as crack. Cocaine mixed with baking-soda and water is literally cooked over a flame from matches or a lighter to produce pebble-sized 'rocks' of crack that sell on the street for about $10. Larger rocks go for about $40.[13] Crack, which is smoked, 'slams through the lung walls and burns like gasoline on water, all slithery blue fire in the blood.'[14] Within thirty minutes, a hard crash follows the drug's short-lived euphoria, leaving the user hungry for more.

Cocaine, snorted in white-powder form or injected in liquid form, also produces an ephemeral high that vanishes quickly. As a result, some addicts feed their hungry veins several times an hour. A heroin high, by contrast, can last several hours a hit. The search for an affordable drug capable of delivering a long-lasting buzz has created an opening for crack's latest competitor, ice. A fiercely addictive rock form of speed, ice is smoked or converted into a liquid that can be injected. It offers a two- to fourteen-hour high.[15]

While it takes about five months for a heroin user, and eighteen months for a 'cokehead,' to get hooked, a crack fan, or 'rock-head,' can become addicted at first use or within the first two weeks of use. Addicts like Crystal often use their drug of choice – or, drugs of choice, in cases of cross-dependencies on heroin and alcohol, for example – for five years or more before they bottom out, overdose, or seek treatment. An alcoholic may not hit bottom for decades. A crack user, by contrast, is more likely to overdose or burn out within six months.[16]

The 1989 Ontario Drug Use Survey done by the Addiction Research Foundation (ARF) showed drug use among students down from 1987 and at a twelve-year low. By contrast, alcohol and tobacco lessened their grip only a little.[17] Among homeless drop-outs, however, the picture differs radically. ARF's 1990 survey of 145 Ontario street kids, average age nineteen, found that almost 90 per cent have drug problems.[18] Forty-one per cent inject their drugs. Sixty-four per cent had used cocaine in the previous year; 39 per cent had used crack. Six per cent of cocaine and crack users did drugs daily. According to the study, alcoholic drug use, depression, and suicide attempts are extremely high among this population. (Yet, ARF found that street kids do not rate substance abuse as their major problem. Rather, they ranked acquisition of basic necessities of food, shelter, and clothing as more pressing.)

Although the ARF survey concentrates on Toronto, its findings may signal significant increases in drug use in just two years since the Canada and Youth AIDS Study.[19] In its 1988 country-wide poll of 38,000 people age eleven to twenty-one, including 656 street youths, the study reported prevalent, but lower rates of drug use among drop-outs and disenfranchised young people. Fifty per cent of street kids in the sample confessed to daily or weekly use. Twenty-nine per cent took cocaine, and 51 per cent LSD.

In the street, drug use is not an aberration. Rather, it is normal, an accepted part of everyday life. In such a toxic culture, non-users are made conspicuous by their abstinence. Far from being chary of drugs, street kids count on them to etherize consciousness.

Down-and-out kids will take whatever their particular streets offer up. Hash and grass, habit-forming but not addictive, are as commonplace as cigarettes. The 'butt out' campaign, winning over impressive numbers of self-respecting Canadians to health consciousness, would be laughed off the street. There, self-esteem and health care are luxuries. Street kids couldn't care less that smoking is the primary cause of preventable death in North America. They couldn't care less that the Canadian Medical Association claims smoking-related diseases take 35,000 Canadian lives a year.[20]

Alcohol is another of their favourite anaesthetics. In ARF's survey, for example, 46 per cent admitted they had serious alcohol problems.[21] In 1988, 23,886 youths were charged with alcohol-related criminal offences in Canada.[22] Pharmaceutical drugs are popular too. On the West Coast, Talwin and Ritalin, 'T and RS' in street parlance, are preferred. Ingested or injected, Talwin and Ritalin in combination produce a heroin-like high.

Kids get these drugs, just as Crystal did, by 'double doctoring,' scamming a circuit of doctors known to prescribe liberally. Or, they buy them in the street from addicts, pushers, and gangsters who, the College of Physicians and Surgeons says, break into medical offices after hours and write out prescriptions. Well-versed in the necessary Larin, crafty forgers scrawl a doctor's signature, then fill the bogus prescription at pharmacies outside the doctor's neighbourhood. According to the RCMP, organized gangs run this lucrative business. In August 1989, in Toronto, for example, 144 fraudulent prescriptions netted criminals nearly $73,000 worth of narcotics, much of it destined for street sales.[23]

INTRAVENOUS DRUGS AND AIDS

An estimated 25,000 to 50,000 Canadians inject themselves with illegal drugs.[24] Many IV drug users get hooked on the needle first time they try it. Like Patsy, whom you met in chapter 5, some 'hypes' feel as attached to the needle as to the drug. Many 'hit up' or 'crank up' on a shared 'rig,' which also happens to be a principal conveyor of the HIV virus. 'In one cockroach-infested flat (in Montreal) that reeked of body odor, urine and rotting garbage, the police found nine young men lying on the floor nodding off in a heroin-induced stupor. The junkies, who ranged in age from sixteen to twenty-five, had shot up moments before, yet there were only three syringes on the blood-splattered living-room floor.'[25] Eleven per cent of street kids in ARF's study said they shared needles.[26]

With recreational and hard-core cocaine use on the rise, fear of an epidemic spread of AIDS among addicts, plus a cross-over into mainstream society, runs very high. Canada already has the second-highest total cases of AIDS among developed countries.[27] One in every 10,000 Canadians has been diagnosed with the disease. In addition to the 2,800 confirmed cases, an estimated 50,000 other people are infected. Some medics are warning that AIDS cases could double and triple rapidly among IV drug users in Vancouver, Toronto, and Montreal, the main drug-use, -distribution, and banking centres.

This epidemic curve has already been documented in cities around the world, in countries as far-flung as Thailand, Spain, and the United States.[28] Most medical thinking seems to concur with that expressed by the president of Toronto's Donwood Institute for drug and alcohol rehabilitation: 'It is simply a matter of time until [IV drug] users become a major bridge for spread of the disease to the general community.'[29]

The Canada and Youth AIDS Study concluded that street kids are particularly vulnerable to contracting AIDS because of their diverse sexual partners and use of needles.[30] Twelve per cent of the drug users, half of them prostitutes, said they injected amphetamines, narcotics, and prescription drugs. Nearly half of the self-confessed intravenous drug users admitted to sharing needles.

In January 1989, when Toronto announced its pilot-project year of exchanging dirty needles for clean ones, it was the first Canadian city officially to do so. A month earlier, a bold Vancouver street outreach organization with deep roots on the down side of town started up its own campaign among high-risk junkies. Tired of watching the disease spread while city council was bogged down in moral debates, the Downtown Eastside Youth Activities Society (DEYAS) financed an AIDS education and prevention project out of staff pockets and private donations. During the first four months of its crusade, DEYAS handed out more than 9,000 plastic bags containing hypodermic needles, cotton swabs, and miniature bottles of bleach and water for sterilizing needles. The kit also included a card explaining that shared needles and unprotected sex are the primary carriers of a fatal disease, AIDS.

Dr Des Jarlais, AIDS-research co-ordinator at the New York State Division of Substance Abuse Services, says that 'common fears that a large-scale, syringe-exchange program would lead to new drug use or to an increase in drug use by current users have not been borne out by the Amsterdam experience ... Instead the programmes ... tend to reduce drug use and increase demand for drug abuse treatment.'[31] DEYAS reported that some addicts signed up for treatment programs as a result of needle give-aways, and that many others took free AIDS tests.

Through DEYAS, the City of Vancouver implemented a needle exchange in March 1989. Montreal launched an exchange program in July 1989. Needle exchanges may slow the spread of AIDS but until addicts, most of whom are poor, gain access to the countervailing advantages of being clean, the drug epidemic will continue to flourish.

Billie and Chris: Parenting their addicted parents

My interview was set with Chris, an esthetic young man with finely chiselled features and natural copper highlights in his shock of chestnut hair. Even from a distance, Chris's body language says quiet, refined, and fragile. Not so the young woman standing next to him as I approach. She is exuberance itself. Bristling with energy, every inch of her, head to toe, is a carefully constructed black-on-black statement of artsy-punk. On her, wacky fashion translates into style.

Billie herself is gorgeous. I guess Eurasian. Wrong. 'I'm native Indian, Tsimshiam, but I hear some wild guesses: Mediterranean, South American, Iranian – you name it.' She smiles widely, her slightly prominent front teeth the only imperfection in a heart-shaped face. Her dyed-blacker black hair is pulled tightly off her face in a tousled pony-tail. A shaved stripe of scalp runs from temple to temple around the base of her hairline.

Billie interrupts my silent survey of this odd couple.

'Can I sit in while you talk to Chris?' she asks, eager.

'Okay with me. It's up to Chris.'

'We're best friends, we go everywhere and do everything together,' Chris says quietly.

A strange symbiosis. Billie attracts as much attention as a deliberately outrageous kid can, while Chris seems to crave anonymity. As we three make our way along Broadway – Chris and I stroll, Billie struts – Billie's journey is interrupted every few yards by friends. She hugs them effusively and has a little chat with each one before racing to catch up with me and Chris.

In our idling time, Chris interprets the passing scene this autumn Friday in Victoria. Sidewalks on both sides of the wide city-centre street are alive with kids, many of them pre- or early teens, caroming wildly through the crowds on skateboards. In Victoria, they are called 'curb kids.' Some are rich, as evidenced by their St Michael's private-school jackets. Most are latchkey kids from working poor and welfare families. They go home on the last bus, abandoning downtown to the two hundred to three hundred street kids who make their permanent home there, numbers that swell in the summer.

The hard core is a mixed lot of youngsters, some as young as twelve, others as old as twenty-one, the majority age fifteen to seventeen. A handful, including some from middle-income broken homes, are nouveau punkers into LSD and style. A smattering are skinheads, making a fascist rather than a fashion statement. Another subgroup of poseurs, on the periphery of Victoria's secretive satanic cults, hangs out in cemeteries, studies horoscopes, and practises drug rituals. (After Stockholm and San Francisco, Victoria is considered an international capital of satanic cults. It is popular with other fringe religious groups as well. The Moonies, for example, have their indoctrination school here, and several stores specialize in occult books and memorabilia.)

Another subgroup comes from a background like Billie's: doped-out, left-over hippies whose do-your-own-thing philosophy includes letting their kids make their own rules and raise themselves. The bulk, however, come from the background typical of most street kids across Canada: devastated and abusive families like Chris's.

Billie catches up with us at a sedate restaurant where we spend our first few hours together. By now I know a bit about each of them, enough to realize that parallel threads in their lives have pulled them together.

'By the time I was two years old, before I was adopted,' Billie, now seventeen, says, 'I had been sexually abused, been through eight foster homes, and I was anaemic and mute: I didn't speak or appear to hear. How's that for a welcome to the world?' She discovered her early history when she was thirteen. 'My boyfriend was trying to make out with me. I let him take off my shirt but then I panicked, yanked my top back on, and ran home to tell my dad because I used to tell him everything. That's when he first told me what my life had been like before the adoption.

'He didn't know that his first wife, my first adoptive mom, sexually abused me too. He wasn't clued in because it happened before I was five, when I was living with her after they split up. I didn't realize it myself until I was fifteen. Then, one time when I was visiting her, I began remembering what she'd done to me as a child. The memories came when she and I were sleeping in the same bed. She was sound asleep and I was wide awake, paranoid, all scrunched up in a corner of the bed, making sure our bodies didn't touch. I didn't know why I felt that way; it was the first time I had had these weird feelings.

'Later, when I went back home, I started having flashbacks, images of me as a little kid in the bath being rubbed down there by my mom. Worse, I remembered that she'd stick her tongue in my mouth when she kissed me goodnight. As a child, I wouldn't have understood that it's not right for a mom to French her kid ... As far as I can recall, she never touched me after I was five and living with my dad, but I'm sure she did when I was little. It figures too; I think her own mom and dad, my grandparents, split up because her father sexually abused my mother.'

Chris listens intently, as if hearing of these familiar episodes for the first time. He squeezes Billie's hand empathically before adding his own confession. 'The sex abuse didn't happen in my life till I was older, the ripe old age of twelve. My sister's boyfriend, who was twenty-one, raped me,' he says, eyes glazing. 'Three days later, he raped my sister.'

Billie could turn to her ex–prison guard father for sympathy and support; Chris could not turn to his ex-cop father. Both families were crippled in their parenting roles, but in different ways.

From age three to five, Billie lived with her adoptive mother and grandmother in Prince Albert. But her adoptive father, then a hotel co-owner/operator in Nelson, BC, fought for custody. Father, by then remarried, won the battle. Billie moved to Nelson and fell in love with him. Already a strong-willed and sassy youngster, she rebuffed attempts by travelling salesmen, 'scuzzy old drunks,' and other hotel frequenters who tried to lure her into their rooms with candy and coins. 'I could always tell the ones who really liked me because I was a fun kid from the ones that wanted to get their hands in my panties.'

By age seven, as far as she and her parents were concerned, she was smart enough to make her own decisions. By then, her parents had sold the hotel and started a more lucrative enterprise, growing marijuana and harvesting magic mushrooms in Vernon, BC. Her dad, 'who looks like an executive and dresses like a yuppie,' had learned how to scam from ten years working in corrections. 'For a front, he got a straight job in construction, worked very hard, made sure he had lots of cop and lawyer friends, and otherwise kept his nose clean,' Billie says.

But everyone in town knew how their garden was growing. At school, Billie was called the 'pot queen' because she generously supplied friends with joints. Parents of many of her classmates were 'shineheads' (makers and consumers of moonshine). Billie's father warned her away from alcohol and chemical drugs but 'as long as I stuck to soft drugs, the "naturals," it was okay by him.' By grade seven, Billie was stoned 'all the time. I'd crawl out of my waterbed and go immediately downstairs in my nightie to my private stash of marijuana.'

At home, she lived free from discipline, happily galloping her horse through open fields. Her mother (adoptive mother number two) tried unsuccessfully to rein her in. 'It's funny about my mom. She married my dad because he was such a straight-up guy, hotel-owning businessman, respectable, and all that. She'd come from a rich family and gone bad on drugs. My dad was supposedly taking her away from that scene, but instead he led her back into it. She turned into a lay-about home-body, doing dope and pretending to be an artist.'

Billie admits she herself was a 'real little instigator' who, goaded on by adoptive mom number one, with whom she spent holidays, treated adoptive mom number two like an 'invader.' 'I deliberately tried to get her edge up so she'd leave me and my dad.' Eventually, number two complied.

After her mom left, a relieved Billie took over parenting in the family by taking care of her father. 'My dad's a real smart guy but he's no judge of character. He let all these scummy types turn our dream house into a drop-in centre. I'd come home from school – where I was fucking up majorly – to find some bad-assed bikers helping themselves to beer and reefers [marijuana cigarettes]. I used to tell Dad that he had to stop letting these leeches suck off him, and stop them from turning our home into a hang-out for all this vile energy.

'I got tired of shooing these types away and having them dump on me like I was some saucy little snot ... One day my dad and I were at the table, eating a nice dinner I'd made, and here's this burly pig doing four lines of blow [snorting cocaine] right off the table! Worse yet, he's offering it to me. My dad didn't want me to get into chemicals, but I made all my own decisions. After seeing my mom [number two] on coke, I knew it was a greedy scene and a power trip; I didn't want anything to do with it.'

What does she think about a parent who would blithely accept his thirteen-year-old choosing to do coke? 'He was incompetent as a parent. I know that. But he loved me and provided for me. He believed in letting me handle my own situations. That was his way of child-rearing. I think his whole life was a spit in his own mother's face because she was a Bible-thumping bitch and a real Nazi on discipline.'

Throughout the interview, Billie speaks like a parent responsible for a child. 'After my mom left, I wanted him to feel that there was still something solid in his life, someone who loved him, who would be there for him, take care of him.' But Billie's mother (number two), as she pulled her own life together in Victoria, started to worry whether anyone was taking care of Billie. Mom returned to Vernon and begged Billie to leave.

'She tried to convince me that I was wrecking my life on drugs and that my dad wasn't the saint I thought he was. She told me about his womanizing and about the hell he'd put her through. I couldn't believe it at first. I mean, my dad was my idol and my best friend. Eventually, though, I realized he was forty-five years old, maybe time for him to take care of himself and time for me to start thinking about myself. Besides, I was tired of trying to reach into his heart and make a real connection. He closes himself off from that kind of emotion.'

After Billie left, her father sold his marijuana and mushroom fields and moved to a Caribbean island, where, according to Billie, 'he grows tomatoes and smokes ganga with his new girlfriend who's using him like everyone always has.'

Leaving her dad when she was in grade eight was 'the hardest decision of my life so far.'

When Billie describes the emotional wrench of leaving home, Chris nods vigorously. Yet, to hear his story, it is hard to imagine how he stayed so long, to age seventeen, with his fractured family in North Battleford, Saskatchewan. 'My dad's a burly, alcoholic ex-cop who loves to play the tough guy.' Chris, quietly and without recrimination, describes a dangerously violent man.

'You want typical examples of how he treated me? One time he pinned me to the ground, dug his finger in my ear and, cut me badly with his broken wedding-ring.' Chris shows me the scar. 'When blood gushed from my ear, it made him madder. He twisted my face to the ground and dragged it through the earth till we hit a cement block in the garden. He wouldn't have stopped then except my sister came screaming from the house. Another time, we were baling hay and the baler went on the fritz while I was driving the tractor. As usual, my dad blamed me for the screw-up. For punishment he dragged me through the alfalfa field till my face was all raked-up and bleeding.' He points to a forehead scar.

'One day when my bedroom was a mess, he stormed in, ripped the bedclothes off, put the dresser through the wall, lifted me to the ceiling by my neck and was choking me when my sister came to the rescue again. He dropped me and went after her. My mom intervened that time and told him to get out of the house, but the minute he was out the door, she started screaming at me, blaming me for all the family problems.'

Chris sighs, then looks to Billie for sympathy. 'Is that enough, or do you want more examples? I have lots more ... Even seven months ago when I told him I was leaving home, that I couldn't take the violence any more, he beat me for that.'

Did his dad beat his mother? 'No, he never touched her, but together they used to beat up my sister. One time they tore out her hair, and they always abused her emotionally, called her a tramp. To this day, she doesn't like herself, and now she has a bad marriage and a young daughter she abuses. My sister is struggling to change, but in the meantime it's pretty scary watching how she's raising her child.'

Like Billie, Chris felt responsible for taking care of his family. 'Someone had to keep the family going. I did everything for everyone: got the groceries, cleaned the house, did the chores. Someone had to be the parent or partner, and neither of my parents could do it. I felt I had to be mother and father to my sister. I was always protecting her from my father; in fact, the only times he was scared of me was when I'd get in the middle of a beating he was putting on her. I was always in the middle of vicious fights between my mother and my sister, too. Other times, I felt I had to be a husband to my mother. Even though she was abusing my sister, my mom was very weak and couldn't stand up to my father.'

Chris had his own problems standing up to abuse. Aware of his homosexuality from a very early age – 'I always preferred girls for play-mates, I had a high voice and feminine movements, and all the school-yard bullies called me a "faggot" long before I knew what that meant' – from age thirteen, Chris was involved in a series of abusive relationships. 'I spent eighteen months with an older coke-addict biker who was into cutting me up. I was lying to everyone. I didn't want kids at school to know I was being beaten up at home, and I didn't want my family to know I was being beaten up by my boyfriend, especially since they didn't know that I had a boyfriend, though they may have suspected I was gay. My excuse to everyone for all the bruises and cuts was that I was in gang fights.'

To escape pain and perplexing feelings, Chris followed his dad's example: he started to drink. He also followed his lover's example by getting into drugs. As hard as he was trying to prevent the breakdown of his family unit, he could not keep his own life together.

'I know exactly how he felt,' Billie interjects. 'Responsible. Guilty. As if everything happening around him was his fault. As if he could somehow be the perfect kid who would patch it all up. I always felt that my imperfections were to blame for losing three families: my natural parents, my first and second adoptive mothers. In recent years, I've felt guilty about the way I flaunted drugs at school; I exposed my dad to the risk of police detection. He wasn't busted, but still I feel that I should have been more responsible in protecting him from risk.'

Chris is nodding. 'When bad things happen to you or in your family, you think it's your fault, and if you do better everything will get fixed. Despite my home life and all the badgering I got at school, I busted my ass to get top grades: I was a straight-A student till grade eight!'

When neither Billie nor Chris could be perfect enough to fix their deficient families, they left home. At least Billie had an interested stepmother waiting for her in Victoria. But the mothering came too late. 'It was okay at first. She had really changed. No drugs. Hard work. Supporting herself with a little help from her parents, plus a settlement from my dad. But by the time I got through grade ten, all the old stuff between us started coming up again. We'd fight like cats or stew around in our fixed opinions of my dad. At fifteen, I walked out.'

For a while, she lived with a girlfriend of her mother's. Mom paid the rent. Billie quit school and worked as a domestic. She used her earnings to buy drugs. Not her usual grass and hash, but acid and 'my best discovery – MDA. When I did 'DA, poof! my crazy life lightened. I soon had a habit, needed my daily flap of 'DA. It got so bad that I stole from a family where I baby-sat.' Soon her mom's friend booted her out and Billie was 'crashing with friends or sleeping in the street. For about a year, I became a street kid supporting my drug habit any way I could. I don't know if I was addicted, but I sure loved MDA. I also loved street life; it was wild and fun.'

Wild and fun soon soured, mostly from the effects of drug abuse. 'I was wired all the time, felt like a real fuck-up, fell apart, started thinking about suicide. I even had a plan. I scored some sleeping-pills from a doctor, bought a canister of gin, and thought about a permanent holiday.'

Around that time, Chris was toying with the same idea. 'Victoria wasn't working out too well. I kept getting into abusive relationships with friends and lovers who made me feel worthless and who degraded me. We were living above a store in a real slum that stunk of trash and dirty laundry, paying $300 a month on my earnings from washing dishes. That's where I met Billie; she was crashing with friends in another rented room down the hall. We didn't actually meet in the building; we met slam-dancing in a slam pit. We did a lot of drugs together. By then I was an alcoholic and a heavy drug user, and I was seriously suicidal.'

Billie's mother, who kept in touch, guessed her daughter was on the edge. Feeling powerless to rescue her, her mom put Billie in CAS care. Since then, Billie, unaccustomed to constraints, has been living in a group home she 'hates.' However, she has begun to build a new life that may soon take the form of supported, independent living. She is back in school and building a stronger bond with her mother. She is off MDA and other chemicals, although still doing what she calls soft drugs.

Chris didn't give in to his suicidal thoughts. Instead, with the help of a streetworker he trusts, he extricated himself from his most recent abusive relationship. 'One month, one week, and two days ago,' he quit alcohol and drugs. 'Right now, I'm dependent on counselling. Trying to get rid of the "tapes" my parents put in my head is hard work. Trying to take control of my life, stop myself from being a target for abusers and self-hatred, is my full-time work right now.'

As part of a healing process, he decided to go home and to confront his parents about his sexuality. 'At first, my mom told me I was "testing her," but I think she's facing it now. My father can't talk about it at all. Both my parents, but especially my father, are very narrow-minded. They think Indians are a curse on mankind, so you can imagine what they think of gays.'

During the brief visit, Chris's dad almost hit him. 'Hit me and I'm gone; I'll never come back again,' Chris blurted out. He was surprised that his father had the self-restraint to stop himself. 'The guy is still a tyrant and he's made my mother's life even more miserable since I've left. She finally admits that he's an alcoholic, not that he'll do anything about it ... But he'll never make my life miserable again. Never.'

Billie and Chris are strong young people. Unlike so many street kids, they still have a lightness of spirit, and an energetic optimism suffuses their speech. They come across as exceptionally intelligent, thoughtful, and articulate, with a steel-like inner core. Billie draws a lot of self-worth from being a loved child; the bond between her and her adoring, though parenting-disabled, father serves as her bridge to a life that doesn't need to be destroyed by drugs.

While Chris was much more severely abused and didn't have a life-line of parental love, he fled early enough to discover that he is a person, not a punching-bag. It's less than a year since he left home. He has spent relatively little time in the street and in the thrall of abusers. He managed to find Billie, a determined fellow traveller, and he managed to connect with a supportive outreach worker. He is only eighteen and, despite a frail, doe-eyed appearance, he's a survivor. They both are.

The Quick Fix

There are probably hundreds of reasons – each a sad tale as unique as its teller – why so many people young and old depend on alcohol and other drugs to get them through the day and through life. People have demons – some real, some imagined – from which they long to escape. Alcohol and drugs fill up the holes in tattered lives, bolstering the desperate and emboldening the weak.

Whatever tangle of tragedies drive people to substance abuse, they develop their crutches in a commercial culture that exalts recreational drinking and pharmaceutical drugging. In 1987, 1.3 million adults used tranquillizers and 1.7 million took sleeping-pills.[32] In 1985, Canada ranked fourth world-wide in per-capita consumption of codeine, a pain-killer.[33]

Cop shows and evening soaps build plots around drug- and alcohol-abusers on both sides of the law and on both sides of the fence. The rich and famous make international headlines with their visits to the Betty Ford drug-rehab centre, tinting abuse with glamour, wealth, social acceptability, and the prospect of getting straight when the habit is no longer convenient. Our solution-by-commodity society sells drugs as the quick fix, and consumption and escape as the cure-alls.

More than typical adolescents, street kids are beset with oppressive problems, both those they bring from home and those they acquire in the street. They have more than the average need to escape. Killing the pain of their existence – getting high as a get-away – is the most compelling lure drugs offer. Addictions develop naturally out of the vulgar business of living in the street because some kids can cope with what is being done to their bodies only by being out of their minds. Drugs offer the illusion of being off the street while you are still on it.

An ex-hooker explains why she got 'desperate for the glow': 'When my body was being used I felt nothing: I wasn't connected to it ... I stayed high on pills, booze, and marijuana. I just wanted a blank. Feeling was too high a premium to pay.'[34] To feel blank, many street kids adopt scoring and doing drugs as their life's daily mission. Evelyn Lau's *Runaway: Diary of a Street Kid* portrays the drug obsession that can so easily possess lost teenagers.

Not only are street kids tied up in more complex psychological knots and practical conundrums than are average teenagers and therefore more susceptible to drugs, but they also live in an environment saturated with these hazardous substances. If alcohol and drugs tantalize many 'normal' kids, they magnetize troubled kids chasing a magical escape.

Factors known to predispose youths to substance abuse include low self-esteem, serious home or school problems, early use, a family history of addiction, parental conflict, feelings of helplessness and hopelessness, and physical and sexual abuse[35] – in other words, the runaway mould. The high risk that a child subjected to abuse may become a substance abuser leaps out from data collected at drug-treatment programs such as Portage, in Ontario. Staff there have found that 100 per cent of addicted young female offenders they treat have been abused sexually. Boys in the program tend also to have been sexually or physically assaulted.

Some runaways, like Billie and Chris, are family-cultivated substance abusers by the time they leave home. But as you saw from glimpses they provided of their lives, alcohol and drugs were only partially to blame for their descent into the street. More often, as you have seen from the profiles throughout this book, initiation to the street itself involves drug indoctrination. Excessive use of illicit substances, which begins as a symptom, quickly degenerates into a self-prescribed 'cure' for hellish reality. But the cure compounds the curse of street life. Kids sinking in narcotic quicksand cannot construct or grab life-lines that might tug them away from ruin. Like chronic alcoholics, drug abusers court death, even as they frantically cobble together the cash for their next hit.

The drug industry is one of few easy access points to a 'free-market' experience that street kids, and poor kids in general, have. Crack, in particular, is an entrepreneurial godsend to aspiring young businessmen from poor neighbourhoods for whom pushers may represent success models. It is hardly surprising, therefore, that a tour of Toronto housing projects reveals a drug bazaar that is nothing less than a 'wide-open, brazen hustle.'[36]

Driving around in an unmarked police car from one government-subsidized ghetto to the next, *Merchants of Misery* author Victor Malarek witnessed the same scene over and over, 'a non-stop choreography of dealing, desire, and despair being played out in glassed-in foyers, dimly lit parking lots, deserted asphalt basketball courts and forbidding underground garages.'[37] More and more youngsters now play their bit parts in the boom industry of cocaine. Minors, under age twelve, exempt from prosecution under the Young Offenders Act, are in demand as 'mules.' They act as look-outs and couriers, delivering drugs and collecting payments. Kids are paid for their services in pot, basketball sneakers, and skateboards – and in crack. Some mules become enterprising little businessmen themselves, subcontracting work to other pubescent truants as young as ten and eleven, eager to please even a fourteen-year-old 'boss.'

By summer 1990, thirty-three Canadians, many of them young women, were in Jamaican jails after attempting to smuggle drugs for their Jamaican-Canadian 'boyfriends.' Among them were two Metro Toronto girls age twelve and fifteen.[38] Traffickers also recruit disinherited young males to guard crack houses, sometimes arming adolescents with automatic weapons. This situation is endemic to Montreal, and to Toronto, which has an estimated 200 outlets scattered around the metropolitan area. Neighbourhood residents easily detect these round-the-clock 'shooting galleries.' Shortly after a crack house opens for business, used syringes litter nearby parks, sidewalks, and laneways. Children pick up and play with these contaminated needles. To outwit watchful police, crack houses regularly close down and move elsewhere.

These blind-pig set-ups are not confined to houses. Cocaine traffickers also operate from private apartments, often in densely populated housing projects where lives mired in misery guarantee a steady clientele. Residents have rallied together in housing projects, such as Regent Park in Toronto, organizing themselves into drug busters determined to clear pushers from their stairwells and sidewalks. In addition, they aim to help distraught families terrified for members who use cocaine or terrorized by addicted family members who peddle drugs.

Up until a few years ago, juvenile pushers sold 'soft drugs,' hash and grass. Canada-wide in 1983, 70 boys and 25 girls aged fifteen to nineteen were convicted of cocaine offences. In 1987, the numbers had risen to 162 and 36, respectively, representing 79 per cent of all drug convictions handed down to boys and 63 per cent of those to girls. In 1978, 15.4 per cent of all drug crimes were cocaine-related. By 1987, 48.4 per cent involved cocaine.[39]

As a consequence of cocaine, according to police, street crime in major cities country-wide has been increasing.[40] Violence in the commission of those crimes has shot up. In 1989, Metro Toronto police, for example, recorded a 30 per cent rise in armed hold-ups over the previous year.[41] About 90 per cent of the robberies were the work of cocaine addicts.[42] Although drug abuse in Canada has not wrought the blood and madness of the American scene, the country has cause to chivvy under the threat of a new cabal of cocaine, and, especially, crack dealers.

Ray: Childhood memories a blur of drunkenness and violence

'Where ya from, lady?' asked the cabby who taxied me down-town from the airport. 'Toronto, eh. Lucky. At least you don't got these no-good Indians.' The tourist brochure in my hotel room offered a mini-history of Regina, extolling it as an old North-

West Mounted Police headquarters. The brochure's only references to native presence or contributions were two plugs for
Louis Riel as a 'controversial folk hero.' I asked the desk clerk
which galleries exhibit aboriginal art. 'I don't know if any of
them do, but it doesn't matter anyway,' he assured me, 'because
Indians don't produce much that's worth seeing.' Also, during
my first hour in Regina, I asked a local resident about population
size. The answer: 186,000. 'How many native?' I enquired. 'About
30,000, but they don't count,' he answered with a jocular lilt,
assuming I'd share his little joke.

My second cabby, who delivered me to Ray's office, warned me
that it was 'welfare week': 'The Indians got their cheques last
night and they're showing their colours this morning.'

Ray's homespun office is an organized clutter of books, pamph-
lets, and papers devoted to rediscovering native culture and to
kicking drug and alcohol habits. Ray, now twenty-five, works
with native and non-native children though mostly the former
since so many troubled youngsters here are Indian.

Small but sturdily built, Ray has a handsome, pock-marked face
framed in a long raven-coloured hair. His manner is soft and self-
effacing, his face a window to his deepest emotions. Born on a
Saskatchewan reserve, he grew up without ties to or trace of
anything proud from his past.

*That's not to say that I didn't understand my people's way of life on
the reserve. I understood it all right: alcoholism. From my grandparents on down, all my relatives were alcoholic. Through my eyes, as a
child, that seemed normal. I never felt different from the other children
and families around me.*

*But I felt lonely and scared almost all the time. My parents would go
out on drunks – for several days to a week at a time. We had no super-
vision at all. As the eldest of four children, and only a very young
child myself, I was expected to take care of the little ones. I don't think
anyone ever warned me about authorities, but I knew exactly what to
do if a car pulled up with white people in it: hide my brothers and my
sister, fast.*

*My father was a skilled carpenter but there was hardly ever any
work on the reserve. He moved us around to other reserves, looking for
jobs, but it never got him anywhere. Instead of working, he drank and
abused us: very severe, regular lickings with electrical cords. At the*

time, I had no concept of abuse, though I hated the way he treated us and started running away when I was very young.

One time, my younger brother and I took off together. Police dogs tracked us down. I remember how glad my parents seemed when we were delivered safely back home. Next morning, my father asked why we had run away. 'Because I don't like the way you treat us,' I bravely told him. We both got bad beatings for having run. I associate that licking with a decision never to express my feelings. After that incident, I became silent and distant. The anger was hard to suppress, especially when he beat my mother. I couldn't condone what he did to her; I had to strain to distance myself from her pain and my anger.

In spite of the way he abused us all, he was – somehow – my hero. I genuinely admired him. He was a big, strong man; he'd been a boxer and weight-lifter, and had served in the militia. One time, when I was just a little kid, I'd watched as he single-handedly beat up three guys during a party at our house. As I looked on, I felt very excited. I was impressed by his strength. I also admired his artistry; he could play any musical instrument you put in his hands.

I didn't inherit his gift for music but I had a talent for learning. I always did well in school, despite the racism that started in the first small-town school I was bussed to and lasted throughout my education. Defending myself from racist attacks at primary school was my first lesson in self-defence.

I was nine when the Children's Aid shipped me off the reserve to my first foster family, white Mormons in Calgary. I didn't understand why I had to go, though my mother did everything she could to prepare me and help me feel excited about the idea of leaving my family. She made it seem like a big treat – until the day I actually left with a broken heart.

It's only recently that my mother and I discussed why she let them take me away. She knew I couldn't get ahead from the reserve. She thought I'd have a better chance to finish school if I lived with a white family in the city. I know her explanation is true because I've always felt my mother's love and affection in spite of her drinking.

However good her motivation, it was not a good situation for me. I was totally out of place. Right off the bat, one of the sons told me his mom was worried that I might not speak English or know what a toilet was. The family did try – at least, the parents tried – to make me feel a part of their home, but even without knowing it, they separated me.

At the neighbourhood school, I was the only native. The other kids never missed an opportunity to punish me for my difference. Everyday someone would call me a 'dirty Indian.' Sometimes, they said and did worse. Like the time a gang of guys, including two of my foster brothers, danced a mock pow-wow around me. All the anger that was stored up in me taught me how to fight at that moment. I attacked without mercy; when a guy was down, I'd kick him in the face. I was literally bursting with rage.

Rage against my natural parents for putting me in this place, anger with my foster parents who couldn't understand why I fought so much. They could not accept that I had no choice but to fight back, that I was alone, unsupported, isolated. They felt, as everyone at school did, that the fights were my fault. I was too aggressive, they said. By then, there was some truth to that statement.

I wrote pleading letters begging my mother to let me come home. Soon I realized that my foster mother was opening my mail because one day she confronted me. 'How can you say these things about us? You know they're not true.' This, of course, wasn't fair, but I'd already learned that life wasn't fair. I felt cheated and despised. Alone. Empty. Bitter. The only way I had of feeling good about myself was by getting good grades.

It was obvious that I couldn't stay with that family; there was too much friction. I was almost eleven when I got shipped off to a farm in Red Deer. The problems I had with the farm family were essentially the same as I had with the Mormons, but I was a bit happier out in the country because I had the freedom of space. After school and after chores, you'd always find me roaming the fields by myself.

I was twelve when I heard the news I'd longed to hear every day of my absence from my family: I was finally allowed to go home. Home, I learned, was now in Regina, where my mother had resettled with my brothers and sisters – more kids had been born since I'd left – and without my father. She'd finally left him and was struggling to sober up and keep her family together.

But going home was not the salvation I'd imagined. I was back with my family, but it wasn't the same anymore. I wasn't able to feel close. I wasn't able to feel much of anything.

By the time I was fourteen, I needed more than good grades to make me feel good. I needed drugs and alcohol. I was already blacking out from booze. Always on the run, skipping school, skipping home, staying away longer and longer stretches, learning to support myself in the way of the street – shoplifting, B&Es, scrapping. Much of those survival skills I learned from an older brother, my mother's son from before our family.

I had the inevitable run-ins with the law, and by fifteen, I was on probation. Only then did my grades really start to slip. I couldn't handle living at home, but I couldn't handle the streets either; they were too mean. The only out I saw at the time was getting myself thrown into a boys' school, a detention centre outside Regina for mostly native juveniles. My brother agreed, so we set ourselves up for a bust by smashing windows at a liquor store and waiting for the cops to arrive.

The lock-up was no better than the street. In fact, it was so bad that we couldn't wait to get out. When we were released, I was so relieved to be outside that I put everything into making it at home and into staying in school. But it was too late on both scores. I was better raw material for street gangs, where my brother and I found that, when we hung together, a circle would always form around us.

I started failing at school. Even my prowess as an athlete couldn't keep me straight. I'd ranked high in the province as a long-distance runner, a gift from my forefathers, certainly not from training. I used to be the only smoker and drinker on the school bus when the boys went to competitions.

I wasn't a total loss though; at least I was willing to work. I got a job as a stock boy and worked my way up to a clerk. Then, because of their incentive program for hiring natives, I landed a clerical job at a Canada Employment Centre. My wages, about $1,200 a month, kept me in booze and drugs. I often showed up to work drunk or stoned or hung over or just moody, but since I was their token Indian, they didn't fire me.

I think of those days now with a lot of shame, especially the way I dealt with girlfriends. I never kept one more than a few months. I just used girls for sex and for bragging to the guys. At least I can say for myself that I was never physically violent. From the first time I saw my father beat my mother, I could not stand the idea of men beating women.

As long as my sisters lived in the same house with my father, I always worried that they might be abused. I was twenty-one when I found out for sure that he'd beaten them and sexually molested them.

[At the memory, fury sears across Ray's face; his eyes fix on a distant pain, and he lowers his head. With great effort, he pulls out of his reverie ...] That discovery threw me over some imaginary line between coping and falling apart. It broke the thin thread of my ordered life – a job, a wage, a little normalcy, even with the booze and drugs.

To this day, I cannot explain what snapped inside me. I just stopped caring – about myself, about everything. I hit the streets.

I ended up in Saskatoon deeply involved in a drug ring. My brother and I worked as enforcers. It was our job to beat up on people who owed the dealers money. We took the assignment seriously, bludgeoning our victims almost to death. It wasn't long before we had a reputation for our violence, and before we were heavy drug users ourselves. Cocaine mostly. That's how they paid us: a little cash, a lot of coke.

We got pretty puffed up about our big name, bold enough to do a little moonlighting. Someone would tell us their sister was getting it from her old man, and we'd pick up a free-lance job beating him up. I didn't understand at that time about the kind of dependency that keeps women in relationships where they're abused. I just hated the beater and was glad of a chance to whip on a Balaclava and bash in his head. I guess it was my father I was really trying to beat.

Half the time, I was in black-outs, unable to recall where I'd been or what I'd done. One time, in a conscious moment I found myself pinning this guy to a bed, one of my hands covering his eyes, the other on his throat. Terrible anger burned inside me. I needed to really squeeze this man. But he pleaded with me to let him go. To this day, I still hear his words: 'Take whatever you want, I haven't got much, I'm on welfare. But please, don't hurt me.'

I don't know why that moment, but suddenly it struck me hard: 'Why am I doing this?' I asked myself. I lifted my hands from his throat and his face, and I fled.

Next morning, someone took me to my brother, who was in hiding from some hoods. I didn't recognize him; he'd been so badly stabbed and beaten. It was the last straw for me, the shove to get my life in order. The first thing I had to attend to was getting him medical attention, except it wasn't safe to take him to a hospital. If we'd gone into an emergency department, they would have called the cops and my brother would have ended up in jail – and dead from guys inside who would have done their hood friends outside a favour.

I called my mother, told her about our crisis. By this time, she was in Regina, studying at the Indian Federated College and doing well. She helped us get to an Indian elder. As far as I'm concerned, the elder performed a miracle. Using herbal remedies, his pipe, and prayers, he had my brother on his feet in three days.

During the bedside vigil, I swore to myself that, if my brother got up, I'd clean up. The day he got out of bed, I contacted the Poundmaker Centre in Edmonton, a twelve-step addiction-treatment program that includes native cultural awareness. I first cleaned up there, then came back to Regina to recover in a program where I could begin to face all the pain hanging onto me from my childhood.

For the past two years, Ray has worked for a small voluntary agency. Seeing himself as a role-model for kids facing the same depredations and temptations that derailed his life, he is hell-bent on staying on track. He feels he can't afford to stray, not when vulnerable kids look up to him and see their future in his accomplishments.

'I'm gifted with the ability to talk to young children at their level. I want always to see myself as their friend, not as the traditional authority model of social work that I grew up with.'

We met just after his 'two-year-old birthday' at Narcotics Anonymous. Among people at the party who paid tribute to Ray's progress was his room-mate, a thirty-year-old 'addict' (members call themselves 'addicts' the way AA subscribers refer to themselves as 'alcoholics') who is 'making amends for abusing his children. I learned a lot about my own father from him. I learned how it feels to beat children, to live with the screaming in your head that tells you not to do it even while some inner force won't let you stop.'

Ray's father was also among the circle of well-wishers who spoke about what Ray means to them. 'For the first time in my life, he told me he loves me,' Ray says with pride. 'I care about him a lot now, too. I know he's sorry for what he did to me, to us. I know he lost his role as a father and the loss of dignity robbed all meaning from his life. And I know he's struggling to sober up, even going to meetings. Now he has periods of sobriety, followed by fall-backs. Maybe my being clean will encourage him.'

I listen with uneasy disbelief as Ray speaks compassionately about his father, a man who abandoned him, beat him, beat his mother and his siblings, raped his sisters ... 'I cannot fathom your forgiveness. I've heard it before from other survivors of abuse. I feel now as I have felt every time. I cannot accept that you can forgive anyone who brutalizes you the way your father did – whatever devastating circumstances in his own life drove him to do it.'

Ray considers my words. It takes him a while to speak. It is still rough territory for him. 'I can't hang onto the feelings I had about him; if I don't let them go, they will drag me down. So I guess you could say that I forgive him for my own selfish reasons, to free myself from bitterness.

'I just took part in my first rain dance, which requires four days of fasting, praying, and sacred observances. After two days, my focus on myself became so overwhelming, I felt I couldn't go on. I only managed to by reflecting on problems other people face, like what my dad went through instead of what I went through. He served a jail term for sexual assault; think about that.'

'Your sisters will serve life sentences for what he did to them. Think about that,' my silent inner voice replies. Yet, there is no denying how deep runs the drive of abused children to forgive their parents. Maybe for people like Ray, himself the perpetrator of terrible hurts, it is easier to summon sympathy.

Treating Addicts

Male drug addicts outnumber females three to one,[43] though the ratio may shift if the number of young women using narcotics continues to climb, a trend the Addiction Research Foundation has already documented in Ontario.[44] In 1984, the average age of men entering the Salvation Army's Harbour Light mission for addiction treatment in Toronto was fifty-two. By 1989, the average age had dropped to twenty-seven.[45] That year, 40 per cent of their patients (about 400 people) were treated for addiction or cross-addiction to cocaine.

Only the wealthy can afford to buy back their lives. The foremost private clinics in the country, such as Bellwood in Toronto, charge up to $9,000 for a three-month cure in a country-club setting that boasts an 80 per cent success rate.[46] Canadian doctors help affluent addicts gain access to private U.S. clinics. In 1987–8, more than 2,000 Ontarians were treated in the United Stated at a cost of almost $10 million to Canadian taxpayers.[47] This therapeutic stint, geographically removed from the temptations and problems of daily life that precipitated drug abuse in the first place, often does not work. Counselling that excludes family members or other significant people in the addict's life also reduces the chance of a cure. An estimated 80 per cent of cocaine addicts of all nationalities who clean up in U.S. programs succumb to cravings within two to three months.[48]

Most addicts in Canada, typically destitute and not receiving medical care, are forced to wait months for a spot in overcrowded, short-term counselling programs. 'Asking an addict to behave himself without help for that period of time [the three to six months it takes to get into many Toronto treatment programs] is ridiculous,' says the head of the Toronto police force's morality squad.[49] What's more, graduates of these programs face very high risk of relapse. In the absence of extended supports and new opportunities, reformed addicts yo-yo in and out of treatment programs the way psychiatric patients without community supports ping-pong in and out of psychiatric hospitals.

Joy Reid, who directs a Toronto drop-in for homeless and socially isolated women, says the 'treatment for our people doesn't work ... because after they're out, then what? They're back on the streets again – same friends, same life.'[50] The inescapable reality of dead-end lives and dealers conspire for their relapse.

People who work with addicts across the country seem to agree that severe failings, especially in decent, publicly funded treatment facilities, sabotage effective turn-arounds. For one, there simply are not enough spaces to meet demand. For another, unequal access to existing beds discriminates against young, old, disabled, and 'multicultural' addicts, according to a program evaluator at the Addiction Research Foundation. He claims that services are most available to white, English-speaking Canadians.[51] The Toronto mayor's task force on drugs released in 1990 confirmed that this is the case in Metro where middle-age, middle- and upper-class men enjoy almost exclusive access to treatment.[52]

The task force report also pointed out that no detoxification services to youths under sixteen exist, and that only eighteen residential beds are open for kids age sixteen to eighteen. Yet, of a hundred drug addicts who sought treatment in 1989 from Toronto's Hospital for Sick Children, eighty were under sixteen.[53] A decade ago, the Addiction Research Foundation's Youth Clinic treated kids who began experimenting with drugs at age fourteen on average. Today's clinic patients first try drugs at age eleven to thirteen.[54] Of 465 addicts who went to the clinic in 1988, nearly one in five was under eighteen. One in twenty was fourteen or fifteen.[55]

This wide discrepancy between need and services is not unique to Canada's largest city. Margaret Michaud, a Vancouver youth worker and author of *Dead End: Homeless Teenagers, a Multi-Service Approach*, visited clinics coast to coast. She did not find one adequate drug and alcohol rehabilitation program for adolescents. In an angry commentary one hears repeatedly from youth workers, Michaud says, 'Drugs kill. What's it going to take to get some funding for decent programs? More kids dying?'[56]

Drug dealers, from the king-pins in poor countries, to the linch-pins on the street in rich countries, are parasites on poverty and its attendant misery. Poverty and profit, more than other factors, drive drug abuse. They drive producers to produce, pushers to push, and users to use. Therefore, the say-'no'-to-drugs education campaign is probably doomed to fail among kids who most need to be spirited away from pusher and peer pressure.

While cold facts about consequences may help steer kids who possess a sense of purpose and hope in their lives away from serious drug involvements, scare tactics are unlikely to dissuade kids who feel directionless and hopeless. Kids who sense they have little to lose because all is already lost to molesting fathers, acrimonious families, or crippling poverty will not be beguiled by simple appeals to self-preservation. Kids seduced by cultural nihilism and hedonism or the innate cynicism of life on a threatened planet will probably remain cavalier about drugs.

Saying no attacks the drug pandemic at the level of individual responsibility, without accounting for the benefits and losses drugs represent to different individuals. Saying no to drugs is not about fighting material or spiritual poverty, nor is it about opposing the degenerate culture promoted by merchants of escape. It is not about attacking causes.

Among the swelling ranks of up-scale cocaine users, saying no to drugs does not address the emptiness at the core of their being. That kind of deprivation – one of purpose and commitment – is also a significant driving force behind the lemming-like plunge into chemical consciousness that characterizes Western cultures.

To date, drug education and campaigns by law-enforcement agencies have been the mainstays of the Canadian government's 'war' on drugs. By 1989, after two years of operation, the $210 million national drug strategy had 'produced little beyond a smattering of billboards, an educational video aimed at school children ... and some minor legal reforms.'[57] In *Merchants of Misery*, Victor Malarek argues that 'police forces could double and triple their expenditures and it would not make an appreciable dent in the [drug] supply. The drug war will not be won by police ramming down doors, arresting dealers and throwing them behind bars ... The drug problem will not be solved by building more prisons and filling them with drug dealers. It will only be resolved by a serious and concerted effort in the areas of prevention, education and treatment.'[58]

Prevention in the form of educating schoolchildren to drug hazards garners attention these days. At the same time, our government continues to overlook the economic and social breeding grounds for drug abuse. Underlying causes remain as remote from the state's so-called war on drugs as do desperately needed treatment programs. The war has not delivered accessible, affordable, local programs with follow-up support and built-in opportunities for altered life-styles.

Instead, the anti-drug campaign has focused on suppliers, as if curtailing supply could stem demand. Even on this ill-chosen front that makes law enforcement the war's first priority, success rarely outsdistances symbolism.

As one distraught Victoria, BC, father of a boy charged with trafficking LSD discovered, law enforcement means little more than sweeping the streets for bit players in a big-time game. After a day in court, which began with his feeling remorseful for his ' "unspeakable crimes" of parental neglect that made my son who he is, a troubled young man with many excellent qualities that aren't quite fitting the mold of mainstream society,' the father's remorse turned to rage. He wrote:

> What I saw was a justice system clogged to the point of breakdown with all the expendable little people in our massive drug war, the nickel-and-dime users and sellers at the bottom of the heap ... Where are the big businessmen of drugs? What I saw in the courtroom were a lot of poor, weak, vulnerable young men ... This current frenzy of scapegoating that is filling up our courts and jails with human sacrifices is the most retrograde excuse for a solution that anyone could imagine.[59]

More police, more prisons, and saying no are no substitute for substances that transport troubled kids to a carefree planet where they feel invincible. Wholesale rejection of drugs will occur only if kids have access to meaningful alternatives. The challenge of infusing young lives with mental health and spiritual hope goes beyond family responsibility and individual choice, to the very nature of our society and our values.

7

Beating the Street

Street kids and other imperilled youngsters need the same things all children thrive on. More than anything, they need love: one-to-one and unconditional from a dependable adult, their very own family of sorts. They need roots, security, protection, commitment, understanding, and a great deal more patience than the most trying of typical kids. They need opportunities and choices.

They also need special services and supports that youth workers, child advocates, some professionals, and the kids themselves have been demanding for a decade. Safe houses top the list. To prevent new runaways who don't already live in the inner city from migrating to dangerous downtowns, these sanctuaries must be located in the kids' home neighbourhoods. They must be truly welcoming places – not warehouses – small and intimate, acceptable to residents, and staffed by counsellors kids trust.

Safe houses can only succeed in helping distraught teens (and pre-teens) make realistic plans for independent living, for family substitutes, or for family reconciliation if they have access to community resources that neither judge nor coerce kids. These resources include medical and mental-health services, such as hassle-free all-night clinics, and drug and alcohol rehab programs designed specifically for adolescents. Counselling and support services, both material and moral, must extend over the long haul until young people gain control over their chaotic lives.

Troubled, delinquent kids need diversion instead of detention. They need reschooling in alternative-education programs and student welfare rates that undercut the necessity for them to sell their bodies for supplemental income. They need to graduate into jobs with living wages and housing with affordable rents.

En route, they need relationships with healthy adult caregivers and role-models who genuinely like young people and empathize with the special problems of children who feel despised and discarded. They need available, dependable adult allies. Ritualized caring does not count here. Street-wise juveniles easily sift the sham from the authentic. Over time, wary youngsters will admit an adult friend into their lives, but they will shun do-gooders who turn concern on and off like a faucet.

According to the kids themselves, what they don't need are bureaucratic authorities, the whole 'conspiracy of do-gooders and mind-fuckers.'[1] Kids often experience representatives of child-protection and correction services as enemy agents bent on locking them up or sending them back to incapable, uncaring or abusive parents, or to unacceptable substitute families assigned by the state.

It is important to point out here that kids' antipathy for traditional helpers, and indeed widespread public doubt about the efficacy of child-protection and correction services, almost invariably focus on front-line social workers. Whether dedicated or indifferent, front-liners take the flack and the fall for systems that fail families and kids. Relatively powerless individuals, they become the targets, the shock troopers, between flawed systems and an angry, confused public.

It is little wonder that child protection and corrections often inspire fear and hostility in those they seek to help. As Martyn Kendrick shows in *Nobody's Children: The Foster Care Crisis in Canada*, children in state care 'share a universe of discredited rights, and scarred emotions, which the system caused, exacerbated, and even at the best of times, failed to heal.'[2]

He explains that instead of matching children carefully with loving families adequately financed, supported, trained, and able to redress or buffer damage done by birth families, the child-protection system tends to compound the misery and alienation of its young charges. By warning foster parents not to bond with their foster children, the state sabotages even the most dedicated substitute caregivers. The child-protection system collects children – about 12,000 a year[3] – desperate for love, then systematically denies them fulfilment of their greatest need: attachment.

Hence, many kids in care trade the nightmare of their original homes – loveless or violent or paralysed by poverty and distress – for the equal or worse heartache of homes the state provides. In Canada, foster parents tend already to be overburdened with below-average incomes and above-average numbers of children, and to be handicapped by weak education.[4] Government pays them about $15 a day, plus expenses,[5] to nurture the neediest youngsters. In 1988, Canada's foster parents threatened to strike for higher rates, complaining they were treated as a 'cheap dumping ground for society's problem children.'[6]

Disturbing experiences in state care galvanized wards to band together in 1986 into the Canadian Youth in Care Network.[7]

While this necessary action for self-help is greatly to their credit, the necessity for children to organize in the interests of self-protection is a revealing discredit to the system.

Yet, as you have seen from many profiles in this book, kids in care have to look after themselves. They can count on the system only to shunt them, at bureaucratic convenience, through a series of homes, including some controlled by abusive parents. Foster kids run away, often repeatedly, ricocheting back and forth from society's margins where they join other scatterlings of state care holed up in the street.

The grudge street kids commonly carry against the system often extends to institutional treatment programs as well, particularly if they are provided in locked facilities. In Montreal, two teenage girls locked up, allegedly for their own protection – though they had not been charged with a crime – in a bid to escape set fire to their detention home. Four other girls, at least three forcibly held, died in the December 1989 blaze.[8]

Some professionals defend locked detention. The interim director of Ville Marie Social Service Centre, which placed the Montreal girls, said, 'An adult sees it as a punitive measure, but [adolescents often] say that someone cares enough to go that far to make sure they're safe.'[9] Other professionals inside the system, and most, if not all, streetworkers oppose force on the basis that it only forces kids to run away.

In *Solomon Says: A Speakout on Foster Care*,[10] author Louise Armstrong slams all uses of force in the treatment of children who've lost their families, from use of restraints to withdrawing privileges as punishments. 'For the [abused] child, then, this "treatment facility" is simply the apotheosis of, the clincher for, all that has gone before.'[11]

What are the chances that Canada's street kids and other children trapped in high-risk environments can expect a new, concerted drive to rescue them and to help restore their lives? The answer varies, depending on who you ask.

Social reformers, many among them in the helping professions, believe government can be forced to assume its responsibility to protect and nurture children. They believe the state can be pressed to adopt and implement what they call 'enlightened social policy' to be achieved by restructuring health, education, and welfare services. For them, the solution is a matter of public lobbying and political will.

In response to simultaneous growing poverty and a shrinking social net, and especially in reaction to food banks, hostels, and homelessness, anti-poverty and children's rights groups have been resurrecting reform's buzz phrases – 'government planning,' 'greater service co-ordination,' 'interagency co-operation,' 're-organization of relationships between existing services,' and the like. Champions of street youths, in particular, have stepped up pressure for results. 'The issue of homeless teenagers must be addressed through prevention, crisis intervention and healthy alternatives, and these steps must be a coordinated effort at all levels of government' reads the jacket promotion copy on *Dead End*, a book about helping homeless adolescents through a 'multiservice approach.'[12]

Clearly, a responsible government would tackle the urgent task of building a fail-safe rescue net to help kids at risk bypass the street. It would provide every possible support to distressed families, especially to those headed by sole-support mothers. It would help shore up crumbling families so that far fewer kids end up in state care.

Few people would question the moral rightness of demanding that our government make sure the basic needs of our youth, and, indeed, of all Canadians, are met. A great gulf, however, separates agitating for what is right from understanding what is possible in a society that worships wealth and tolerates poverty. If one listens to voices in the street, those of the homeless and those of streetworkers in venturesome voluntary agencies, one does not hear expressions of faith that government initiatives will ever rescue the kids. A few small programs here and there to keep the lid on, a lot of noise about a little social spending – that happens, they say; but widescale prevention, early intervention, and a serious rescue campaign, they fear, will never happen. They fear it will never happen because of who hard-core street kids – mostly, but not exclusively – are: from poor, or near-poor families, and therefore devalued and disposable.

In the trenches, one hears an unrelenting tirade against public systems of help, and a weary cynicism about any officially assisted detours around the dead ends. When government ignores hunger, forcing private charities and private citizens to substitute for public justice, what can anyone expect it will do for homeless kids? people ask.

On the down side of town, beyond anger and seething frustration, one hears more about helping kids find individual solutions for massive social problems.

A scattering of alternative social services struggle to do just that, to help kids after they hit the street. Everyone agrees that intervention at this point comes too late. Yet it is necessary because so little help exists to bolster families and to rescue kids before they hit bottom. Once kids find themselves in desperate circumstances, straightening out their lives becomes trickier than it would have been earlier in their downward spiral. In addition, once kids are jettisoned into the street, their chances of escape diminish proportionally to the time they spend trapped in the inner-city sewer. The longer they are down, the harder they fall and the smaller the chance of their getting up or coming out alive.

Despite discouraging odds, both established and fledgling programs operate in various cities across the country.[13] Some of these small but visionary projects are run by mainstream bodies such as school-boards and municipal governments. By far, the majority are non-governmental enterprises so badly underfunded that their doors open and close – and sometimes reopen – according to the vagaries of short-term grants and fund-raising drives. They run on the dedication of underpaid and overworked staff, many of whom burn out within a couple of years. Scores of volunteers help keep these undertakings alive. Although these outreach, often store-front, organizations are small in number coast to coast, they usually have high visibility among disaffected youth.

Despite philosophical divides and vastly differing services, these organizations seem to share similar beliefs about working with kids. Their principles and practices stand in marked contrast to those evident in most mainstream social and education services.

It's tough to do, but street organizations accept youngsters as they find them with their burrs on, all brash and bombast to mask their numbing pessimism. Outreach organizations are not put off by pariahs with their belligerent behaviour and crude mouths. They don't expect discarded children to be compliant and grateful and well-behaved.

These organizations understand that change is not propelled by a single clairvoyant moment in which a youth decides once and for all to quit prostitution or drugs or crime and to mount an unimaginably bold foray back into the straight world. Sometimes one particular crisis amid the endless horrors of street life works as the breaking-point. More often, the gradual accumulation of disasters, disappointments, and dead ends coalesces into a drive to break away. The child's decision 'manifests itself less in words than in the tone of voice, and in a curious change of pace and energy. Fantasy often equals energy, and truth fatigue.'[14]

In order to detect this change in pace and energy, youth workers have to be attuned to subtle shifts among their flock in temperament and in tolerance for street life. That means they have to understand the kids they work with, really know them, not simply recognize them as a file number and a face that shows up occasionally. That's why outreach agencies position themselves for maximum contact with minimum discomfort for teenagers, whereas public agencies tend to be set up for minimum contact under conditions of maximum discomfort.

It is not by accident that non-traditional agencies work in the streets, literally, and from unintimidating offices on or near the strip. Nor is it by accident that they don't expect street kids to keep daily diaries and adhere to exact schedules. By contrast, conventional helpers are usually ensconced in offices removed from the action. Kids usually have to take buses to see them, by appointment, in anonymous cubicles in inhospitable public buildings, after waiting in reception areas where they feel like they are on display.

Alternative organizations take for granted that, even for the most determined, breaking with street life and integrating into straight or quasi-straight life proceeds gradually. The process often leads to imperfect endings. More often than not, getting off the street represents a relative, not an absolute accomplishment. Someone who manages to quit today, maybe for months, even years, may well be back on the street when his or her shaky fortunes in the mainstream falter. Objectively, getting off the street may not mean getting very far, but subjectively, it may mean the difference between having a half-decent life and having no life at all.

In the progress towards a mainstream life, lapses may be many and advances few. Outreach workers do not give up on people easily, or blame them when they backslide. Rather, they understand how deep run the needs, insecurities, and misfortunes of young people desperate enough to seek out the streets as a home. They know they are dealing with challenging kids driven to persistently test adults who seem to care about them. They realize that building relationships with youngsters who profoundly distrust adults is a tedious, time-consuming effort. The attempt may – or may not – eventually stretch a ready youngster to think about tomorrow, about education, about a job, about a room of his or her own.

Street agencies realize that kids who've never had able parenting need reparenting. Outreach workers accept that they must hang in, without conditions, over the long term. They may have to scurry around more than once, mobilizing resources for a kid who swears she'll make it this time. But kids party and lose their rented rooms. Cash-hungry, they turn back to tricking. Lost without habitual crutches, they turn back to crack.

This untidy flip-flopping behaviour unnerves rigid social-service bureaucracies already burdened with huge caseloads and threadbare budgets. If kids want help, they are expected to behave civilly and conform to the rules: show up for appointments, fill out forms, produce receipts. More flexible outreach programs, by contrast, expect erratic behaviour. Rather than demanding that kids fit the system, they strive to individualize service, depending on the distinct needs of different kids.

Plans are worked out according to goals young people articulate themselves. The plan is neither pre-set nor imposed. Rather, the adolescent, not the agency or the worker, makes the choices and controls the process. Wise counsellors understand that 'a sense of personal power that allows the individual teen to choose to be free is the first step in constructing a sense of direction.'[15]

Street services operate on the premise that coercion alienates young people from adults who might be able to help them. Kids cannot be guilted into changing. Change is voluntary, a universal principle particularly true of street kids. As every agency that scores successes with troubled teenagers knows, 'attempts to restrict and restrain them and to ignore their needs and issues are futile, because this is precisely what they have run away from.'[16]

Besides, most street kids have been on their own for ages. They are not candidates authorities can manipulate. If typical teens resent heavy-handed authority, street teens are uncompromising in their rejection of controlling approaches. It is telling that ex–street prostitutes in one study reported feeling most powerless in their interactions with social-service agencies. They felt ignored, misunderstood, disbelieved, rejected, and pushed around.[17]

By contrast, kids can feel empowered by social agencies and caring adults who help them bridge the chasm between hostile and healing worlds. While their own intrinsic motivation to beat the street is critical to crossing over, kids need passage people who can help them get to first base. They need people willing to act as stepping-stones, to get close, invest a lot, risk a lot, probably endure a lot of abuse and still be there. It is a kind of professionalism that is not crisp, detached, or efficient. As Peter McKenna, a Halifax priest and streetworker described it to me, it's a 'getting-your-hands-dirty' professionalism, and it is not for everyone.

Advocates willing to forge strong links with kids they serve come from a variety of backgrounds and work in a variety of settings, often at odds with their own agencies. Some are trained in helping disciplines: education, childcare, health care, social work, community development, psychology, and theology, among them. Others have the expert training of experience: they are ex-street kids, ex-offenders, welfare recipients, survivors of incest and abuse. If they work outside bureaucracies, they network with allies inside. Many are organizers and outspoken activists, trouble-makers in the best sense. However, relative to the need for child advocates, they are few. Their abilities and accomplishments, however impressive, are dwarfed by the sorry state of government commitment to Canada's neediest children.

It is hard to imagine that Canada would continue to eject children into the gutter if their parents had, among other supports, access to basics for a stable life: decent jobs and liveable wages; adequate, secure housing; quality, affordable childcare; healthy food and life-styles, to name but some of the ingredients missing from the survival kits of more and more families in this country.

It is hard to imagine many kids would be in the street if schools were committed to educating and guiding students at greatest risk for personal ruin; if public-assistance programs extended realistic financial support to families and individuals, including adolescents in need; if social services provided family counselling and community-based mental-health clinics to help disturbed youngsters before they hit bottom; if the state guaranteed kids loving alternatives to dangerous homes; and if the corrections system were dedicated to rerouting budding delinquents. It is hard to imagine a serious street-kid problem would exist if male violence against women and children did not.

Prerequisites such as these for sound, safe child-rearing reify into pipe-dreams as society pursues the skewed social outcomes of our 'free' society, in which people are free to be un- , or under-, educated, employed, and paid; in which the scions of commerce and culture are free to sell, at a high price, nihilism and decadence as the highest values. Certainly, our dollar democracy is very free and fruitful for some, full with the perks of precious individual rights that supersede the common good.

From the vantage point, however, of dispossessed Canadians – whether the one and a half million poor kids or the hundreds of thousands of impoverished mother-led families, to name but two among many excluded populations – freedom is just another luxury only money can buy. To the thousands of homeless kids, it must appear as it does to Eugene, a street kid you met in chapter 1: 'It's a free society, man. We're free to die down here and nobody give a shit.'

Notes

1 STREET KIDS

1 Bruce Ritter, *Covenant House: Lifeline to the Street* (New York: Doubleday, 1987), p. 210
2 Ruth Morris and Colleen Heffren, *Street People Speak* (Oakville: Mosaic Press, 1988), p. 23
3 Elly Danica, *Don't: A Woman's Word* (Charlottetown: Gynergy Books, 1988), p. 66
4 Warner Troyer, *Divorced Kids* (Toronto: Clarke, Irwin, 1979)
5 Evelyn Lau, *Runaway: Diary of a Street Kid* (Toronto: Harper & Collins, 1989), p. 91
6 B.C. Public Interest Research Group, *Off the Street*, conference proceedings prepared for the Victoria Association for Street Kids, September 1987, p. 26
7 Ritter, *Covenant House*, p. 143
8 Morris and Heffren, *Street People Speak*, p. 51
9 See, for example, the summary of views in Mark-David Janus, Arlene McCormack, Ann Wolbert Burgess, and Carol Hartman, *Adolescent Runaways: Causes and Consequences* (Lexington, MA: Lexington Books, 1987), chapter 8.
10 Martyn Kendrick, *Nobody's Children: The Foster Care Crisis in Canada* (Toronto: Macmillan of Canada, 1990)
11 Cited in 'Dark victory,' *Toronto Star*, 17 December 1989, p. B1

2 DESTROYED AND DESTROYING FAMILIES

1 Rix G. Rogers, 'An Overview of Issues and Concerns Related to the Sexual Abuse of Children in Canada,' discussion paper prepared for the Ministry of National Health and Welfare on Child Sexual Abuse, October 1988, p. 29
2 'Child sex abuse a crisis, study says,' *Toronto Star*, 16 June 1990, p. A14
3 'Disabled abused "almost daily," group charges,' *Toronto Star*, 2 May 1990, p. A9
4 'Child molesters: Out of the shadows,' *Toronto Star*, 21 November 1989, p. C1
5 Myrna Kostash, *No Kidding: Inside the World of Teenage Girls* (Toronto: McClelland and Stewart, 1987), p. 133
6 Gitta Sereny, *The Invisible Children* (London: Pan Books, 1986), p. 252
7 Mark-David Janus, Arlene McCormack, Ann Wolbert Burgess, and Carol Hartman, *Adolescent Runaways: Causes and Consequences* (Lexington, MA: Lexington Books, 1987), p. 103
8 Sereny, *The Invisible Children*, p. 18

9 Allan Gould and Maggie MacDonald, *The Violent Years of Maggie MacDonald* (Scarborough: Prentice-Hall, 1987), pp. 52–3

10 Information in this paragraph is based on examination of child-abuse data, in particular 1986 and 1987 child-abuse figures, from Nova Scotia, Quebec, and Manitoba. Sources for all abuse figures cited from Nova Scotia: Family and Children's Services (calendar years 1983–7); Quebec: Comité de la protection de la jeunesse (fiscal years 1986–9); Ontario: Ministry of Community and Social Services (calendar years 1986–8); Manitoba: Child and Family Support (calendar years 1983–7); and British Columbia: Ministry of Social Services and Housing (fiscal years 1987–8).

11 'Extra funds to fight child abuse ruled out,' *Toronto Star*, 2 July 1989, p. B6

12 Robin F. Badgley, *Sexual Offences against Children: A Report of the Committee on Sexual Offences against Children and Youth* (Ottawa: Supply and Services Canada, 1984), p. 175

13 Cited in ibid., p. 198

14 'Child molesters: Out of the shadows'

15 Research done by Finkel cited in Rogers, *An Overview*, p. 22

16 Janus et al, *Adolescent Runaways*, p. 57

17 Research done by Ross Dawson, cited in Martyn Kendrick, *Nobody's Children: The Foster Care Crisis in Canada* (Toronto: Macmillan of Canada), p. 46

18 Rogers, *An Overview*, p. 77

19 '8 in 10 native girls sexually abused, study finds,' *Toronto Star*, 28 January 1989, p. A1

20 Data in this paragraph are taken from Nicholas Bala, *Review of the Ontario Child Abuse Register*, prepared for the Ontario Ministry of Community and Social Services by the Social Evaluation Group (Kingston: Queen's University, 30 September 1987), pp. 5 and 56.

21 Linda Gordon, *Heroes of Their Own Lives: The Politics and History of Family Violence* (New York: Penguin Books, 1988), p. 4

22 See, for example, 'Introduction' and 'Child battery' in Connie Guberman and Margie Wolfe, eds., *No Safe Place: Violence against Women and Children* (Toronto: Women's Press, 1985).

23 Guberman and Wolfe, eds., *No Safe Place*, p. 102

24 'Victims of Nfld sex scandal "could have said no," Bishop says,' *Toronto Star*, 11 August 1989, P. A1

25 Gordon, *Heroes of Their Own Lives*, p. vii

26 Holly Levine, producer and director, *I Am One of Them: Mothers Speak Out about Incest*, a video sponsored by YWCA of Metropolitan Toronto, 1988

27 Pat Ohlendorf-Moffat, 'Wives of men who commit incest,' *Chatelaine*, March 1989, pp. 59–63, 129–31

28 'Girl, 3, partly blamed in Vancouver sex case,' *Toronto Star*, 25 November 1989, p. A6

29 'Multiple personalities,' *Toronto Star*, 3 March 1989, p. B1

30 Margo Rivera, quoted in 'Multiple personalities'

31 Martin Daly and Margo Wilson, 'Child abuse and other risks of not living with both parents,' *Ethnology and Sociobiology* 6 (1985): 197–210

32 Dr Alan Gilmour, *Innocent Victims: The Question of Child Abuse* (London: Penguin Group, 1988), p. 29

33 Maria Roy, ed., *Battered Women: A Psychological Study of Domestic Violence* (New York: Van Nostrand Reinhold, 1980), p. 30

34 Gilmour, *Innocent Victims*, p. 105

35 According to Linda MacLeod, author of *Battered but Not Beaten: Preventing Wife Battering in Canada* (Ottawa: Canadian Advisory Council on the Status of Women, 1987), speaking on CBC-TV, 'The Journal,' 11 October 1989

36 Gilmour, *Innocent Victims*, p. 105

37 Guberman and Wolfe, eds., *No Safe Place*

38 Gilmour, *Innocent Victims*, p. 24

39 P. Jaffe, D. Wolfe, S. Wilson, and L. Zack, 'Similarities in behavioral and social maladjustment among child victims and witnesses of family violence,' *American Journal of Orthopsychiatry* 56 (1986): 142

40 Neil Boyd, *The Last Dance: Murder in Canada* (Scarborough: Prentice-Hall, 1988), p. 209

41 MacLeod, *Battered but Not Beaten*, p. 38

42 Cited in Guberman and Wolfe, eds., *No Safe Place*, p. 46

43 MacLeod, *Battered but Not Beaten*, p. 38

44 Gordon, *Heroes of Their Own Lives*

45 Peter Jaffe and Carole Anne Burris, *An Integrated Response to Wife Assault: A Community Approach Model* (Ottawa: Solicitor General of Canada, 1984), p. vi

46 Michele Landsberg, 'Only in male justice system does primary care count so little,' *Globe and Mail*, 15 March 1986, p. A2 (emphasis added)

47 MacLeod, *Battered but Not Beaten*, p. 32

48 Ibid.

49 Ibid., p. 33

50 Ibid.

51 Eilleen Spillane-Grieco, 'Characteristics of a helpful relationship: A study of empathic understanding and positive regard between runaways and their parents,' *Adolescence*, 19 (73; 1984): 63–75

52 Ibid., p. 74

53 Sereny, *The Invisible Children*, p. 251

54 Roger C. Loeb, Theresa A. Burke, and Cheryl A. Boglarsky, 'A large-scale comparison of perspectives on parenting between teenage runaways and non-runaways,' *Adolescence* 21 (84): 921–9

55 Donald G. Fisher, cited in MacLeod, *Battered but Not Beaten*, p. 33

3 SEXUALLY EXPLOITED KIDS

1 See Canadian Child Welfare Association, 'Consultation summary,' in *Proceedings of the National Consultation on Adolescent Prostitution* (Ottawa: Canadian Child Welfare Association, 1987).

2 Gitta Sereny, *The Invisible Children* (London: Pan Books, 1986), p. 254

3 Laird Stevens, *The Stroll* (Toronto: New Canada Publications, 1986)

4 Ibid., p. 164

5 'New study confirms anti-hooker law isn't working,' *Calgary Herald*, 27 November 1988, p. C1

6 'Soliciting law hasn't reduced street prostitution, study shows,' *Toronto Star*, 1 August 1989, p. A3

7 Sereny, *The Invisible Children*, p. 254

8 Sylvia Barrett and W.L. Marshall, 'Shattering myths,' *Saturday Night*, June 1990, p. 21

9 Patricia Marshall, quoted in Barrett and Marshall, 'Shattering myths'

10 Annie Ample, *The Bare Facts: My Life as a Stripper* (Toronto: Key Porter Books, 1988), p. 164

11 Ibid., p. 165

12 These figures are cited without reference in Frédérique Delacoste and Priscilla Alexander, 'Prostitution: A difficult issue for feminists,' in *Sex Work: Writings by Women in the Sex Trade Industry* (London: Virago Press, 1988), p. 205.

13 Street Outreach Services, *Monthly Totals of Significant Contacts by Program Component, January–December 1988* (Toronto: Street Outreach Services, 1989)

14 Sereny, *The Invisible Children*, p. 250

15 Robin F. Badgley, *Sexual Offences against Children: A Report of the Committee on Sexual Offences against Children and Youths* (Ottawa: Supply and Services Canada, 1984), p. 983

16 Margaret A. Michaud, *Dead End: Homeless Teenagers, A Multi-Service Approach* (Calgary: Detselig Enterprises, 1988), p. 8

17 Evelyn Lau, *Runaway: Diary of a Street Kid* (Toronto: Harper & Collins, 1989)

18 John Lowman, 'Taking young prostitutes seriously,' *Canadian Review of Sociology and Anthropology* 24 (1; 1987): 103

19 Sereny, *The Invisible Children*

20 Ibid., pp. 27–8

21 Dr Alan Gilmour, *Innocent Victims: The Question of Child Abuse* (London: The Penguin Group, 1988), p. 103

22 Canadian Association of Elizabeth Fry Societies, *Response to the Fraser Report on Prostitution* (Ottawa: Canadian Association of Elizabeth Fry Societies, January 1986)

23 Sylvia Fraser, *My Father's House* (Toronto: Doubleday Canada, 1987)

24 Elly Danica, *Don't: A Woman's Word* (Charlottetown: Gynergy Books, 1988)
25 'Who's killing B.C. hookers?' *Toronto Star*, 13 July 1989, p. A2
26 Bruce Ritter, *Covenant House: Lifeline to the Street* (New York: Doubleday, 1987), p. 58
27 Myrna Kostash, *No Kidding: Inside the World of Teenage Girls* (Toronto: McClelland and Stewart, 1987), p. 153
28 'Sheila,' quoted in Victor Malarek, *Merchants of Misery: Inside Canada's Illegal Drug Scene* (Toronto: Macmillan of Canada, 1989), p. 47
29 Wendy Lever, 'Juvenile prostitution and the law,' *Symposium on Street Youth: Symposium Proceedings 1986* (Toronto: Covenant House, 1986), p. 135
30 'Who's killing B.C. hookers?'
31 Marie Arrington, quoted in 'Who's killing B.C. hookers?'
32 'Who's killing B.C. hookers?'
33 'Sex, violence swamp city park,' *Winnipeg Sun*, 22 November 1988, p. 2
34 'Highlights of what our street team found,' *Youth Horizons*, Issue 33 (Montreal: Youth Horizons Foundation, December 1989)
35 Patricia Hersch, 'Coming of age on city streets,' *Psychology Today*, January 1988, p. 31
36 'A tale of self-destruction: Ex-hooker talks of life with drugs and AIDS,' *Toronto Star*, 18 October 1988, p. C1
37 Roy Reid, 'A Time for a Change,' unpublished paper (1986), p. 11
38 For a more detailed account of the complex relationship between pimps and young prostitutes, plus the problems girls face 'signing on' their pimps, see Tom MacDonnell, *Never Let Go: The Tragedy of Kristy McFarlane* (Toronto: Macmillan of Canada, 1987).
39 Lau, *Runaway*, p. 165
40 Trudee Able-Peterson, *Children of the Evening* (New York: G.P. Putnam's Sons, 1981), p. 165
41 Ibid., p. 184
42 Femia-Wiseman quoted in 'Toronto's SOS heroine: Femia-Wiseman reaches out to street prostitutes,' *Metropolis*, 15 December 1987, pp. 7–8
43 Femia-Wiseman, quoted in Wendy Dennis, 'Street fight,' *Toronto Life*, November 1988, p. 136
44 See, for example, 'From the floor,' in Laurie Bell, ed., *Good Girls, Bad Girls* (Toronto: The Women's Press, 1987), p. 48.
45 Delacoste and Alexander, eds., *Sex Work*, p. 174
46 Lau, *Runaway*, p. 237

4 HOMELESS AND HUNGRY

1 Sandy Craig and Chris Schwartz, *Down and Out: Orwell's Paris and London Revisited* (Harmondsworth: Penguin Books, 1984)

2 Jim Ward, *Organizing for the Homeless* (Ottawa: Canadian Council on Social Development, 1989), p. 2

3 Ibid.

4 'U.N. code posits kids' rights,' *Toronto Star*, 27 May 1989, p. D5

5 'Crucial U.N. vote on children's rights,' *Toronto Star*, 19 November 1989, p. A1

6 Data on U.S. homelessness and poverty taken from 'Ordinary People' and 'Overview' in Jonathan Kozol, *Rachel and Her Children* (New York: Crown, 1988)

7 Heather Lang Runtz, 'Housing for our women,' *Canadian Housing* 4 (1; 1987): 18

8 According to former NDP leader Ed Broadbent, quoted in 'Broadbent seeks end to poverty,' *Toronto Star*, 25 November 1989, p. A3

9 'Facts on Homelessness' flyer (Ottawa: Canadian Council on Social Development)

10 'Fractured families are forced to live "underground,"' *Globe and Mail*, 4 February 1989, p. D2

11 Ibid.

12 Spokesperson Ellen Adelberg, quoted in 'Housing: A slippery treadmill,' *Globe and Mail*, 28 January 1989, p. D5

13 Craig and Schwartz, *Down and Out*, last page of preface

14 Ward, *Organizing for the Homeless*, p. 5

15 According to John Jagt, Metro Toronto's director of hostel operations, quoted in 'Shelters leave families out in the cold,' *Toronto Star*, 22 December 1989, p. F1

16 Ibid.

17 Grant Wanzel, 'Home wreckers,' *Housing – A Right*, a collection of essays published on the occasion of the exhibition 'Housing – A Right,' organized by The Power Plant – Contemporary Art at Harbourfront, Toronto, 22 June to 3 September 1990, p. 4

18 Tom Follard, Editorial, *Housing – A Right*, p. 3

19 Ibid.

20 'Analysis of campaign contributions reveals links to development industry,' *Globe and Mail*, 9 August 1989, p. A10

21 Neil Smith and Peter Williams, *Gentrification of the City* (Boston: Allen and Unwin, 1986), p. 17

22 'Housing: No place to grow,' *Toronto Star*, 23 January 1989, p. B1

23 'Housing crisis blamed as child abuse cases soar,' *Toronto Star*, 26 April 1989, p. A3

24 Parkdale Community Legal Services, 'Homelessness and the right to shelter: A view from Parkdale,' *Journal of Law and Social Policy* 4 (1988): 43

25 Bairstow, Bairstow and Associates Limited, *Reaching Out for Help: Manitoba's Homeless in 1987*, p. 41
26 Edmonton Coalition on Homelessness, *Homelessness in Edmonton: No Place Like Home* (Edmonton: Edmonton Coalition On Homelessness, May 1987), p. 71
27 According to Anna Lenk, policy and programs officer, Market Housing Branch, Department of Housing and Property, City of Ottawa, in interview with Steve Endes (for author), 11 November 1989
28 'New by-law worries group aiding homeless,' *Globe and Mail*, 23 March 1988, p. A14
29 'Housing: A slippery treadmill,' *Globe and Mail*, 28 January 1988, p. D5
30 '4 of 5 can't afford metro bungalow, bank says,' *Toronto Star*, 13 June 1989, p. A1
31 Ibid.
32 'How to live in metro on $40,000 a year,' *Toronto Star*, 27 May 1989, p. A1
33 *Progress against Poverty* (Ottawa: National Council of Welfare, April 1987), p. 7
34 Cited in Linda MacLeod, *Battered but Not Beaten: Preventing Wife Battering in Canada* (Ottawa: Canadian Advisory Council on the Status of Women, 1987), p. 44
35 Brenda Doyle Farge, 'Position Paper on Women and Housing,' prepared for the National Action Committee on the Status of Women, May 1986
36 Ward, *Organizing for the Homeless*, p. 8
37 Ibid., p. 8
38 Mark Nichols and Ann Finlayson, 'The search for a future,' *Maclean's*, 16 February 1987, p. 34
39 Reva Gerstein, *The Final Report of the Mayor's Action Task Force on Discharged Psychiatric Patients* (Toronto: Mayor's Action Task Force on Discharged Psychiatric Patients, 1984), p. 30
40 Data in this paragraph taken from Bairstow, Bairstow and Associates Limited, *Reaching out for Help*, p. 53
41 David Cohen, *Forgotten Millions* (London: Paladin, 1988)
42 'No vacancy: Canada's homeless in a helpless search for shelter,' *Globe and Mail*, 3 October 1987, p. D1
43 Craig and Schwartz, *Down and Out*, pp. 68–9
44 Lesley D. Harman, *When a Hostel Becomes a Home: Experiences of Women* (Toronto: Garamond Press, 1989)
45 Jonathan Kozol, *Rachel and Her Children* (New York: Crown, 1988)
46 Ruth Morris and Colleen Heffren, *Street People Speak* (Oakville: Mosaic Press, 1988), pp. 92–3
47 Ward, *Organizing for the Homeless*, p. 6
48 'Closing down the food banks,' *Toronto Star*, 8 April 1990, p. B1

49 'Food banks close to collapse,' *Toronto Star*, 17 June 1990, p. B1
50 'Closing down the food banks'
51 Ibid.
52 Ibid.
53 Ibid.
54 'Thousands going hungry amid plenty,' *Toronto Star*, 31 October 1989, p. A1
55 Physician Task Force on Hunger in America, *Hunger in America: The Growing Experience* (Middletown: Wesleyan University Press, 1985), pp. 128–9
56 Cohen, *Forgotten Millions*, p. 103

5 CRIME TRAPS

1 'Plight of single parent families a national tragedy,' *Toronto Star*, 31 August 1989, p. A21
2 National Council of Welfare, *Progress against Poverty*, rev. ed. (Ottawa, April 1987)
3 'Plight of single parents a national tragedy'
4 'Housing: A slippery treadmill,' *Globe and Mail*, 28 January 1988, p. D5
5 Sylvia Farrant, quoted in 'Women's poverty called inevitable,' *Toronto Star*, 6 June 1990, p. A24
6 'Women's poverty called inevitable'
7 Melanie Chandler, 'The unexpected face of the homeless,' *Chatelaine*, September 1987, p. 51
8 Sheila Baxter, *No Way to Live: Poor Women Speak Out* (Vancouver: New Star Books, 1988), p. 220
9 'Little point debating merits of minimum wage,' *Toronto Star*, 21 April 1989, p. A27
10 National Council of Welfare, *Welfare in Canada: The Tangled Safety Net* (Ottawa, November 1987)
11 'Little point debating the merits of minimum wage'
12 Statistics Canada, *Income Distribution by Size 1988*, Cat. no. 13-207 (Ottawa: Supply and Services Canada, 1989), Table 70, p. 173
13 National Council of Welfare, *1989 Poverty Lines* (Ottawa: Supply and Services Canada, 1989), p. 6
14 Ibid., p. 9
15 See Ruth Morris and Colleen Heffren, *Street People Speak* (Oakville: Mosaic Press, 1988), chapter 1.
16 'Advocates fear budget will harm poor most,' *Toronto Star*, 16 April 1989, p. A1
17 Cited in 'Don't make poor pay for cuts, Ottawa urged,' *Toronto Star*, 19 April 1989, p. A16
18 Pro Canada Network Research and Analysis Team, *Federal Budget '89:*

Prebudget Briefing Notes (Ottawa: Pro Canada Network, 17 April 1989), p. 7

19 Cited in '93,000 firms with net profits paid no taxes in 1987: Report,' *Financial Post*, 16 November 1989, p. 3

20 'Tory UI changes both cruel and inept,' *Toronto Star*, 12 November 1989, p. B3

21 John Crosbie, quoted in 'Why Wilson faces nationwide tax revolt,' *Toronto Star*, 12 August 1989, p. D1

22 Cited in 'The campaign for welfare reform,' *Toronto Star*, 28 February 1989, p. A22

23 'Senator's passionate attack on poverty,' *Toronto Star*, 13 January 1990, p. D4

24 Cited in 'Two paths to a healthy community,' *Toronto Star*, 1 June 1989, p. A25

25 Cited in 'Nutrition: An unhealthy start,' *Toronto Star*, 26 January 1989, p. L1

26 Cited in 'Psychology: A tough time in childhood,' *Toronto Star*, 28 January 1989, p. H1

27 Peter Calamai, *Broken Words: Why Five Million Canadians are Illiterate* (Toronto: Southam Newspaper Group, 1987)

28 Ibid., p. 71

29 George Radwanski, *Ontario Study of the Relevance of Education, and the Issue of Drop Outs* (Toronto: Ministry of Education, 1987), p. 76

30 Jeannie Oakes, *Keeping Track: How Schools Structure Inequality* (New Haven: Yale University Press, 1985), p. 40

31 Maureen Baker, *What Will Tomorrow Bring?* ... (Ottawa: Canadian Advisory Council on the Status of Women, 1985), p. 21

32 Myrna Kostash, *No Kidding: Inside the World of Teenage Girls* (Toronto: McClelland and Stewart, 1987), p. 82

33 Calamai, *Broken Words*, p. 9

34 Ibid., p. 18

35 'Behind native hunger strike,' *Toronto Star*, 22 April 1989, p. A2

36 'Minister refuses to meet Indians on hunger strike,' *Toronto Star*, 8 April 1989, p. A3

37 Canadian Business Task Force on Literacy, *Measuring the Cost of Illiteracy in Canada* (Toronto: Woods Gordon, 1988)

38 Ibid.

39 Statistics Canada, *Canadian Economic Observer* (Ottawa: Supply and Services Canada, August 1989), p. 4.11

40 Calamai, *Broken Words*, pp. 16, 17, 31

41 'Finding support for kids in crisis,' *Toronto Star*, 21 March 1990, p. A26

42 'Out-of-control kids put schools in crisis,' *Toronto Star*, 10 March 1990, p. A1

43 'Finding support for kids in crisis'

44 See, for example, Stan Wojick, 'Some factors affecting the employability of disadvantaged youth,' *Symposium on Street Youth: Symposium Proceedings*

1986 (Toronto: Covenant House, 1986), pp. 227–35, and/or Calamai, *Broken Words*, p. 33.

45 Calamai, *Broken Words*, p. 13

46 Quoted in ibid., p. 68

47 Ibid., pp. 67–8

48 Cited in 'Drumbeats of anger,' *Maclean's*, 2 July 1990, p. 28

49 Neil Boyd, *The Last Dance: Murder in Canada* (Scarborough: Prentice-Hall, 1988)

50 Statutes of Canada, 'Juvenile Delinquents Act,' in *Revised Statutes of Canada 1970*, Vol. v (Ottawa: Queen's Printer for Canada, 1970), Chapter J-3, s. 38

51 Nicholas Bala, 'The Y.O.A.: A new era in juvenile justice?' in Barbara Landau, ed, *Children's Rights in the Practice of Family Law* (Toronto: Carswell, 1986), pp. 238–54

52 According to justice minister Doug Lewis, attributed in 'Provinces told consensus needed to alter Young Offenders Act,' *Toronto Star*, 3 March 1989, p. A13

53 'Getting tough with teenage crime,' *Toronto Star*, 26 February 1989, p. B1

54 Cited in ibid.

55 For a more detailed discussion of disposition options under the YOA, see 'Criminal prosecutions under the Young Offenders legislation,' in Margaret A. Michaud, *Dead End: Homeless Teenagers, a Multi-Service Approach* (Calgary: Detselig Enterprises 1988).

56 'Children of crime,' *Maclean's*, 30 January 1989, p. 44

57 Cited in 'Violent crimes by youths rise 10% in 3 years, figures show,' *Toronto Star*, 21 April 1990, p. A12

58 Cited in 'Ottawa seeks 5-year term for killers,' *Toronto Star*, 21 December 1989, p. A3

59 Quoted in 'Inside Willingdon,' *Vancouver Sun*, 2 February 1989, p. B1

60 Elliott Leyton, *The Myth of Delinquency: An Anatomy of Juvenile Nihilism* (Toronto: McClelland and Stewart Limited, 1986), p. 193

61 See, for example, William Ryan, *Blaming the Victim* (New York: Vintage Books, 1976), chapter 5.

62 Leyton, *The Myth of Delinquency*, p. 204

63 Ibid., pp. 25–6

64 'Like families, cultures teach kids by example,' *Toronto Star*, 23 May 1989, p. A21

65 Health and Welfare Canada, *Suicide in Canada: Report of the National Task Force on Suicide in Canada* (Ottawa: Health and Welfare Canada, 1987)

66 John Kirkbride, quoted in 'Inside Willingdon'

67 'A day in the life at Willingdon,' *Vancouver Sun*, 2 February 1989, p. B5

68 Ombudsman of British Columbia, *Willingdon Youth Detention Centre: Public*

Report No. 17 (Victoria: Queen's Printer for British Columbia, 1989)

69 Dr Robert Menzies, quoted in 'Kids need sense of self-worth,' *The Province*, 20 January 1989, p. 26

70 James Tyman, *Inside Out: An Autobiography by a Native Canadian* (Saskatoon: Fifth House Publishers, 1989), p. 102

6 DRUGS: KILLING THE PAIN

1 Victor Malarek, *Merchants of Misery* (Toronto: Macmillan of Canada, 1989), pp. x and 161

2 Ibid.

3 'Canada flooded with illegal drugs,' *Toronto Star*, 7 May 1989, p. C5

4 Malarek, *Merchants of Misery*, pp. 78–9

5 Diane Francis, 'Harsh measures against drugs,' *Maclean's*, 12 September 1988, p. 9

6 'Canada flooded with illegal drugs'

7 'A global struggle: Drug police are fighting the odds,' *Maclean's*, 3 April 1989, p. 48

8 Cited in Malarek, *Merchants of Misery*, p. 114

9 Cited in 'Cocaine offences jumped 36.3% in 1988, agency says,' *Toronto Star*, 30 September 1989, p. A3

10 'Stats-Facts: Alcohol and other drug use in Canada,' *The Journal*, 1 September 1988, pp. 5–8

11 'Legalizing drugs: The case for and against,' *Toronto Star*, 4 November 1989, p. D1

12 According to Toronto police superintendent James Clark, quoted in 'Drug seizures double as charges jump 36%,' *Toronto Star*, 1 February 1990, p. A1

13 Chris Wood, 'A deadly plague of drugs,' *Maclean's*, 3 April 1989, p. 44

14 Carsten Stroud, 'Drugs in the city,' *Toronto Life*, June 1989, p. 50

15 According to Ontario's chief coroner, Dr James Young, quoted in 'Metro deaths from cocaine an epidemic, coroner says,' *Toronto Star*, 4 May 1990, p. A1

16 'Cocaine rules as new king of drug jungle,' *Toronto Star*, 7 May 1989, p. C10

17 Cited in 'Gettin' high goes down,' *Metropolis*, 12 October 1989, p. 6

18 Cited in 'Almost 90% of homeless youths have drug problem, survey finds,' *Globe and Mail*, 9 June 1990, p. A8

19 Social Program Evaluation Group, *Canada Youth and AIDS Study* (Kingston: Queen's University, 1988)

20 Cited in Malarek, *Merchants of Misery*, p. 24

21 Cited in 'Almost 90% of homeless youths have drug problem, survey finds'

22 Statistics Canada, 'Police reported crime by offence and the provinces/

territories, 1988,' *Canadian Crime Statistics 1988*, Cat. no. 85-205 (Ottawa: Ministry of Supply and Services, 1988)

23 ' 'Prescription squad" battles drug crime wave,' *Toronto Star*, 16 October 1989, p. A3

24 'Arrest addiction,' *Now*, 5–11 October 1989, p. 9

25 Malarek, *Merchants of Misery*, P. 51

26 Cited in 'Almost 90% of homeless youths have drug problems, survey finds'

27 'Needle exchanges help fight AIDS,' *Toronto Star*, 23 July 1989, p. B2

28 See, for example, 'AIDS/IV drug use on "epidemic curve," ' *The Journal*, 1 July 1988, p. 1, and 'AIDS set to hit general public,' *The Journal*, 1 September 1988, p. 1.

29 Dr David Korn, quoted in 'AIDS set to hit general public'

30 Social Program Evaluation Group, *Canada Youth and AIDS Study*

31 Quoted in 'Needle exchange can reduce drug use,' *The Journal*, 1 April 1989, p. 3

32 'Stats-facts: Alcohol and other drug use in Canada' p. 5

33 Ibid.

34 Trudee Able-Peterson, *Children of the Evening* (New York: G.P. Putnam's Sons, 1981), p. 133

35 According to Dr Kathy Sdao-Jarvie, quoted in 'Addicts find no easy way to kick habit,' *Toronto Star*, 7 May 1989, p. C8

36 Malarek, *Merchants of Misery*, p. 143

37 Ibid., p. 143

38 'Jamaica holds 33 Canadians for drugs,' *Toronto Star*, 19 June 1990, p. A1

39 Health Protection Branch, Department of National Health and Welfare, *Narcotic Controlled and Restricted Drug Statistics 1987* (Ottawa: National Health and Welfare, 1987), Table 11, and p. 3, figure 1, respectively

40 'Profiteering and violence are at the heart of the drug world,' *Maclean's*, 3 April 1989, p. 46

41 'Drugs blamed as store holdups rise,' *Toronto Star*, 16 January 1990, p. A1

42 Ibid.

43 According to a spokesman for Bry-Lin, a private Buffalo hospital for addicts, quoted in 'Addicts find no easy way to kick habit'

44 Cited in 'Sharp increase reported in cocaine addiction,' *Toronto Star*, 27 November 1989, p. A1

45 'Addicts find no easy way to kick habit'

46 Ibid.

47 'Why addicts seek help in U.S.,' *Toronto Star*, 5 September 1989, p. A21

48 According to Dr Peter Wu of the Addiction Research Foundation, quoted in 'How a "miracle drug" turned into a killer,' *Toronto Star*, 7 May 1989, p. C9

49 Staff Inspector Jim Clark, quoted in 'Cocaine rules as new king of drug jungle'

50 Joy Reid, quoted in 'Addicts find no easy way to kick habit'
51 Brian Rush, quoted in 'Addicts find no easy way to kick habit'
52 Cited in '150,000 addicts need treatment task force finds,' *Toronto Star*, 10 May 1990, p. A9
53 'Addict children refugees of war on drugs,' *Toronto Star*, 18 December 1989, p. A1
54 According to Elsbeth Tupker, head of the Youth Clinic at Toronto's Hospital for Sick Children, quoted in 'Addict children refugees of war on drugs'
55 'Addict children refugees of war on drugs'
56 Margaret Michaud, quoted in Marcia Kaye, 'Kids on the street,' *Canadian Living*, June 1989, p. 53
57 Wood, 'A Deadly Plague of Drugs'
58 Malarek, *Merchants of Misery*, pp. xi and xii
59 'Father's plea: Let's stop this street-sweeping of drug users,' letter to the editor, *Toronto Star*, 30 September 1989, p. D3

7 BEATING THE STREET

1 Myrna Kostash, *No Kidding: Inside the World of Teenage Girls* (Toronto: McClelland and Stewart, 1987), p. 163
2 Martyn Kendrick, *Nobody's Children: The Foster Care Crisis in Canada* (Toronto: Macmillan of Canada, 1990), p. 127
3 Ibid., p. 109
4 Ibid., p. 43–4
5 Ibid., p. 4
6 Ibid.
7 See ibid., chapter 7.
8 'Locking up runaways no guarantee of survival,' *Globe and Mail*, 1 August 1990, p. A5
9 Helen Downey, quoted in 'Locking up runaways no guarantee of survival'
10 Louise Armstrong, *Solomon Says: A Speakout on Foster Care* (New York: Pocket Books, 1989)
11 Ibid., p. 184
12 Margaret A. Michaud, *Dead End: Helping Teenagers, A Multi-Service Approach* (Calgary: Detselig Enterprises, 1988)
13 Some examples are discussed in Michaud, *Dead End*, chapters 6–10 inclusive, and in Kendrick, *Nobody's Children*, chapter 8.
14 Gitta Sereny, *The Invisible Children* (London: Pan Books, 1986), p. 88
15 Sharon E. Williams, 'Mapping the way out: An introductory overview,' in Michaud, *Dead End*, last page of overview
16 Ray Edney, 'Successful experiences,' in Michaud, *Dead End*, p. 69
17 Ibid., p. 68